D1634622

SARAH MURRAY

Sarah Murray (nee Maese) was born in 1744 and at the age of thirty-seven married Captain William Murray RN, third son of the Earl of Dunmore. It was a short marriage, for on Christmas Day 1786, just over three years later, William Murray died. The affection of his widow for her husband and his homeland can be clearly seen in her references to Perthshire and her enthusiasm for the Scottish Highlands. When she was 52, Sarah Murray made the tour of almost two thousand miles which forms the bulk of her *Companion and Useful Guide* and she emerges from her writing as a strong and indefatigable woman, rarely daunted by danger or desolation and with a perceptive eye for the country and its people, their traditions and legends. In 1802 she married again, to George Aust, a career civil servant and first permanent under-secretary of state for Foreign Affairs. Sarah Murray died, on November 5th 1811 at Noel House, Kensington, but through the pages of her principal work she lives on — her scorn for the *shavers* who meddle with nature's beauty a warning against ill-considered developments, her enthusiasm for Scotland encouraging us to follow the tracks of her chaise to this day, over mountain pass or through leafy glen to the waterfalls she so abundantly loved, to the shrines and memorials of the past, to *The Beauties of Scotland*.

The Beauties of Scotland

A Companion and Useful Guide to

The Beauties
of Scotland

Sarah Murray

Edited by William F. Laughlan

Byways

First Published 1982 by Byway Books
9 Maxton Court, Hawick, Roxburghshire TD9 7QN

© **Byway Books**

ISBN 0 907448 02 X

Phototypeset in Compugraphic English 18
and Printed in Scotland by Kelso Graphics,
The Knowes, Kelso, Roxburghshire

**This book is published with the financial assistance of
the Scottish Arts Council**

Contents

Illustrations cont.

All illustrations are courtesy of the Borders Regional Library Service. Those of Staffa, Buochaile, Canna and Skye are taken from *Pennant's Tour,* the others are by Cattermole, Allom, Brown, Stewart, Billings, Sanby, McLea, Skene, Fraser and Daniel.

Introduction

TO THE EDITORS OF THE LITERARY REVIEWS

Gentlemen — I am an Author neither for fame (my subject being too common a one to gain it), nor for bread. I do not publish from the persuasions of friends, or to please myself. I write because I think my Guide will be really useful to travellers, who may follow my steps through Scotland; by informing them of these objects which are worthy of notice and at the same time acquainting them where, and by what means, they can get at them in the safest and most comfortable manner. A plan, I believe, never attended to (in the way I have done) by any of my predecessors in Tour writing.

I have no wings to soar Parnassus' height; no talents to tread the wild path of imagination; but having (as the great Frederick termed it) a little of "ce gros bon sens qui court les rues", I am able to relate, in my own fashion, what my eyes have seen.

But you, Gentlemen, frighten me. Should you discover faults — and faults in abundance I fear there are — be generous, as the mastiff is to the babbling lap-dog, who looks with calm dignity at the Lilliputian, passes on, and takes no notice: so that if your conscience will not permit you to give me a word of encouragement, I entreat you to be silent. On the contrary, should my child be thought in the least worthy of your approbation, I shall rejoice and ever think myself obliged to you.

I am, Gentlemen, with great respect, your most obedient humble servant,

Sarah Murray   *Kensington, March the 30th 1799.*

~

Gentlemen — Had you put an extinguisher upon my former feeble light, there would have been an end of my *Guideship:* but as you and the indulgent Public have sanctioned, by your approbation, my endeavours to be of use to travellers in Scotland, I again venture to appear before you: not quite with the same anxiety as I did in the year 1799, because your critical remarks on my first Guide have made me look up to you with rather more confidence.

The wish to deserve and obtain commendation, has been the chief stimulus of my actions through life and, when I read the very flattering observations on my Guide, in the *British Critic* for October 1799 and in the *Monthly Review* for May 1800, my heart exulted in the praise you were pleased to bestow upon my

7

performance and it determined to exert once more my endeavours to produce a second Volume, which I trust will make my Guide more complete, as it includes the Hebrides. Should this Second Volume meet with the same indulgence its predecessor has obtained, I shall feel proud indeed. My heart will ever retain a grateful sense of your very favourable report of my first bantling. I am hopeful my second will not be found degenerated and therefore equally deserving of your attention; but, at all events, I must beg that you will have the goodness to accept of my thanks for your opinion already given.

I should be inclined to comply with the advice offered in the *British Critic,* concerning a Map; but two reasons deter me from adopting it. Small maps are very erroneous, consequently of little use, and the other is that a copper-plate of a map suitable to my work would cost at least ten pounds. My Guide is an humble pocket or chaise-companion, not intended for a book-case, consequently its wear and tear must be considerable and daily and perhaps sometimes it may be left to perish in an inn, on a rock, or by the side of a cataract; I would therefore wish travellers to have it in their power to replace their Companion on as easy terms as the increased price of paper and printing will permit.

I beg pardon for being thus prolix, but I wish to name my reasons for not following good advice.

I am, Gentlemen, with great respect, your obliged and most humble servant,

Sarah Murray   *Kensington, October the 25th, 1803*

~

Gentlemen, and Ladies — In offering you this revised edition of Mrs. Sarah Murray's *Companion and Useful Guide to the Beauties of Scotland,* we have sought to follow in her footsteps — not only literally, but also in spirit. Just as she was concerned that her Guide should not be prohibitively costly, so we have endeavoured to ensure that this edition can be as much a Companion to-day. We have, however, been able to insert several maps — small maps — agreeing with the British Critic that "a small map of the places visited by this entertaining traveller seems to be the only thing necessary to make the publication, in a high degree, entitled to attention." One step further, we have added engravings illustrative of many of the charming scenes so ably described by Mrs. Murray.

Her lively style, quick eye and determination to see everything, regardless of danger, coupled with a sharp perception — particularly evident in her shrewd analysis of the causes of the Clearances — put her well ahead of her time, both as a traveller and as a writer.

Certainly Sarah Murray's *Companion and Useful Guide* is of

value to-day — both for its initial purpose, to act as a guide to everything that is worth seeing, for so many of the places to which she beat her path are now recognised as attractions for any tourist; and as a contribution to social history, for it acts as a snap-shot, giving to-day's reader a clear picture of the Scotland through which she travelled alone (accompanied for the most part by her maid, her manservant, a post-boy or James Allen, the doughty driver from Perth, or, in the summers of 1801 and 1802, Angus Cameron of Rannoch).

Why did not Walter Scott dedicate *The Lady of the Lake* to Mrs. Murray? She felt that he ought to have, in recognition of her discovery of the beauties of the Trossachs — an assertion hotly debated but perhaps the basis for Wordsworth's claim to locals, in justifying his interest in the area, that it was a beauty well-known in London.

And so, Gentlemen — and Ladies — we offer you her *Companion and Useful Guide to the Beauties of Scotland* and trust that it will prove as successful and popular as in 1799. It is published with the assistance of the Scottish Arts Council, of the Borders Regional Library Service and of Hugh Mackay, Hawick, whose skill at detection must never be underrated. I remain, on behalf of the Publishers, your most humble and obedient servant,

William Laughlan　　　　　　　　*Hawick, April the 24th 1982*

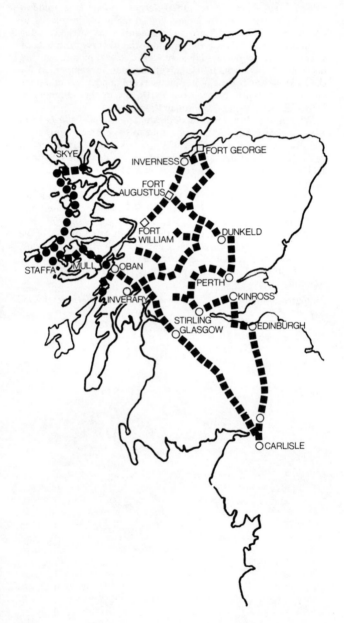

SKYE

FORT GEORGE

INVERNESS

FORT
AUGUSTUS

FORT
WILLIAM

DUNKELD

STAFFA

MULL

OBAN

PERTH

INVERARY

KINROSS

STIRLING

EDINBURGH

GLASGOW

CARLISLE

Advice for the Traveller

Provide yourself with a strong roomy carriage, and have the springs well corded; have also a stop-pole and strong chain to the chaise. Take with you linch-pins, and four shackles, which hold up the braces of the body of the carriage; a turn-screw, fit for fastening the nuts belonging to the shackles; a hammer, and some straps.

For inside of the carriage, get a light flat box, the corners must be taken off, next the doors, for the more conveniently getting in and out. This box should hang on the front of the chaise, instead of the pocket, and be as long as the whole front, and as deep as the size of the carriage will admit: the side next the travellers should fall down by hinges, at the height of their knees, to form a table on their laps; the part of the box below the hinges should be divided into holes for wine bottles, to stand upright in. The part above the bottles, to hold tea, sugar, bread, and meat; a tumbler glass, knife and fork, and salt-cellar, with two or three napkins: the box to have a very good lock. I would also advise to be taken, bed-linen, and half a dozen towels at least, a blanket, thin quilt, and two pillows; these articles will set a traveller quite at ease, with respect to accommodation; the blanket and quilt will be very seldom wanted; however, when they are, it is very pleasant to have such conveniences in one's power. If a traveller would like to save a great deal of money, and render a servant more useful than on horseback, put a seat for him behind the carriage. Let two strong hooks be screwed on the body of the chaise, and a standing piece of iron from each hind spring, and a bar of iron across, to support the perpendicular pieces. The canvas or leather seat may, with straps, be so fastened to the hooks in the body of the carriage, and the upright irons, as to make it a very comfortable easy seat; and the servant being thus a part of the equipage, is always at hand for use, either in opening gates, or in the case of accidents; besides, he never can be left behind at the inns where you stop, or elsewhere, which is for ever the case when a servant is on horseback: he is hardly ever with you, when you most want him; and often comes galloping after you, at the risk of his own neck, and to the great detriment of the poor post-horse. You will say, perhaps — if the servant be stuck to our backs, how inconvenient! not to be able to send *on* for horses. If you travel for pleasure, you need not be in such haste; and besides, how few men are able to ride a hundred or more miles a day, for two or three days together? also, when you get into the countries where you are obliged to take your horses wherever you go, there can be no sending on for fresh horses. But the most solid reason with many for adopting this mode of conveyance for a manservant is the very considerable sum of money it saves. To me the convenience is not to be described, as by my man's being at all times at hand, he was ready to discover if anything was amiss, and to assist in setting it to rights.

In a journey of near two thousand miles, my carriage was only *once* near being down, and would certainly have been so, had the servant been anywhere but on the seats behind. He felt and saw the shackle belonging to one of the hind springs break, and instantly called to the postillion. Had the carriage not stopped immediately, I do not know what might have happened; but as it was, a new shackle was taken out of the pocket of the chaise, and it was set upright again in a very short time: which, in my mind, afforded a strong proof of the utility of carrying a set of shackles, and having the servant on the chaise. This accident happened on the road near Loch Awe, far from assistance of any kind, and in torrents of rain.

Thus much for the first set off. I will now run over the ground I travelled in 1796, and I will begin my Guideship, equipped as above, from my own house; and you will soon reach the first post in the great North road.

With my maid by my side, and my man on the seat behind the carriage, I set off, May the 28th, 1796. Mr. Edes, of Stratton-street, Piccadilly, provided me with a good pair of horses; and a very civil man he is: those who have occasion for post-horses do well for themselves if they employ him. In all probability you have travelled much of the road in England before, therefore you may wish to get on, as I did, as fast as you can. But in Scotland it may be new to you; I will therefore notice what you may see in your way, or at least mention what I saw with pleasure; also the inns most convenient to sleep at, with their distances from each other; and I will endeavour to point out a route that will give you an opportunity of seeing most of the natural beauties of the Highlands, etc. It will be a zig-zag route, but it will be much to the purpose, if you really wish to *see* Scotland, and not merely to *say* you have made the tour of that country.

If you are keen to travel for pleasure, and are willing to be safe, make a resolution, (and keep to it strictly) *never* to be out after dark. If you will adhere to my plan, and be early in a morning in your chaise, you may see each day's portion of beauty, and have daylight to lodge you safe, in your intended quarters, unless some unforeseen delay should occur.

If you have no friend's house to go to at Edinburgh, there are several fine hotels in the New Town; but to remain at them, is very expensive. You must at any rate stay some time at Edinburgh, because many charming things are to be visited in its neighbourhood. As far as Perth you can get post-horses all the way; but when you arrive at that town, if you do not proceed on the coast road, which I did not, you must hire horses by the day, to go through the Highlands, or wherever you please to be carried. For example, if you hire them to go to Blair Atholl, Taymouth, or any other part, where you propose paying a visit of days or weeks, you must either retain the horses, and pay so much each day for them; or send them back to Perth, and order them to come again for you; paying for the time they take in getting from you to Perth, and from Perth to you again; as I was obliged to do from Blair, and from Rannoch, besides other shorter distances.

If you wish to travel through the Highlands in as perfect security as is possible, from good horses and careful driver, you must apply to Mr. Millar, at the Salutation inn, for horses, and James Allen, his driver, to take care of you; for I verily believe he will drive you (and with perfect safety too), through roads that no other man can drive, without accident, unless he be as careful, and as skilful, as James was when he drove me. I think there are very few such driver as Allen; and because he was sober and careful, I gave him half-a-crown a day for himself, which he well deserved; for whilst he drove me (and I am sure for many a mile where my carriage went under his conduct, never carriage had gone before), I felt perfectly easy; though sometimes, on the one hand, I beheld a deep lake below, and on the other, stupendous rocks, out of which the road, only the width of the carriage below, is blown; yet still I was, and even thought myself safe, with James Allen, and his steady black horses.

Hay, in the summer of 1796, was very dear, consequently Mr. Millar was obliged to charge higher, than in former seasons, for the horses. I gave him twenty shillings a-day, and had nothing more to pay for them or the driver, except the daily present of half-a-crown to Allen.

If you have no friends at Perth, I recommend to you the Salutation inn for your headquarters; for though it not be reckoned the first inn, yet you will find your account in the civility of Mr. Millar, and the superior cleanliness of his house.

When you leave Perth, provide bread to last you until you get to Inverness; and wine, and cold meat for your dinners; for you will find it much more comfortable to dine in your chaise while your horses are baiting, than take what you may find at the inns. Good water you may at all times, and in all places, procure. I ate and drank what I could get at the inns, where I passed the night, it being right to give the inn-keepers some profit for the use of their beds; but in the middle of the day, I found it

Part One

CHAPTER ONE

Carlisle has been so often described, and is so well known, that it is needless to say a word of that ancient town. I will therefore begin my peregrination from the division of the road; the one leading to Annan and Moffat; the other to Langholm, which I took. From Longtown to Langholm is a drive that must give pleasure and satisfaction to anyone who has a taste for beauty in its natural state. Almost the whole of the road runs by the side of the River Esk, which is rolling beneath; sometimes seen through the stems of trees, deep, and close below the carriage; at others, at some distance, with verdant meadows sweeping to its edge on one side, and on the other, high rocks clothed with wood; the river loudly tumbling through the arches of picturesque bridges of soft grey stone, over black rocks, partly whitened by the dashing of the rapid stream.

Unfortunately I arrived at Langholm in a pouring rain, consequently saw that place very imperfectly. Another unfortunate circumstance attended me, that of following the steps of a great man, and upon his own territory too. The Duke of Buccleuch had, about an hour or two before my arrival at Langholm, left that place in his way to Dalkeith, and had taken from the inn all the horses, except one wretched pair. The landlady said, she did not like the fashion of the servant's going behind the carriage; — would I not have a saddle-horse for him? — No. For I had determined a negative to that point on every occasion. Had the good woman been in possession of another pair of horses at home, she, I plainly perceived, would not have taken me to Hawick, without four; luckily for me she had them not, and the two poor miserable beasts were brought out to be put to the chaise. As the inn had nothing inviting to me to stay there, I hastened into the carriage, it still raining prodigiously hard. As soon as I was seated, I perceived a fine honest-faced old Scot, twisting a cord from one fore spring to the other. — "Friend, what are you doing?" — "Making a seat, My Lady; the one horse being hardly able to stand, for rheumatism and broken knees; and the other will not suffer me to ride him, being woefully balled on the back." — "Well, but surely such poor creatures will never carry us to Hawick?" — "Never you heed my Lady, have patience, and they will carry you on cannily: I will be bound for it, they'll gang the last mile better than the first."

Necessity has no law, I was therfore obliged to be silent.

Presently I observed the good old man at the head of the horses, twirling his fingers at their snaffles, with pieces of slender pack-thread. "What is all that for, friend, what are you doing now?" — "Only making reins, my Lady." — "We cannot, surely, go with safety, with reins of that twine, up such hills as are before us?" — "Never you heed, my Lady, I'll answer for your safety: after a wee bit we shall gang weel and cannily." When this very slender tackle was completed, the honest man mounted his seat, and we soon crossed the bridge over the Ewes, which at Langholm joins the Esk, and came to a prodigiously steep hill; here my heart failed me, not being able to walk, by reason of the hard rain and almost a hurricane of wind. The old Scot, however, quitted his perch, and took hold of the head of the should-be riding beast; I ordered my man to lead off the horse; and, what with whipping, hooting and coaxing, the poor lame creatures at length got the chaise up that first hill, where they stopped to recover a little the dreadful pull. The talkative conductor again took his station, and went on safely, but slowly. As soon as I was convinced the horses were likely to proceed, I began to look about me in Ewesdale, in which we were. Ewesdale is a very contracted valley, and part of it, only the bed of the river; and the road between stupendous mountains, covered with verdure to the summits. The road is cut out of the sides of the hills, sometimes a vast height above the charming rolling water, at others, close to its edge; every step affording a variety of scenery.

The road follows this delightful river nearly to its source at Mosspole, from whose lofty hills it issues, at various springs. The ground at Mosspole must be high, as two fine rivers there rise, and take their course different ways. At Mosspole there is only one house, which would make a very convenient stage for changing horses, as it is nearly half-way between Langholm and Hawick. I observed to the man who kept the house, that as I understood the Duke of Buccleuch wished to promote the use of that road, his Grace should encourage an inn at Mosspole, for changing horses. I received in answer to my observation, that they could not keep horses in that wild place, having no food for them. To be sure, it is situated amongst such a chain of mountains, that it does appear that no number of animals, except sheep, could be fed from the produce of that district. A little meal and water was the only refreshment my poor, lame, and galled beasts found at Mosspole; which when they had swallowed, we proceeded. Having just entered Roxburghshire, we met with a branch of the Tiviot, which we crossed; about four miles further, we joined the main Tiviot water, and entered Tiviotdale, contracted like that of Ewesdale, and in some degree, in its beauties, similar; but more diversified, by every charming scene that water, hills, rocks, and wood, can produce. All I could see through torrents of rain, was delightful, particularly below the junction of the branches of the Tiviot with the main stream; which came rolling down amongst rocks and wood, in a very charming style. Any one, less delighted than I am with wild nature, would, perhaps, be somewhat alarmed at such a road, and such scenery, in a violent rainy day. The road too, rough and steep, and not wider than a carriage; with huge clefted rocks on the right, sometimes covered with wood, at others, bare, and frowning through the shade of other overhanging precipices; and water gushing in spouts from innumerable apertures. On the left, the river deep below, foaming, and rolling down its close bed of rocks and precipices; varied by, now and then, a mile of a beautiful winding flat verdure; but still rocks and wood confining the view, on every side. No fields, no corn, no produce, except feed for sheep and goats. Such was the scene till I reached Hawick, where the Slettrick water joins the Tiviot.

The Town of Hawick is, in itself, a very middling place, but its situation, and its surrounding beauties, are enchanting. Its bridges, and its views, from almost every part of it, are picturesque, and highly gratifying to those who love nature in its true simplicity. Lord Napier's house and woods, seen through the arch of the bridge over the Tiviot, are well worth a wet walk, which I had, to get a view of them.

My old Scot's prediction of his horses, was truly verified; for, notwithstanding both they and their master were like drowned rats, we really performed the last two miles better than any of the foregoing twenty; which, however, took eight hours to accomplish; consequently gave me less time at Hawick, than I intended, as I much wished to have seen more of that part of Tiviotdale, than I could do, by arriving so late as eight o'clock in the evening. — When I got out of the chaise, the inn looked large, but the inside of it was very dirty and uncomfortable, and rendered doubly so by the extremely wet day. There was a long demur, whether I could get either a sitting room, or a good bed-chamber; because company from the South had sent on to secure rooms, which their servant had done. Fortunately for me, I soon learnt this company was expected from Langholm: from which place, we convinced the landlord, they could not stir for want of horses. I was therefore let into the apartment occupied (as I was informed) by the Duke and Duchess of Buccleuch, whenever they came that way. His Grace (another piece of good luck for me) had stopped short of Hawick that day, at his factor's, Mr. Ogilvie's. Glad should I have been, and quiet too, had his Grace's servants been with him. They and their friends made a jolly evening of it at Hawick, and got completely intoxicated. Their noise, in the next room to mine, was very uncomfortable; and would have been alarming too, had I not taken good care of the fastenings between the two rooms. The town of Hawick is old and shabby, at least that part of it which a short half hour of cessation of rain gave me an opportunity of seeing. I walked over the bridges, and below them to the water's edge, and into the churchyard. Curiosity soon collected a small group about me, and I was somewhat mortified to find their language unintelligible to me; I learnt. however, there was a manufactory in the town of carpets, etc., but could not acquire a knowledge of particulars. Here I was confirmed in what I had often before observed, that those who find they cannot be understood, immediately conclude the person spoken to must be deaf. Some young lads passing through the churchyard at Hawick, whilst I was in it, with dogs, and some strange looking things on their backs; I inquired what they were, and what they were going to do with them; but their language, to me, was as Arabic. On my shaking my head, as a token of not understanding them, they began screaming in the highest notes of their voices; taking me, I suppose, for a deaf woman: and at last we separated, laughing at our inability of understanding each other.

The morning after my arrival at Hawick was fine, and I left the uncomfortable inn with pleasure very early. My eyes followed the Tiviot, in its course towards Kelso, and the Tweed, in its sweet dale, as far as the road to Selkirk would permit me; but it was not long before it carried me to a very hilly dreary country; for nothing can be more so, than the greatest part of the way from Hawick to Selkirk. As for Selkirk town, its appearance is truly deplorable. The houses are mostly old, falling to pieces, and deserted: nothing but dirt and misery to be seen. I had not breakfasted, therefore entered the inn; and being, at that time, an inexperienced traveller, I was totally unprovided with necessities for that meal. Every being, and thing in that house, disgusted me at first sight; the extreme dirt, and the smell of the whole, was nauseating in the highest degree. I in consequence made but a very slender breakfast; and was happy to re-enter the chaise.

I got from Selkirk a very good pair of horses, and just such another honest-hearted, good-humoured Scot, as he drove me from Langholm to Hawick. Before I left the inn door, I told the driver I had nearly overturned into a ditch, from the Hawick boy's carelessness, in coming down one of the hills; I therefore hoped his horses were steady. "Ay; and as gude horses as ere gang, my Lady: they wad trot down a ridge of a house, and nae fa'." Indeed I was never better carried; although the stage between Selkirk and Bank House be extremely hilly and fatiguing for horses. The descent from the town of Selkirk is something similar to the ridge of a house, very narrow, and paved; not withstanding, the horses actually did trot briskly down it, without the wheel of my heavy carriage being dragged. The bridge over the Ettrick and Yarrow united, is at the foot of the descent; and the road winds sweetly round its banks, for a mile or two; then leaves it rolling on, to the Tweed, into which it empties itself a few miles below.

I had been wonderfully pleased with Eskdale, Ewesdale and Tiviotdale: but I cannot describe my sensations of delight, when I came in sight of that part of Tweeddale, around Yair, and Fairnalie. The road, after it quits the banks of Ettrick, takes a quick turn, and winds round the bases of the hills; when on a sudden, it comes close on the Tweed; and within sight of a simple bridge, and scenery more enchanting than can be described. As soon as I crossed the bridge, Yair was to my left, on the other side of the river; and Fairnalie, on my right; I knew not which to admire most; the river; its banks; the hills; the rocks; or the wood, (which is here in abundance). All are beautiful. The fancy, in Arcadia, cannot paint a more soft, more sweet, or more lovely scene, than that part of Tweedale. It is pastoral beauty completely perfect. Not an object than can hurt the eye, or ruffle the mind. The soul, for four miles, must be lost to every other sensation but that of soft delight, heightened by an elevation of sentiment, which nothing but such enchanting scenes as those on the Tweed, at Yair, can produce.

When the chaise turned from the sweet flowing Tweed to mount the steep hill, by a rapidly tumbling water's side, I felt as if I were leaving Paradise. Two miles after I had turned my back upon this pastoral Paradise, the road came down upon the banks of the Galla water, joining the road to Galla Shiels: and then I entered Edinburghshire.

The first sight of Edinburgh, from the Middleton road, is, for an extensive view, very grand. Arthur's Seat, and Salisbury Crags, rise high on the side of the town: the Castle in front; Calton Hill; the Forth; and the Bass in the back-ground: all together forming a very grand and extensive prospect. From Laswade Bridge is a view of Melville Castle, in a thick wood: it is white, and conspicuous; but some buildings, with furious red tiles (stables and washing houses, I suppose) break, and spoil the view of it. — I would blow up all such vile erections. — It is a sin against nature, thus to disfigure its works, "by such tiles and bricks, threatening to set fire to the Glen." I was not at the Castle; but these buildings must inevitably spoil the view from it to Laswade bridge and town, which would be extremely pretty, were it not broken by such eye sores.

CHAPTER TWO

James the First of England was born in a small room, or rather closet, in Edinburgh Castle; in which, when I saw it, soldiers were drinking porter. There is a dwelling-house in the castle for the governor; but almost the whole of the edifice is now converted into barracks.

Edinburgh is built upon the declivities of a hill, on the west side of which is the castle erected on the summit of a huge perpendicular rough rock, inaccessible on every side but one. The Abbey, or Palace of Holyroodhouse, is at the bottom of the hill, at the distance of a mile from the Castle. The High-street, which is wide, is a regular descent; and is the communication from the Castle to the Abbey. The rest of the town lies sloping on each side of the High-street, continuing to the flat ground, or more properly the hollows, at the foot of the hill. Many of the houses in the High-street have, from their sloping situation, three or four more stories at the back part of them, than in the front. The houses, in general, in the old town, are very high; some in the High-street have fourteen or more stories, or, as they are termed in Scotland, flats. Each flat contains a family, and is completely shut up from the staircase, of which there is but one leading to all the flats in the house; and it may easily be imagined in what condition this common, corkscrew, stone staircase, must always be. There is but a very small winding flat space, or rather hollow, between the low parts of the town, around the Abbey, and the sharp rise of Salisbury Crags, Arthur's Seat, and Calton Hill; so that the situation of Edinburgh is unique; for it is built upon the various irregularities of a huge rock, sloping to the flat ground on one side, and on the others to hollows, from whence rise lofty mountains, both in the near and distant prospect.

The violent gusts of wind, continually to be felt in the streets of Edinburgh are, I imagine, owing to its situation, and must be the cause of health to its inhabitants (they are very healthy; for had not the atmosphere of that city some powerful refiner, such as a constant high wind, it would, by its nauseous scents, poison the race of beings living in it.

About the middle of the High-street it is intersected by two wide streets, the one leading to the north bridge, over the dry trench to the new town; the other to the south bridge, over the Cowgate, a street so called. In passing over the south bridge, it may not be observed to be a bridge, as it is very wide, with handsome shops on each side, except over the arch. Near the south bridge is the old university, and an exceedingly handsome new college, begun some time since; but when I was at Edinburgh, it was at a stand for want of money. The very large pillars, in front of the building, are each of one huge stone. It was with infinite labour, and danger, they were brought and fixed in their places; for they were hewn at the quarry, and afterwards conveyed to the college. George's square, in the old town, is very pleasant; nearly equal, I think, to any place in the new town.

In one of the old churches I had the great satisfaction of hearing the good and venerable Dr. Blair, whose sermons have been edifying the world for some years past.

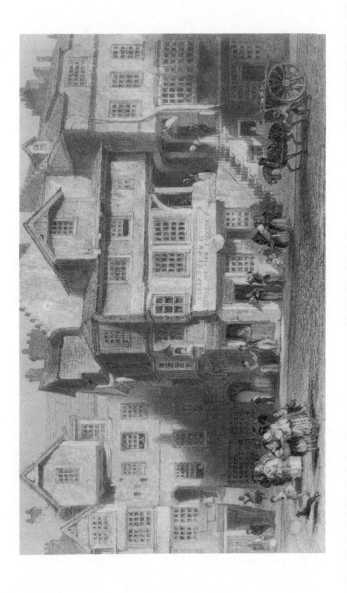

The register-office, in the new town, is a fine building. Princes-street is a noble street, or rather row of houses, looking over the dry trench up to the backs of houses in the old town; some of them, as I have before observed, fourteen stories high, on that side of the High-street; having almost all of them little sloping gardens, with pieces of rocks, and trees interspersed among them. From Princes-street too is seen, at the extremity of the High-street to the west, the Castle, and the irregular perpendicular side of the bold projecting rock on which it stands.

Most of the new town is built with free-stone, hewn, something like that of Bath. St. Andrew's square is grand; but Queen-street, for view, beats all the other parts of the town. It is a row, rather than a street; it being in front open to everything that is beautiful, towards Belle Veue, Leith, the Forth, and the lofty hills of Fifeshire beyond it. The fronts of the houses, however, in Queen-street, are not so complete as those in St. Andrew's square, because they are not all finished of hewn stone. The rough stone looks unhandsome; much like a comely face fitted with the small pox.

Lord Moray's house stands pleasantly, and under the bank on which it is built is St. Barnard's well, a romantic little spot; but the simplicity of it is spoiled by a temple in the style of the Sybil's temple at Tivoli.

There cannot be much passing and repassing in the new town in summer, for in almost every street the grass grows.

The Canongate joins, and in fact makes a part of the High-street, in the old town, and leads to the Abbey; and a fine place it is, for every thing that is disagreeable. The houses are high, and chiefly inhabited by the lower order of people. As the street narrows on the left in going down, is a tottering bow-window to a house, whence the reformer Knox thundered his addresses to the people.

I never saw anything like the swarms of children in the Canongate. I believe they do everything but sleep in the street. It may be truly said that they are fat, ragged, and saucy: and it is not to be wondered at; for what can be expected from an education begun and ended in the street. I was one fine evening walking up this *inviting* Canongate, nicely dressed, in white muslin: an arch boy eyed me, and laid his scheme; — for when I arrived opposite a pool, in the golden gutter, in he dashed a large stone, and, like a monkey, ran off chuckling at his mischief.

Though the whole of the town of Edinburgh is far more cleanly, in one article, than it used to be, yet the Canongate still bears strong marks of its old customs; for *haud your haund, haud your haund,* is still very necessary to cry out; and even that will not do in the Canongate now, if perchance one should be there after ten o'clock in the evening: for at that hour one

begins to hear, *slop* — here, there, and everywhere. Even in the middle of the street, where decent folks generally walk for fear of accidents, they are not exempt from splashes, unless they are in high good luck.

At times one's nose recalls to the mind Sawney's soliloquy on coming within the distance of twenty miles of the capital of Scotland, when he exclaimed, "Ah! canny Edinburgh, I smeel thee nooe!" At the bottom of the Canongate is the Abbey: its first appearance, at present, is not amiss. The tower of Duke Hamilton's apartment, that of Lord Adam Gordon's, and the gateway under the Holy Cross, to the quadrangle, with a grass plat in front, contribute to make it look somewhat palace-like; but twelve years back, I remember it resembling a state-prison. It formerly bore the name of the Monastery of Coenobium; of Santae Crucis; and the Abbey of Holyroodhouse. The chapel of the Abbey was erected by David the First, in the year 1128, in memory (as it is said) of his miraculous deliverance from the horns of an enraged hart, by the interposition of Heaven in the form of a cross. It was converted into a palace by James the Fifth, in the year 1528, who built the north wing of the present front. The form in which it now stands was completed by Charles the Second, in 1664. Whoever erected the side of the square now standing, from Duke Hamilton's apartment to the chapel, must have been a barbarian, and a murderer of taste. Look at the west front of the ruined chapel, and you will be of my opinion. The grand door of entrance was certainly there, facing the beautiful large window to the east. The whole of the west side of the chapel, judging from what remains of it, must have been in the highest style of Gothic architecture, and was certainly at first in the exact form of a cross; but by the erection of that vile north side of the quadrangle, one part of the cross, and half the grand door, are entirely taken away. Without doubt, originally, that fine door must have been perfect and entire; and to complete the front, a square tower, similar to the one which now stands to the north of the door, must also have existed on the south of it, forming, on the whole, the exact shape of the cross. The out-building now called Mary's kitchen, was certainly erected long since the chapel; and all the outlets belonging to the apartments of Duke Hamilton and Lord Dunmore, with the ground on which Queen Mary's Kitchen stands, were probably in David the First's time, an area before the grand entrance into the chapel. The outside of the fine ruin is at present better worth looking at, than the inside; though a stranger may as well see both. Poor Darnley's bones (if they be his) are often disturbed by the rude hand of the shewer of them. The beautiful roof of this chapel fell down in the year 1768.

For the accommodation of the Comte d'Artois, Government

The children are ragged, fat and saucy!

has wonderfully improved the Abbey, both external and internal. The long gallery is new floored, and painted white; and the suite of rooms on the same story with it, are all new sashed, painted, papered, and fitted up and furnished in the modern taste, and in the neatest manner. Amongst the French of fashion in Holyrood-house in 1796, the venerable and most respectable appearance of the unfortunate Duc de Serrent struck me the most: all that is good and amiable is strongly marked in his countenance, rendered more interesting by his flowing hairs, and the sweet though melancholy tone of his voice; and a manner that must be a magnet to every heart susceptible of affection, or conversant with the feelings of paternal suffering; for poor man, he was, when I saw him, still weeping for his murdered sons, his only children; who, I have been informed, were both very amiable and accomplished.

I was told, during my visit to the Abbey, that the first day of every month the Bank of Scotland, by order of the Government, sent down to Monsieur one thousand guineas for his maintenance. How far it was true, I cannot say. His Royal Highness was glad to take refuge in the liberty of Holyroodhouse, from whence he could not safely stir, by reason of large debts contracted in England, probably before the French Revolution. A *chere amie* of the Prince had a house in the park; he made her a visit every morning at eleven o'clock, and again at eight in the afternoon, and supped with her. A gentleman of his suite always attended him to her door, and again at his return to his apartment. Monsieur is a fine man in person, and looks far younger than he can be. His manner is very graceful and gracious.

There scarcely can be a finer view than that from the Calton Hill, which rises from the town of Edinburgh. I have never seen the view from Naples, to its Bay, but I am told, those who have seen both, are in doubt to which of the two to give the preference.

On gaining the summit of Calton Hill, a grand view presents itself to the North, over the flat ground of a mile and a half, between Edinburgh and Leith, enriched by villas, gardens, woods, and fine land; over which is seen the town of Leith; its road, crowded with ships, and the Forth, like an arm of the sea, seven miles broad, flowing from Stirling to the German ocean; with the mountains of Fife closing the scene. To the east is the course of the river, with islands adding to its beauty; and a rich vale towards Musselburgh, Preston Pans, and Haddington, bounded by the great rock in the sea, called the Bass. To the south-east, Arthur's Seat and Salisbury Crags rise boldly, sheltering the palace of Holyroodhouse. On the west is the town, the castle, and a rich vale beyond, bounded by gigantic mountains; and the Pentland Hills finely close the scene to the south-west. Such is the charming prospect from Calton Hill. But as that hill is common, daily, and nightly lounge of all the

vagabonds and loose tribe of the town, the walk over it must be taken with a gentleman in company, else women of decency will be insulted.

The view from Arthur's Seat is very extensive, and worth the trouble of a fatiguing walk to it. It is called by that name from a tradition, that Arthur, King of England, sat at the top of this mountain to behold a sea-fight. In going up to Arthur's Seat, I passed by St. Anton's, or St. Anthony's well, of extremely pure water, also the ruins of St. Anthony's Chapel, or Restalrig Church.

At a short mile in the Musselburgh road are new barracks; the square before them forms a spacious fine parade, and the apartments within are very convenient. I walked around Salisbury Crags, in the middle path by the quarries, which requires a tolerably steady head; for had I taken a roll down the precipice, there would have been an end of me. At the quarries I saw vast heaps of the hard rock divided into small pieces, ready for shipping; and I was told great quantities of that crag were sent to London for paving the streets. After I had descended Salisbury Crags, and crossed the road by which the carts carry the broken stones into town, I came to some fragments of rocks, where I made my servant try to discover the fine echo, in which he at length succeeded; and I thought it the most distinct I had ever heard. By continuing the track I was in, I came to a new foot-way round the base of Arthur's seat. The large pieces of rock strewed on the green below the path, a few years back, broke away from the mountain with a tremendous noise, to the great terror of the washerwomen and bleachers, constantly busy on that green; but very fortunately, as a talkative *gude* wife told me, none of them were very near the spot at the moment the huge pieces of rock separated from the mountain. From that foot-way I had a distant view of Crag Miller Castle, the favourite retirement of Queen Mary, when in love with Bothwell. Proceeding on my way, the first sight of Dediston small lake and house much pleased me; and, indeed, the whole walk, from Dediston round to the Abbey, including the delightful prospects towards Preston Pans; the Barracks; the Forth; the Bass; and the mountains of Fifeshire.

The town of Dalkeith is a dirty, shabby place; and the Duke of Buccleuch has done wisely to build a bridge very near his house; by which the approach to it will be, and I suppose now is, far handsomer that that I arrived at, through the town. I did not go to Scotland to see fine houses, nor dressed places. The simple beauty of nature is my hobby-horse; and where can a hobby-horse of that breed find greater scope than in Scotland? particularly in the Highlands. I did not attempt to enter the house at Dalkeith, but contented myself with seeing the pleasure grounds, park etc. The bridge, viewed from the house, must be a fine object; it is of one arch; a semicircle of 70 feet; thrown from rock to rock. The wood, and banks of the river about the

bridge, are very romantic; and, to me, beautifully rough and broken.

On expressing my admiration of all I saw, I was answered by an overseer of the bridge, then not finished, that by and by it would be much finer; for the bed of the river was to be *cleared;* and the banks *smoothed,* and *dressed.* Fye on the shavers, as Mr. Knight calls them, how unmercifully do they "shave the Goddess whom they come to dress!" And will they not spare even the lovely North Esk? Dalkeith on the whole is a place well worth seeing. I was conducted to a spot in the Duke's grounds, to admire a frightful animal of the monkey kind; a disgusting little black beast. I was glad to turn from his nauseous prison, to the fine woods and grounds in which he is confined.

Roslin! sweet Roslin! — I was enchanted, with its beauties. The chapel was the first thing seen, being very near the inn. Its outside appeared to me like a common looking kirk, with a tiny side door for an entrance. Certainly a larger one, at the end, must have once existed, though now walled up. At present there are only two small Gothic doors, opposite each other. No sooner had I passed the threshold, and entered the side aile, than I was struck with astonishment, at the beautiful structure and workmanship of the ceiling, and pillars; which, I suppose, were originally of a reddish stone, which time and weather have changed and softened to a variety of most beautiful tints. This chapel was built in the purest age of Gothic architecture, by a Sinclair of Caithness, who married the daughter of Robert Bruce, King of Scotland. The chapel of Roslin has been the burying-place of the Sinclairs of Caithness for ages; but at present they have no property at Roslin.

As one generally learns the legend of the spot one visits, from some garrulous guide, that of Roslin chapel must not be forgotten; but it was told in language so unintelligible, by the good wife who shewed it, that I fear my tale will be but imperfect. An abridgement, however, may not be amiss. I shall, therefore, only take up her tale from the apprentice's pillar; which is certainly very different from all the others.

The architect employed to build this chapel could not discover the intent of the plan given him; he was therefore obliged to go to Rome to learn his lesson. In the mean time his apprentice, having more penetration than his master, discovered the design; and in the absence of the architect, wrought the pillar that goes by his name. When the master returned, and found that his lad had more skill than himself, he struck him a violent blow upon his temple, which instantly killed him.

Over what I suppose to have been the great door (opposite the four windows over the altar piece), is carved the broken head of the poor apprentice, and his mother weeping, for his untimely end. After all his trouble, the architect did not succeed, if the

Roslin! Sweet Roslin!

apprentice's pillar was conformable to the original plan of the edifice; for no other part of the work in the chapel resembles it; or the employer did not like the richer, and more complicated style of the apprentice's pillar, so well as the more simple workmanship of the rest of the chapel. — Roslin chapel is not large, but it is reckoned to be a specimen of a very chaste and elegant piece of Gothic architecture. It is a ruin, but the most perfect ruin that can be seen. From the chapel to the castle, is a short quarter of a mile, down a very steep hill. There is but a very small part of the castle standing; a middling modern house being erected on a part of its wall; it is situated upon a small peninsulated promontory of an immense rock, high above the surrounding river, North Esk, which winds round the castle, rushing hoarsely over its rocky bed, imprisoned by perpendicular sides of towering rocks, finely covered with wood; — its noise, and its romantic beauties, increase as it rolls down towards Hawthorndean, and forms a most picturesque view from the turning at the entrance to the castle. The walks by the river's side, cut through the rocks and woods of Roslin, are enchanting beyond description. It is impossible to do justice to the romantic charms of either Roslin, or Hawthorndean; whose ancient walls rise amidst rocks and wood, hanging over the opposite side of the river, within sight of the walks of Roslin. Hawthorndean belongs to Bishop Abernethy Drummond, and was once the habitation of Drummond, the poet.

In going through Laswade, from Dalkeith to Roslin, we met the procession of a country wedding; it was a very fine day, and the parties had just quitted the kirk, and mounted their horses. The bride and bridegroom were on the first horse, and a long cavalcade followed them; some double on a horse, some single, all trotting after the happy pair. As soon as they got down the steep hill from the kirk, they scampered through the town as fast as they could, in order to escape, as quickly as possible, the gaping curiosity of the townsfolks, who all came crowding to their doors. This, probably, was a penny-wedding. In former times, when money was of a far greater value than it is at present, it was the custom, in some parts of Scotland (when a bridegroom was not in circumstances to *treat* the guests at his marriage), for all who were invited to the wedding to pay each one penny, for dinner, dancing, etc. And although a shilling, or more, be now paid on such occasions, still they are called Penny-weddings. I was told that it is no very uncommon thing for the meeting at such weddings to be so numerous, as from the profits of it, to enable the new married pair to furnish their house, or take a small farm.

CHAPTER THREE

I was told, at Edinburgh, I must consult the tide to cross the

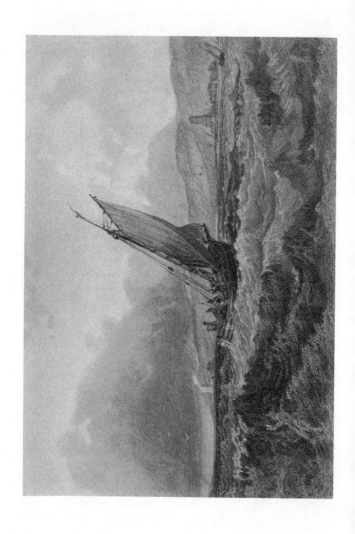

Queensferry: this obliged me to leave the Abbey at five o'clock in the morning. To avoid the steep rise of the Canongate, the postillion drove me up the back street, and through the Cowgate; it was then I saw the wonderful effect of the South Bridge over my head: also by going the back streets, I had an opportunity of seeing, as I drove round the base of it, the whole of the stupendous rock on which the castle is built.

The drive from Edinburgh to Queensferry, is very pleasant; and I was delighted with the appearance, and neatness, of all the houses on the road; every one, without exception, having a garden well stocked with vegetables; and potatoes planted on every bit of waste land, besides many large fields of that vegetable here and there, all the way. I was very agreeably surprised, on arriving at the Ferry, that I was not too late for the tide, of which I had some fears. There is no cause for fears of that sort; for I soon learnt that the tide will serve almost at any hour. Now and then, indeed, at spring tides, it may happen that a carriage must wait an hour or two.

The contrivance they have for hoisting carriages in and out of the ferry-boats, is very clever: my chaise was drawn out pretty far upon a stone pier, and in a very few minutes it was laid safe upon deck; and in a short time relanded, as soon as the ferry-boat touched the shore on the opposite side. I took the precaution of not suffering any brute animals to be on board with me, as they are always troublesome, and sometimes dangerous. Nothing could be more fortunate than I was in my passage; I timed it to a minute. The morning was gloriously fine when I set out from Edinburgh, but it began to cloud and darken for some time before I reached the Ferry: the clouds, however, supported their burden, and Eolus kept close his bags, until I was within ten yards of the end of my passage. It began to rain as I landed, and I had not been in the inn on the north side of the water, three minutes, before it poured; the wind blew a hurricane; and the sea tossed high. I rejoiced I was safe on shore; but I was sorry the storm, and thick mist, prevented my having a view of Hopetounhouse.

As I approached Kinross, Loch Leven on the right of the town, and the fine range of mountains rising from the lake, and sweeping finely away in a gradation, formed a beautiful landscape; the sun too shone out, after its eclipse at the Ferry, in full lustre, and rendered the island in Loch Leven, and the ruined castle upon it, conspicuous; at the same time richly gilding the whole surrounding scenery. From Kinross, I advise all travellers to see the Rumbling Brig, and Cauldron Lin (I was told in the inn, they were not *worth* going to see; so little do the common people of that, or any other country, discriminate what is, or is not worth seeing); I journeyed, therefore, to Craig Town, close to the Lin, the farm of my friend and worthy host, Mr Charles Mercer, and there met his friend the Rev. Mr.

Graham; nor must I forget the civilities of Mr. Lowry Johnston, by whose clever and expert exertions, I was the next day conducted to places where few, if any, women had ever ventured. The Rumbling Brig is a small arch of stone, from rock to rock, almost embracing each other, high above the water. The top of the arch is covered with turf, so that it is like a green bank. Trees grow luxuriantly and thick from every part of the surrounding rocks, bending over the arch, covering the side banks, and feathering down their rugged sides, and so closely entwined down to the deep chasm below, the water is more heard than seen, dashing through its narrow, rough, and winding passage. The whole of the scenery, both at, above, and below this curious bridge, is to a very great degree romantic and beautiful, on each side of the river. There are several very picturesque falls above the bridge; particularly where huge, broken, and projecting rocks impede the course of the water, and luxuriant wood hanging over them, listening, as it were, to the loud thumping of the Devil's Mill. Whatever the name imports, the fall so called, and the scenery around it, is angelic, and fills the mind with harmony and delight. The sound of this fall of the river, at a distance, is certainly similar to that of a mill continually in motion; and the *gude* kirk-folk, who reverence the Sabbath, maintain, that as the mill pays no more respect to the Sunday, than it does to the other days of the week, it must be the Devil's Mill. I was much pleased with a view of the bridge on the south side of the river, above it, and also below it, from a huge rock in the middle of the water, looking close into the chasm under the bridge, where the towering rocks on each side, covered with beautiful wood, form a magnificent and awful shade over the murmuring water, issuing from its dark and confined passage. The later station is a very difficult one to gain, and is still more difficult to be maintained. It is in the middle of the river, on a huge slippery rock, amidst other innumerable fragments, over and against which the impatient water loudly dashes; having huge towering rocks, full of clefts, overrun with wood on each side; and in front, the small arch of the bridge just visible, through the thick shade of the wood and rock, at least one hundred feet above the eye. In such a situation it is almost impossible to preserve one's head from swimming. I attempted to sketch this scenery; but in the attempt I was several times obliged to shut my eyes, and take fast hold of the rock on which I sat, lest I should drop from it into the whirling foaming stream. From the Rumbling Brig the river flows gently down, for about half a mile; and after it escapes from its rough towering sides at the bridge, its banks shew nothing remarkable, till it runs to a narrow chasm formed in a very high rock, rising perpendicularly on each side of the Cauldrons to a considerable height, covered at the top with wood. The passage or gap in the rock may be forty feet in length; I only judged by my eye. The walk to the Cauldrons and Lin, on the south side, is very conveniently and judiciously made, by Mr. Charles Mercer. I came first on the top of the rock, where I looked down, and perceived the river enter the gloomy passage by a low cascade, and fall into one cauldron; from which it enters a second, whence it boils up most furiously, foaming and white. It then falls into a third cauldron, and from that, rushes through its narrow dark passage, till it reaches the end of the chasm, when it precipitates itself over a prodigious mass of rocks, I should imagine, at least two hundred feet high, and dashes perpendicularly down to a bed of huge fragments severed from the main rock. It is a very awful view to look down upon these cauldrons from the small ash-tree hanging over them. The depth of the perforation from which the foaming furious water returns, must be great, to cause such an extreme agitation. It is more a scene of solemnity, surprise, and astonishment, than that of beauty; but on descending to the foot of the Lin, the beautiful is there, in a considerable degree, mixed with the sublime. The huge masses of broken rock on each side of the fall are, here and there, ornamented with branches of trees sprouting from every crevice, and timidly bending their light boughs to the loud roaring and foaming water. The sky that gleams through the chasm, between the almost kissing black rocks which hang over the Cauldrons, is extremely curious; and the little ash-tree on the right trembles, as it were, with affright at its perilous station. The vigorous birch, small oak, and ash-trees, on the left, add much to the beauty of the whole. As soon as the Devon has fought its way through this curious and laborious pass, it becomes tranquil, and flows on in peace towards the Forth.

The road from the Crook of Devon to Stirling runs, at the southern base of the Orchill Hills, or, as they are commonly called, the Eckles. To the north of this range of hills, I was told, no coals are found, at least no coal-pits have ever been worked to the north of those mountains.

In entering the woeful town of Dollar, high amongst gloomy hills and dark firwoods, I perceived the ruin of Castle Campbell. It belongs to the Duke of Argyle. In its time it must have been a very strong hold; it stands upon a peninsula of a mountain, on two sides surrounded by a furious burn (brook); and on the others by deep hollows, between it and other still higher overhanging mountains. The walls of the castle are enormously thick, and the rooms within (by what remains of them), must have been dismal dungeons; but in the times when that castle was inhabited, men were more like wild beasts than human beings. The Grahams had a strong castle on the other side of the Orchills. Two lions, whose dens had only a ridge of hills for a barrier between them, could not be restrained from injurious encroachments on each other's territory. Accordingly when the

Campbells were away, the Grahams stormed and burnt; and, in return, Argyle laid waste and levelled to ruins the castle of Graham, near Auchterarder. There is a small remain of a curious subterraneous passage from the former inhabited part of Castle Campbell, cut in the rock down to the burn; from which the inhabitants of it could get water in safety, and unseen by their enemies from the heights of the surrounding mountains when they were beseiged. There are some pretty falls of the burn, but it is very difficult to get at them.

The old man who keeps the key of the ruin, in giving the history of the castle, added a piece of wit of a lady of the house of Campbell, in very remote times. This poor lady was confined in this solitary castle (her mind was somewhat deranged), and being asked one day what made her so melancholy. — "How can I be otherwise?" she replied; "being born in grief, christened in care, and lodged in the castle of gloom;" — alluding to the town of Dollar, where she was born; the burn of Care, and the hill of Gloom, that hangs over the approach to the Castle. Indeed it may well be called the Castle of Gloom to this day.

The drive from Dollar to Stirling is very pleasant, and the road tolerably good. The hills are chiefly verdant to the summits; and skirted with wood; birch, oak, and all sorts of natural growing forest trees; and there are large fine plantations besides, at Alva, and many other charming places nearer Stirling.

The view of Stirling, enter it which way you will, is fine; but those coming from Dollar, from Auchterarder, and Callender, are particularly so. The Castle is on a stupendous rock, like that at Edinburgh, inaccessible on every side but one, where the town rises to it. The surrounding mountains and crags, with the rich winding vales, through which the Forth meanders, altogether exhibit a view delightfully fine; and from the castle, in a clear day, is a prospect both towards the north-west, and south-east, that is far beyond description; taking in the rich extensive vales from the sources of the Forth, to the firth of it, beyond Edinburgh. The walk round the base of the rock on which Stirling Castle is built, is very fine; but the coach road between that rock and river, has something very terrifying in it. The width of the road is the only space between the shivered rock, and the broad winding river. To look up, huge fragments hang over the head suspended in a loose soil; appearing in such a state, as if the jolting of a carriage were sufficient to shake them from their very slender hold; and that they would come tumbling down, crushing to atoms, and whirling to the middle of the river, everything in their way! — To look at, it was the most frightful pass I had seen. But the pieces of rock must undoubtedly adhere much more firmly to the great mass than they seem to do, for I heard of no mischief ever being done by them; though sometimes pieces do fall, as numerous fragments lie

side of the river. — The whole drive from Doune to Callender, is in a pleasant fruitful valley, and the distant views from it are extremely wild and sublime. The fore-ground is the vale: the back-ground, the mountains of Ben Lomond, Ben Venue, and Ben Ledi. Ben Venue, is in the middle, and is rather lower than its left and right hand gigantic neighbours. All three, at a distance from them, appear to the eye of a similar conical shape.

Callender, and the town of Killmahog adjoining to it, lie close to the River Teith, which is there very rapid. The situation of these towns is extremely romantic; Ben Ledi being to the north of them, and prodigiously high crags rising directly behind them; these crags are entirely composed of small stones, cemented in a socket of clay, and so hardened, as to be as firm as solid rock; It is called the plum-pudding stone: the towns are entirely built of it. There is a very good bridge over the Teith at Callender, and one at Killmahog, over the branch of it that comes from Loch Lubnaig. I crossed the latter bridge to see the wonders of the Trossachs, around Loch Catherine. It was a gloomy morning; the waters roared, and the mountains looked black, particularly Ben Ledi, scowling over the pass of Lennie. After crossing the bridge, I for some way kept near Ben Ledi, to my right, and soon came in sight of Loch Van-a-choir (the lake of the fair valley).

It is thinly wooded, but fertile in corn, and bounded by high hills. It is said to be called the White, or Fair Valley, from the appearance of the corn; which, when ripe, and waving, gives a fair look to the vale, and is a fine contrast to the black craggy mountains that surround it. Before I got to the end of this valley there came on a very heavy rain, which made me despair of seeing (what I came out of my way a mile to see), the surrounding scenes of Loch Catherine, which, I had been informed, were more romantic than any other in Scotland. I was provided for any wet that I might find on the ground; but it was needless to proceed, when it fell in torrents from the clouds; therefore I had to be sheltered in a barn at a small farm near; trusting that at noon it would clear up. It did so; and I proceeded through a small cluster of huts, and mounted a very steep rough road, cut out of the mountain; and then went winding in labyrinths of crags intermixed with patches of verdure: bogs, rushes, and some wood, with pouring torrents from every quarter: the carriage often hanging over a precipice, and the wheels every moment up and down, over large pieces of rocks and stones, in chasms, torn by the rushing waters down the sides of the crags. Though it ceased to rain, all nature was weeping when I came to the foot of Glen Finlas, and to a river issuing thence; over which is a frail foot bridge of considerable breadth, made of birch wood intertwined, and covered with sod. As I entered the ford, the scene was solemn, gloomy and awful. — I was alone in the chaise: but I had confidence in my driver; therefore my mind was perfectly free from all sensations, but those produced by the extraordinary scenery around me. On the right a few scattered huts, and the river roaring from the deep glen, at that part darkened almost to night, by the high towering crags of the forest of Glenfinlas covered with wood. — The river, though loudly heard, was scarcely to be seen from the abundance of large trees; some tall and straight as the pine, others spreading wide and embracing each other from bank to bank, bending over the broken flood, which was furiously advancing to the green bridge. — To the left, Loch-a-chravy, closely surrounded by hills of every shape, with the river I was crossing flowing into it. In front of the heads of the horses, was a quick short turn from the ford to the road just the width of the chaise, cut close at the edge of the lake, on the left hand; and to the right, rocks rising perpendicularly, with branches of trees, and shrubs of all sizes and description, starting from every crevice of the craggy forest. The awfulness, the solemnity, and the sublimity, of the scene at the ford, and by Loch-a-chravy's side, towards the entrance to the foot of Loch Catherine, is beyond, far beyond description, either of pen or pencil! Nothing but the eye can convey to the mind such scenery: — well may it be called Loch-a-chravy, the lake of the field of devotion. When I quitted the narrow road under the rocks, by the side of Loch-a-chravy, it became amazingly jumbling and winding, amongst various shaped rocks and crags, covered with wood; and rent chasms, deep and dark on every side; no trace of man, or living thing to be seen; every sound reverberated from rock to rock, flying through the gloomy labyrinth, to announce the approach of unhallowed steps. My heart was raised to heaven in awful silence; whilst that of my poor man was depressed to the dread of hell. He was walking somewhat before the horses, who were step by step thumping the carriage over rocks; when he suddenly stoppt the chaise, and coming to me with a long face, said, "Madam, I believe the devil is in this place! do you hear that noise?" — All was echo; the whistle of a bird, the sound of the foot of an animal, the rustling of the wind amongst the trees, the gush of a torrent, or the fall of a pebble, resounded through the solemn pass, as through a ruined cloister. I listened: — it was a sonorous deep noise — dying away; and again regularly resuming the same key. I had no fears, and bid the men advance. But the road getting worse, and the pass narrowing, I got out of the carriage, thinking it more advisable to explore it on my own legs, than shut up in the chaise: I thus became the vanguard of my servants, as the fittest person to encounter the devils, should they have taken possession of the field of devotion.

When I caught the first glance of Loch Catherine, I was astonished, I was delighted! — a faint ray of sun was just then penetrating through the mist, still resting on the tops of the

surrounding mountains and crags, tinging the wood on their sides, and gleaming on the beautiful islands in the lake. The devils too, greatly added to the beauty of the fore-ground. They were in a large boat, throwing from it, upon the shore, logs of wood, which they had brought from the head of the lake. This was a very fortunate circumstance, as it enabled me to be rowed about the lake as much as I chose. It was a mere chance, but a lucky one for me, that a boat should then be at the end of the lake. Whilst the innocent devils were finishing their work, I walked up the road, cut out in steps on the crags, hanging over the lake to the north, to a high point, since called Mrs. Murray's hill, whence I saw the chief part of the Loch; which lies nearly from west to east. The view from that point to the foot of the lake, which is the east end, over the islands, and to the mountains on the south side of the lake, belonging to the Duke of Montrose, is beautiful; but part of it may truly be called sublime, where the lake runs off by a river that conveys the water of it through the awful pass to Loch-a-chravy. I was very sorry I could not see the shape of the Stuic-a-chroin, or the Peak of Rutting, on the south side of Loch Catherine; but it had on it an impenetrable cap of mist. At the south side of the Peak is Loch Chroin, and Choir-a-chroin, the valley of Rutting. From the high point I was upon, I perceived my boatmen had finished their task, and were rowing to take me up. I therefore descended to the edge of the lake, and, with some little scrambling, embarked. They rowed me to the Den of the Ghost, and under the solid rock which rises two hundred feet perpendicular above the level of the lake; also round the beautiful wooded island, and to the foot of the lake. While I was sketching a few of the enchanting beauties of that part of the Loch, I perceived the driver in a wicker sheelin (a kind of shepherd's hut), very busy. I was glad to see it, as a proof that he was not ready for our departure, and therefore would bear the length of time I was on the lake more patiently than he otherwise might have done. I afterwards learnt the real cause of the bustle in the sheelin: he cleaning his horses with the following accident. As soon as I had gratified myself with the first sight of Loch Catherine, I took my servant with me, and walked on, as I have mentioned, to the high point, there to wait for the boat. As soon as I had departed, the driver loosened the horses from the carriage, and, I suppose, began to gaze at the wonders of the Trosachs (the scenery around Loch Catherine being so-called), before he gave them their feed of corn: — what with the admiration of the harmless devils, and the astonishing scenery around him, he forgot his poor horses: they strayed, but not many yards before they were bogged, almost over their backs, and it was with great difficulty they could be extricated. Indeed, I believe it

I was astonished, I was delighted!

hurt them very much, for they soon after became extremely thin and weak. It was impossible to be more wet and dirty than I was; I therefore returned through the pass on foot, picking up singular stones, washed from the mountains, till I came to Loch-a-chravy. I should have been saved an alarm had I continued on foot, and repassed the river Finlas by the turf bridge. — In going into the river, in order to avoid the crumbling bank, the carriage took a somewhat greater sweep, and thereby got into a deeper part of the water, and I believe off the ford; and, to mend the matter, the wheel mounted on an unseen piece of slippery rock, which was within a trifle of tipping me over. But happily the wheel slipped off the stone, and the carriage recovered its equipose, without further harm than making our hearts jump, and a loud *oh!* from me. This might have proved a fatal circumstance, which roused me, for a moment, from my enthusiastic reverie at quitting the Field of Devotion.

It soon after began to rain, and all the scenes I had passed in the morning were obscured by mist and the approach of the night, for it was scarcely driving light when I reached Callender. On entering the inn, I found my rooms stripped of their carpets, to cover new-made or new-making hay ricks, in order to screen them from the rain.

The next day I took a little boy for my guide, and proceeded (by the road that leads from Callender, over the hills, to Comrie) to Brackland Brig. and the cascades there of the water Kelty, (or violent.) I was told it was not a mile to walk thither, but I found it at least two. The glen about the bridge is extremely narrow and deep; and, until I came within the noise of the cascades, I perceived nothing that indicated the romantic horror which had been described to me. But on descending a steep field, close to the top of the falls, I found them grand and beautiful; dashing in different directions, height, and breadths, till the water roars and foams through the deep chasm under the bridge, to the pool just below it, which is, at least, sixty feet beneath the bridge. The path to get at the bridge is about one foot and a half wide, upon the jutting sides of high towering rocks, from which sprout wood, from the depth below to the jagged tops above, in every direction, feathering down to, and hanging over, the rushing water. The only safeguard for the hardy being advancing to this awful Brig. are upright, broken, irregular pieces of rock, which form a winding natural parapet; and having the spray constantly falling upon them, are covered with moss; and fern, and all sorts of aquatic weeds cling to them. It requires some strength of head to creep round this path; the huge mass of rocks to the right is woody to the top; to the left is a precipice of perpend-icular jagged rocks, at the bottom of which the rushing cascades contend with each other which shall first dash through the

It struck me with astonishment and admiration!

chasm, sixty feet beneath the spectator. After passing this winding path, of a foot and a half wide, I came to the bridge, which struck me with astonishment and admiration. The rocky bank on the other side of the bridge, is on a level with the flat projecting part of the rock, on which the path to the bridge is worn. The chasm between the two rocks, over which the bridge is laid, cannot be wider than four or five yards. Before I ventured upon the bridge, I stood trembling to gaze and admire; for I could not help shuddering, though I was highly gratified with the whole scene. Before me lay a bridge made of birch poles, extending from rock to rock, over the deep chasm, and these poles have branches of birch laid thick across them, and turf covers the whole. On the opposite side is a beautiful rocky bank, covered with wood, intermixed with some verdure, coarse grass, rushes, fern, etc., with broken pieces of rock peeping through the stems of trees, weeds, and moss. The bridge appeared so light, and the depth below so terrific, that I was in some doubt whether I should venture to cross it. My little guide, however, stood upon it, whistling with the utmost unconcern. I followed him; but in truth I looked not on either side, for the bridge vibrated, and the waters roared beneath, so that I was glad to skip over as fast as I could. The bridge, to look at it, is a narrow, tottering green path, from rock to rock, not a bit of fence on either side, and about a yard wide.

In order to see this extraordinary bridge and the cascades in every possible point of view, I crept through the wood and broken rocks, until I got upon a huge projecting tower, in front of the chasm, where the pent up water rushes through the narrowest passage. In getting, however, to that point, I was obliged to step over several rents in the rocks, of at least a foot wide, the depth of them not to be seen; but the grand beauties of the cascades, and the deep glen below, seen from that station, made me full amends for my temerity in getting to it. The bridge, on my return, seemed not less tremendous than when I first crossed it; and I was glad to reach my first situation on the side of the rock, with a solid parapet before me.

The next day I admired the Pass of Lennie, through the Grampians, and the fine cascades of the Teith, running from Loch Lubnaig. This pass is as romantic as any through the Grampian mountains, and is particularly woody; which forms a striking contrast with the black sides of Ben Ledi, or Ben-le-Dia, the hill of God; which is 3009 feet perpendicular above the level of the sea. It is in form conical; and its appearance, through the pass of Lennie, is truly black and glossy. In some parts it is craggy, but mostly it is covered with coarse verdure and heath, where sheep, however, will feed. Innumerable springs are found all over the great mountains, which render them always wet and boggy. Somewhat short of the summit of Ben Ledi, is a small lake called Loch-an-nan-corp, the small lake of dead bodies; so named from the catastrophe that happened to the attendants of a funeral, from Glen Finlas to a kirk just to the north of the pass of Lennie. I suppose the corpse was a person of Consequence, as the chief part of the people of the glen attended the funeral, amounting to near two hundred. The lake was frozen and covered with snow; whether that circumstance deceived the procession, or that the ice on the lake was not sufficiently strong to bear the weight of so many people, is not known; but it is asserted, that the whole number sunk in the lake, and never were heard of more.

In approaching to Loch Lubnaig I saw, towering to its north east, Benvorlich, Mealfourwich, and Morben, on the south side of Loch Earn.

On the west side of Loch Lubnaig (the crooked or winding lake), about the middle, rises perpendicularly from the water, a stupendous rock, called Craig-na-coheilg, the rock of the joint hunting. The forest of Glen Finlas, formerly covered with the deer of the kings of Scotland, is in the neighbourhood of the rock of the joint hunting. On the east side of Loch Lubnaig is a house, called Ardhullary, nearly opposite to Craig-na-coheilg; in this house, and in this sequestered region, the Abyssinian Bruce (James Bruce 1730-1794) arranged his papers and finished his account of his *Travels to the source of the Nile.* He could have had no interuption in the desert of Hullany, where nothing is to be seen but high mountains on every side; a winding lake, with dashing rivers issuing from it, and entering into it; and the lofty Ben Ledi, occupying an immense space. From Loch Lubnaig to Loch Earn Head, is not more than seven miles. The inn, and that the only house at Loch Earn Head, commands a fine view of the lake nearly to the foot. On the south bank, and near the head, stands Eden Ample, a white castle looking building, surrounded by trees.

Loch Earn is beautifully surrounded by hills and crags, and at the foot of the lake the eye is charmed with a small island of a beautiful shape, covered with wood; and on the south side, with the high towering crags, the tops of Benvorlich, Mealfourwich, and Morben, where eagles breed. About two miles from the foot of the lake, by a road beautifully variegated with wood, mountains, and the winding Earn river, I came to the most singular spot, I believe, in the world; singular to a degree, by nature, and made beautiful by a little assistance from art. The old name was Movey, (which, I was told, signifies the mouth of hell); now it is called Deneira, and is in the possession of the minister, Mr. Dundas (now Viscount Melville), in whose hands it has been only about fourteen years. The house he built; it is modern, and extremely comfortable; it is whitened over, and erected on a very small plain, in the shape of a large round table, encircled by mountains and masses of rocks, jumbled together in a very picturesque manner; they are of all forms and dimensions, and mostly covered with wood. The round space on which the house stands is perfectly level, and is a grass-plat of rye and clover, neatly kept. The road to and from this insulated habitation, sweeps round the fairy lawn to the right and left, and is quickly lost to the sight, entering into labyrinths of rocks leading to the high road. A shallow burn bounds the lawn to the west, issuing from a very steep, thick wooded, narrow glen; and this burn, at about a mile above the house, rushes through branches of trees, over broken rocks of considerable height, forming a very picturesque fall. The rustic bridge, and the walks to and from this fall, are very judiciously executed. With some fatigue I continued the walk, from the fall of the burn to the top of the mountain, whence I had a view of the lake, and the majestic mountains surrounding it. It was like coming up out of one world, to peep down into another on the contrary side of the mountain. The way back to the green round table is winding, steep and rocky; most of the rocks, when I was there, were covered with heath in full bloom, beautiful and fragrant: others shaded by vast plantations that have flourished amazingly, forming a delightful shade; and through the branches of the trees are heard, unseen, the murmurs of the falling rills. To see all the beauties of Deneira, requires far more time than I had to spare; I did, however, see sufficient to make a very long lasting impression on my mind, particularly of its singular situation. Indeed the whole of that part of Strath Earn, from Drummond Castle to Loch Earn Head, for rich picturesque and sublime scenery, is equal to any other in Scotland. On leaving Deneira, I crossed the Earn to the south side of the river, where the Strath rather widens, and came to Dalchonzie, pronounced Dalwhonie, and Abernhill, both beautifully situated amidst towering and craggy mountains. At Comrie I again crossed the Earn, where I joined a scene of mirth and gaiety, it being the fair. The young lasses were decked out for the show, but their head-dresses struck me as very unbecoming. Their hair was snooded up; that is, bound up with a snood, or band of three-penny breadth ribbon, tied plain round the fore part of the head, leaving the long hair loose and flowing behind; which, in most parts of the Highlands, where it is simply snooded up, is very pretty for young girls; but at Comrie, they added a great bunch of a cushion, in the shape of a potatoe, put low on the forehead, and the front hair turned plain over it, which gave the appearance of a smooth, shining solid lump of hair, stuck on close over the eyebrows. The small town of Comrie is finely situated, and beautifully romantic: for some years past it has been visited with very frequent shocks of earthquakes which at first greatly frightened the people of Comrie, and the surrounding inhabitants, but when I was there, they were so accustomed to the shocks, and had so far lost all dread of them, that they were actually going to build a town on the convulsed spot, which will probably, one day or other, open or form a lake; as the noise under ground is like the gushing of water, making a fresh passage through rocks. The shock has at times been sufficiently strong to displace shovel, tongs, and poker from a fire-place in a room, at Ochtertyre, five miles from Comrie.

Through the whole of this district the houses of the lower class of the people are remarkably neat; and I was pleased to see potatoe stems in bloom on every bit of waste bank. To do justice to the beauties of Ochtertyre, (two miles from Crieff,) requires a far abler pen than mine: — but thus far I can say, the approach to it is lovely; and by the variety of ground, woods, lake, and western boundary of the sublime and picturesque hills around Loch Earn, it is rendered one of the most enchanting spots in Britain. In the woods are two falls of the water of Turret, from Loch Turret. The first and the highest fall is rendered the most beautiful by the scenery about it, which is strikingly picturesque; in short, every thing, both within and without the elegant and hospitable mansion of Ochtertyre, fixes the heart and eye; for the family which that excellent house contains is as superiorly amiable, as its surrounding scenes are beautiful.

CHAPTER FIVE

The town of Crieff, one of the barrier Highland towns, is sweetly situated, just as it were without the jaws of the Highlands; I say jaws, for I observed that in most grand passes there are castle-like hills placed at the entrance, as sturdy guards, to chop off and obstruct the way of obtruders. Those that guard the pass towards Loch Earn, near Crieff, are particularly beautiful, and have been covered with wood; and formerly, in all probability, strong forts, of powerful chiefs, were built thereon, as their Gaelic name denotes. To the south-east of Crieff, on a pretty eminence, the white walls of Drummond Castle rise; it is about two miles from Crieff; and the way to it is by a part of the old Roman road to Stirling, which is a straight line with trees on each side. The approach to Drummond Castle is on the right hand, by a modern lodge, not very suitable to the rest of the place; and then through a most beautiful avenue of fine old trees. Immediately below the house is a bridge, to break the steep ascent to it; from the bridge, the road, canopied by trees, winds round a sloping pleasure-ground to the castle, of which indeed there is but a very small part remaining. The modern habitation is two sides of a square; and the side in which are the best apartments, faces that part of Strath Earn running towards the east; from those rooms is an extensive view, but not half so fine as that to the west, over Crieff, and those beautiful hills that seem to guard the pass, towards the lake, and the stupendous mountains around it, which gave sublimity, magnificence, and beauty to the whole scene. Close by Drummond Castle is a crag, on which Mrs. Drummond, (now Lady Perth,) has erected a fog, or moss-house, commanding a delightful view of the country. Beyond the fog-house crag, Top Turlock raises its brown, though not ill-shaped, high crest.

By Glen Almond is another grand pass through the Grampians. I set out from Ochtertyre to visit that wild region. The view from the road going up the hill over Ochtertyre to the mountains, about Loch Earn, is worth travelling several miles to see. After that view, there was little but distant hills and heath to be seen, till I came to the entrance into Glen Almond. The deep channel of the river I saw winding away to the east, towards Perth; and before me a zig-zag road, creeping down the sides of tremendous hills, leading to a deep narrow glen, so hemmed in by vast mountains, that at first sight a stranger sees no way to escape out of it. The entrance into Glen Almond from Crieff has something uncommonly striking in it; — prodigious craggy mountains rising to the clouds bending their rough head to each other over the Glen through which the water rolls, in a stony bed, murmuring as it flows. In some parts, the craggy precipices sweep to the edge of the river; in others, small patches of velvet-looking verdure smile at the crags, careless of their frowns, and heedless too of the deep murmurs of the stream which gave them birth. I entered this silent solemn pass (where no trace of human habitation is seen, no sound heard, save that of the bleating sheep, and the rushing of the water) with awful pleasure, and wild as the scene appeared, I was delighted with it. The river Almond in floods, and on sudden thaws, is a prodigiously furious water; it rises rapidly to an incredible height, and roars down with such violence that it carries every thing before it with a noise like thunder. It was not in that state when I saw it; but was as clear as chrystal, complaining only of the broken rocks which impeded its course, and formed cascades, the sound of which was echoed by the mountains. The small patches of verdure by the river's side were remarkably beautiful, from the colour and the fine soft texture of the grass, contrasted with the rough sides of the shivered stony mountains. The Glen as far as Newton, two miles, is in width about half an acre. The road, the river, at the edge of which the road runs, and the patches of verdure, fill up the space. It struck me in going down into this Glen, that it probably once might have been a subterraneous cavern, like that now at Castleton, in Derbyshire; and that by some great convulsion it had been torn asunder at the top, and thrown back on each side. The same idea occurred when I saw Dovedale, in Derbyshire.

At Newton, the road to Amulrie leaves Glen Almond, and proceeds to Strath Brand. While my horses were resting at the huts, I walked up about two miles in Glen Almond, and every step opened a new beauty to my sight. The Glen increases in width, and is tolerably well wooded, particularly on the banks of the river; the fields producing grass, barley and oats. On the north side of the river, from the top of a very high mountain, falls a torrent, which in violent rains must be magnificent. It had been many days fine weather when I saw this torrent, notwithstanding it was then grand. I sat down to rest at the entrance of the fall into the Almond, among huge pieces of rocks brought down by its force, admiring the scene with delight; surrounded by birch, alder, mountain ash, with other trees; fern, and all sorts of large aquatic plants and weeds; the torrent tumbling from above, and dashing beneath against the huge stones, on one of which I sat. Such scenes as these raise the soul to the first Cause of all things; and there it is lost to all sensations, but those of gratitude and calm delight. As I sat among the stones, viewing the torrent, Mr. Knight's poem called the Landscape, came into my mind; and I was glad to find in the scene before me, no trace, no slime of the modern *shavers* of dame Nature; the sweet simple goddess there reigned triumphant, and feared neither their trimming razors, nor their sluggish serpentines.

I left Glen Almond with regret; ascended the same zig-zag by which I entered it, and proceeded, through another road, by the course of the Almond, to the Brig of Buchanty; a very singular and romantic spot. The country all around this bridge is an extensive waste of black and brown; but on a sudden the eye is unexpectedly caught by the sight of a mill, and the river running in a very narrow channel to the bridge, with trees hanging over it, and wood feathering down to the water over huge rocks, on which the bridge rests; also the roaring water, bursting through its dark and close passage, to fall with a loud noise under the arch, altogether rendering this spot beautifully picturesque.

I was going on to make a visit at Logie Almond; which within itself, abounds in wood, and the house is situated on the bank of the Almond, very romantically; but of all the spots, for its size, none can compete to the sweet Eden, of Leadnock.

The old Scotch ballad, of Bessy Bell and Mary Gray, gives the history of two affectionate faithful friends; how

"They bigg'd a bower on yon burn brae,

"And theek'd it o'er with rashes," etc.,

And it is the burn that moans through the thickets at Leadnock, by which these friends chose to build their bower, and there to retire to avoid the plague. Their lover followed them; but they did not escape the fatal disease, for all three fell victims to its rage.

About thirty years since, the small estate of Leadnock was purchased by Major Barry, who found it in the rudest state of nature. Like our first parent, he pruned and planted; and with his faithful Eve, morning and evening, saw that it was good;

and for it rejoiced, and were thankful to Him who gives and takes away. Every thing flourished under the fostering hands of this worthy pair.

The woods, the walks, the verdant banks, the blooming rose, and twining woodbine, all proclaimed their taste and industry; not a spot in their Paradise but what was noticed and named emblematically. The house and garden situated on a small plain, are embowered with trees of my friend's planting. In front of the house is a lawn, of an unusual semicircle, at the edge of which is an almost perpendicular rough rocky bank, where deep below rolls the Almond river, more picturesque than can be described, over a wide rocky bed, dashing through its winding way, darkened by high projecting rocks on both sides of it, with wood sprouting from every cliff, and feathering to the roaring stream. On the Leadnock side, upon the lawn, on the rocks, down the rocks, and on every side, are fine trees of every description; particularly those to the left (in appearance impenetrable) towards the old Brig of Almond. To the right is a winding walk to the edge of the rocks hanging over the river; and at the top of a very steep path a stone seat is placed, on which is cut, "rest and be thankful."

The owner and creator of Leadnock was in Lord Ancram's regiment, the 24th, when in the year 1746 that regiment made the road through Glen Croe, in Argyleshire; and put up the stone on the top of the high hill between Glen Croe and Glen Kinglass, called "Rest and be thankful." The Almond, with high rocky banks on one side of it, and flat to a lovely meadow on the other, sweeps round the better half of it; and on the other parts of this pastoral lawn, rising from it, are the thick woods of Leadnock, and the high banks of the Logie Almond, covered with impenetrable underwood, and backed by noble timber trees; with the burn of the fair friends, marking the division of property, moaning in its course down the brae over pieces of rock, and through tufted branches, stumps of trees, and bushes, to join the Almond below. In this Arcadian meadow, under the hanging wood of Leadnock, I came to a bit of ground, walled in, and on a stone in the wall I read this simple inscription, "The tomb of Bessy Bell and Mary Gray." I plainly saw the marks of two graves, by the rising of the sod: the third, that of the lover, said to be at their feet, I could not find. These walls were raised, and within and without planted with all sorts of odoriferous shrubs and flowers, by the Officer, above mentioned, who discovered the graves, unveiled the natural beauties of Leadnock, and brought them to perfection.

The carriage road to Leadnock from Logie Almond is a great way about; and the walks through the woods that were once made and kept open for the convenience of the families of Leadnock and Logie, are now entirely obliterated and choked by thick wood, briers, springs, and every obstacle that rude nature

has combined to destroy them. I was determined, however, to see that admired place. I set out alone, and contrived to lose my way; and into the bargain, got my flesh and my clothing tattered and torn; but I was resolved to accomplish my purpose; I therefore pierced thick wood, climbed stone walls, clambered over ploughed clods knee deep, waded the burn, and at last succeeded. I was hospitably regaled with some nice mutton and potatoes at Leadnock house; a very acceptable refreshment after my laborious, lonely, blundering walk. The good man and his wife belonging to Mr. Graham, attentively shewed me all that could be seen, and then set me in the right road to Logie.

CHAPTER SIX

Perth is a very ancient town; but within these few years it has been increased to a great degree, so that it may be called a new town. Its bridge over the Tay, and its two Inches, ornament it greatly. The Inches are large flat grass fields, one at the south entrance of Perth, the other at the north; and the roads and walks in them are through avenues of trees. There is a view of the town of Perth coming from the south, where the Romans halted to admire, and cried out with one voice, "Ecce Tiberim!" I think they paid a very bad compliment to the Tay, as there can be no comparison between it and the sluggish Tiber. Nothing can be finer than the two views after passing north of the range of mountains called the Oichill hills. The first of these views is the richest part of Strath Earn, and the junction of the River Earn with the Tay; taking in the Brig of Earn, the wooden hill of Moncrief, and the noble plantations of Dupplin, Lord Kinnoull's, for its northern boundary. After climbing the hill of Moncrief, and two miles north of the Brig of Earn, then comes the charming prospect that delighted the marching Romans; and which, on taking a short turn round a hill, at once opens to the sight. To the right hand is the broad sweeping Tay, coming from the north, and winding round the base of the Kinnoull Crags, flowing majestically to the east, and towards the rich Carse of Gowrie and Dundee. In front, is the town of Perth, its noble bridge, the South Inch, the spires; and other edifices in the town; the waving corn, in part of the fertile district of Strathmore, with the grand chain of Grampian mountains, in the back-ground; all conspiring to make this a prodigiously striking view. One of the days I passed by this beautiful spot was a Monday, the day after the sacrament; I perceived a multitude not far from the road's side, with a wooden stand raised in the midst of the throng; some of the congregation were standing; others sitting, forming altogether an amazing concourse of men, women, and children. It was a field-preaching day. It is impossible for *all* to *hear* the sermon: - but, good souls, if they are only within the holy *sough* (or sound), that perfectly satisfies them. As often as the sacrament is administered, there is preaching all day on the Thursday preceding, as well as on the Sunday and the Monday after, attended by hundreds flocking from every quarter, and from a very great distance. In the small towns, as well as in the large ones, this practice too is kept up; and on the sacrament Sunday, one minister is preaching in the church, and another in the adjacent field; the congregation continually going from one to another. In Scotland, in general, the proprietors of the land in each parish pay the stipend of the minister, build the kirk, and the manse (the parsonage), and keep them in repair; they also pay the stipend of the master, or masters, of the schools in a parish; one English, the other Gaelic. At these schools the children of the poor are taught to read and write, for one shilling a quarter. At Gask, nine miles from Perth, I saw more than forty boys and girls in one school.

The fashion of large farms, instead of small ones, has unhappily of late years made its way into Scotland, as well as England, to the great detriment of both countries. The rich farmer goes to the landlord, when the small farmer's lease is nearly expired, and says, "I should be glad to add such a farm to the one, or more, that I have; I can afford to give you more rent for it than such an one can; and besides my opulence will secure you your rent, without delay, danger, or drawback." This tempts the proprietor, and thus farms accumulate: and in every respect, the inconveniences resulting from it, are equal in Scotland to those in England. No poultry, no pork, etc., are raised, as formerly, for market; all is consumed in the great farmer's own family, which increases the price of those articles prodigiously, besides many others. The late worthy possessor of Gask, would on no account destroy the small farms on his estate. Many of his tenants rented at the rate of three or four pounds a year. He never turned a widow off his estate; and if she could not keep on the farm her husband held, some cot or other, with a small piece of ground, was given her. His worthy son, the present Gask, continues the same benevolent plan his father long practised; and in 1796, when he brought home his new married lady, he gave a dinner to his tenants, consisting of more than three hundred.

The ground around Perth, I was told lets from two to three, and five pounds a Scotch acre, which is about one fourth more than an English acre. Butter is about ten-pence a pound, twenty-two ounces. Not only butter, but eggs, and poultry of all sorts, are greatly increased in price since the small farms have decreased in number.

As no coal pits have been worked north of the Eckles, or Oichill Hills, that necessary article is brought by water to Perth; the Tay being navigable for considerable vessels as high as that town; and as many, if not more, of the Newcastle coals are burnt there, than of Scotch coals; because they are procured full as cheap, if not more so, than the coals from Fife and Stirlingshire.

The labourer, at Perth, gets commonly fifteen-pence a day; in harvest, sixteen-pence, with meat and drink.

Mason's wages, twenty-pence a day; their labourer's fourteen-pence.

In the year 1796, I was pleased to find potatoes were so cheap in Scotland. At Campbelton, in Cantire, they sold forty-four pounds for six-pence; and at Crieff, when cheapest, 360 pounds for four shillings.

In the street called the Water-gate in Perth, part of the old Castle of Gowrie is still remaining; some military men were quartered in it when I was there; notwithstanding, there are very fine barracks erected at the west end of the town. In the Castle of Gowrie, James the Sixth of Scotland (afterwards the first of England) was confined by the earl and his brother, but saved from instant death by one of Gowrie's servants, and afterwards rescued by the courage of a very few friends who had come to Perth with him, and regained his palace at Fifeshire.

Near Perth are a great number of extensive fine bleaching grounds, the chief manufacturers there being cottons. Great quantities of men's shoes and boots are also made at Perth, and sent to London market.

From Perth I crossed the Tay, and proceeded to the new bridge of Isla, then scarcely finished; it is very near the junction of the river Isla with the Tay. The old ruin of the Castle of Kinclaven is on the edge of the west bank of the Tay, just below the junction of the two rivers. From off the walls of that ruin, I had in July 1785, some of the finest apricots I ever eat in my life. The ferry of Kinclaven, immediately at the junction of the rivers, before the bridge of Isla was built, was the only means of getting to Mieklour, without going round by Coupar in Angus, and Blair Gowrie.

The palace of Scone, where the Kings of Scotland were wont to be crowned, was the first place of note I passed after leaving Perth. About seven miles from Perth, on the west side of Tay, is Stanley; where are large cotton works, which have injured the beauty of the place, but have made it more profitable to the owner. A mile above Stanley, on the same side of the river, is Taymount, once a lovely spot, and the habitation of superlative virtue, (though a thatched dwelling,) hanging over the noble Lin of Campsie, a very fine fall of the Tay. Under this humble roof lived, with his excellent mother, my late husband, the Honourable William Murray, third son of William Earl of Dunmore. At his death it returned to his brother; and is become a neglected, wretched, shaven farm.

Somewhat above Taymount, on the opposite bank of the Tay, the ancient walls of Stubhall rise, belonging to Lord Perth.

— The house is in the very old style of building, but the situation of it is very romantic and beautiful.

From Stubhall I proceeded to Mieklour-house; it is more like a beautiful English place than any I saw in Scotland. The Tay is there full and deep, and glides on as tamely as any English river.

The woods are extensive; and the hills within sight are not very high. From the front of the mansion is seen, at a distance, Dunsinane Hill (rising from Strathmore), at the top of which Macbeth had a castle; and at the base of it is Dunsinane-house, surrounded by wood; though, I believe, Birnam Wood never took root there. From Mieklour-house, I perceived a large gap in Dunsinane Hill; and the legend tells, that in his flight, Macduff leaped it; and the prints of his horse's feet, on the rock, are still to be seen.

By the assistance of the most excellent inhabitant of Meiklour -house, Mrs. Mercer of Aldie, I was enabled to see Loch Clunie, which is only a small lake; but its banks, and its surrounding mountains of Stormount (in fact, part of the Grampians) render Loch Clunie a place worth seeing. In it is an island, covered with wood; out of which rises a large old castle-like building, belonging to Lord Aryly. On this island was born the *admirable* Crichton; but not a trace of his family is left. Between Loch Clunie and Blair Gowrie, is Marlie, near a small lake, lying low; so does Ard Blair.

Blair Gowrie is a small town upon the west precipitate bank of the river Airdle, and lies at the beginning of another wild pass through the Grampions, by Glen Shee and Glen Beg, to Braemar. A mile from Blair Gowrie, at Lerinty Burn, begins a zig-zag road, to climb, a lofty hill; and again it zig-zags round precipices, down to the Cally Bridge; from thence the traveller scarcely ever loses sight of some fine water or other, till through many a glen he reaches the Castle of Braemar, and Invercauld, on the banks of the Dee.

At Blair Gowrie, I found the river Airdle was called Airoch. About a quarter of a mile above the bridge, which is at the bottom of the town, is a very picturesque salmon leap, called the Keith of Blair Gowrie. The great stones in the river, at the Keith, I believe, are plum pudding stone, the pebbles of which seemed fine, but they were so tight in their sockets, that I could not by any effort in my power procure one of them. The plants, all about the Keith, appeared in the highest luxuriant vigour; but being ignorant of botany, I in that instance lost much pleasure. A few miles above the Keith, on the brink of the same river, is a very singular, sequestered, romantic spot. The house is situated on the edge of a promontory of a huge solid rock, hanging over the river, quite out of the perpendicular line. The rocks touching the river on each side of it, from the chasms and other irregularities in them, occasion the water to dash furiously round them. All the rocks are covered with trees of every sort; some straight as pines, others feathering and branching from the top to the bottom; and the opposite bank is a counterpart of that on which Craig Hall is built. The rock, and the wall of the house, seem a piece; and the eye, from the windows, sees nothing but the precipice, that would turn the head giddy were it not for the stems and branches of trees sprouting from every chink of the jagged rocks. There is a zig-zag path, however, cut by the side of the house, with much art and labour, down the rocks to the margin of the rolling river: this path leads to a scene of rock, wood, and water, not to be described. — I fancied myself at the end of the world, and at the gate of Paradise! This old secluded habitation belongs to the ancient house of Rattry; which, in the iron age of Scotland, possessed a great extent of territory in that part of Perthshire.

From Mieklour we one morning set out to visit the fine fall of Isla, called the Reeky Lin. We passed through Blair Gowrie, the small town of Rattry, and proceeded to Ailyth, amongst the wildest of the Stormount hills. Torrents of rain fell during our drive thither, so that the burn, which comes from the forest of Ailyth, and runs through the town, was rushing down its precipitated bed with the utmost violence, joined by the many streams from every quarter. The town of Ailyth lies upon the declivity of a steep hill; and the streets are so narrow, and sloping, and were rendered so slippery with the wet, that I thought it impossible for the horses to draw the chaise up. After leaving the town of Ailyth, the road became worse and worse; in some parts very steep, with loose ground; in others, boggy, narrow, and rough, beyond belief. At length, however, we arrived on the banks of the Isla, very near the fall. A *gude* wife was our guide, who first conducted us to the top of the great cataract, and then to the bottom of it, down a long, dangerous, and slippery bank; afterwards from one huge stone to another, till we arrived at the pool into which the river falls. Imagine yourself upon vast masses of slippery rock, severed from the mountain, damming up, in some degree, the great body of water in front, precipitating itself from an immense height over jagged heaps of rock upon rock, in every possible form, with a violence that sends out its spray to a very great distance; and falling into a pool, of which no one knows the depth; and then on the right, dashing against towers of rocks, rising majestically to the sky, with sprigs of mountain ash, birch, and oak, thinly and carelessly scattered over them. To the left, is a carved recess of rocks equally high with the opposite towers; in which, either by clefts, or ravages made by the force of the dashing water, caves in numbers, deep and black, appear, to affright the timorous, or the guilty wight. To attempt to get at these caves is almost certain destruction; but what dares he not do, whom guilt has rendered desperate? The legend of the place (and almost every place of curiosity, either in Scotland, or elsewhere, has its legend), says, that an owner, in former times, of Craig upon Isla, having killed a man, fled to the Reeky Lin, and hid himself in one of the caves above described; but conscience would not let him rest there, though he was sure man could not disturb him. He declared, that in the dead of night he saw the de'il in the shape of a black dog, run up the towers of rock just facing the caves; which so terrified him that he quitted his hiding place, preferring the just punishment of his crime, by the hands of man, to the nightly horrors of the devil in the shape of a black dog!

We quitted the charming fall of Isla with much reluctance, to change our wet clothes, and to take the very acceptable repast provided for us by our kind friend at Mieklour, which we eat in the chaise; — nought to be seen or heard except the thundering noise of the Lin, and the wide waste around us of barren russet mountains, with many boggy glens between them; and two solitary huts made of turf; which altogether rendered the scene uncommonly wild. But that could not allay our appetites: which, when we had satisfied, we returned by a road less dangerous but equally rough; happy to re-enter the hospitable walls of Mieklour-house, after a long and fatiguing dripping day.

Part Two

CHAPTER ONE

On the 30th day of July, 1796, with the utmost regret I left
Mieklour, loaded with kindness in every shape; and not an article of convenience or comfort for the long journey before me
was forgotten by the friendly lady of the house, and her amiable
daughters. My chaise was crammed with provisions, wine, and
other things for my use; and, what was more grateful to my
heart, their warm affection and good wishes were with me; so
that when I departed from their hospitable door, I felt what I
cannot express.

As from Mieklour to Dunkeld I was on the north side of the
Tay, I did not go any part of the new road from Perth to Dunkeld, but passed by Delvin, imbowered in wood, on its flat
peninsula. I saw also, on the opposite side of the Tay, Marthly's
ancient walls, and its rich meadows to the edge of the river, and
the rising hill on which Birnam Wood once grew. As I advanced
to Stenton, a piece of beautiful crag, covered with wood,
pleased me much; and the situation of Dungarthill is picturesque. But the view from the high ground before the descent
into Dunkeld is fine beyond description; the cathedral, the
town, and the Duke of Atholl's house, with prodigious surrounding woods; the Tay issuing from avenues of large trees,
from which sweep, to the right, beautiful sloping grass fields
and walks, backed by the noble rough sides of the Craggy
barnes, covered with wood, except now and then where huge
masses of rock bid defiance to the planter's labour, and rear
their bare heads majestically. The left side of the landscape is
occupied by the woods at Inver, the dashing Brand, and the
charming scenes at the Hermitage. As the beauties of Dunkeld
have been so often immortalized by pens far abler than mine, I
shall say little of them: at the same time I cannot omit expressing the pleasure I experienced from everything I there met with.
Every step from the house to the Hermitage is beautiful. After
crossing the Tay ferry, where the banks of that smooth river are
charming, winding, and finely wooded, I entered a shrubbery
that soon led to the river Brand, dashing through a rough bed of
large stones. Opposite the shrubbery are high rocks, covered
with wood, and picturesque to a great degree. As I advanced I
came to lofty projecting rocks on each side of the river, striving,
as it were, to kiss each other; they are united by a simple bridge
of one arch, through which, deep below, by a very confined
rocky channel, the water forces itself; scarcely recovered from

its foaming rage at the falls just above, which is partially seen through the high arch. On entering the Hermitage I was astonished. The contrast between the room, the beautiful cataract, and its scenery, is beyond description striking! — The mirrors in the room, so far from being absurd (as some Tourists say,) multiply every object they reflect, and thereby increase the delight. A large bow window, down to the floor of the room, faces the fall, and indeed hangs over part of it; so that the reeking spray dashes in with violence, if the sashes be open. The noise of the cascade is excessive, and the view of the river above it is charming; rendered so by the great variety of small falls, wood, and projecting rocks.

I much wish to have continued my walk by the Brand side till I came to the Rumbling Brig; and such a walk would be delightful. If the Duke of Atholl should extend his walks beyond their present limits, and carry them on by the river side, up to that romantic part of it over which the Rumbling Brig is thrown, it would be a great improvement: but as this is not yet the case, I went in the carriage to the brig; which should be seen, for it cannot be described with justice, nor in language to be understood.

The view at the junction of the Tumel river with the Tay is very fine; indeed, the whole of the drive, from Dunkeld to Blair Atholl, is beyond description; and it may be termed one of the grandest, as well as the most beautiful of all the passes through the Grampian mountains. In some places of this delightful drive the opening is very narrow, particularly north of the Moulin Hows. The Tumel river is far more violent than the Tay, which smoothly glides the chief part of its course. The Tumel begins to roar very soon after its egress from Loch Rannoch, falling finely and furiously between neighbouring crags of Schihallion, and then running towards Glen Tumel, and a lake of that name; it afterwards pursues its course, and again falls at Fascalie: these two falls of Tumel are not so high as many others in Scotland; but the body of water at them is far greater; for this river comes from a district full of mountains, from whose sides flow never-ceasing torrents.

From the ferry at Logierait, towards Blair, the passage narrows, and nothing is to be seen but the road, the craggy mountains on each side, covered with wood, and the fierce Tumel below, growling through its rough bed, concealed by rocks, and trees of mountain ash, birch, alder, oak and pine, growing among them.

Henry Butter, Esq., is the happy man who now owns Fascalie; and to the civility of his family I am indebted for a complete sight of its beauties. The house lies far below the road, just at the south entrance of the pass of Killycrankie, in a sort of triangular flat space of meadow land, beautifully wooded by very fine

Beyond description striking!

large trees, which also ornament the fields adjoining, and cover the banks of the rivers which there unite; and plantations climb up every crag, which on all sides surround Fascalie. On the easternside at Fascalie, is the road to Blair, with stupendous mountains on the right. At the western angle issues the Tumel from its furious fall, and meets the river Garrie, which rolls precipitately (and in times of rain), foaming and roaring through its deep rough bed at the pass of Killycrankie; but just before its union it throws off all its angry forms and gloomy aspect, and softly mixes with the boisterous Tumel, dressed and ornamented by the genuine hand of nature; thus united, the stream gently winds round the southern side of Fascalie, and then is lost to sight among thick woods and craggy mountains.

The road through the pass of Killycrankie was made by the military; I believe in Wade's time. The old road was tremendous; but now that it is taken higher up the mountain, it has lost all its horrors, and retains its beauties, with additions, from a very great increase of plantations by Mr. Butter. About half a mile above Fascalie is a bridge of one arch, over the deep bed of the Garrie, and a bridle road to Rannock, through Glen Tumel. The bridge is rendered picturesque to a great degree by the scenery near it. At the emersion from the pass of Killycrankie, the view opens finely to the plain of Atholl; in the midst of which stands Atholl-house, very conspicuous, by being white; and at a farther distance is a sham castle, backed by thick woods, and the craggy mountains of the forest of Atholl. Three miles short of Blair I perceived a very large field to the right, and an upright stone standing therein, like one of the smallest at Stone Henge in Wiltshire; I found it was the tombstone of Lord Dundee, who fell in the battle of Killycrankie, by a shot from the house upon the high ground above the field. The action at Killycrankie was the last of any consequence at the Revolution in James the Second's time.

The charms of Blair, and its adjacent country, are better known than most places in Scotland; notwithstanding I must particularize Glen Tilt, and Glen Bruar, in which his Grace the Duke of Atholl has lodges. The one in Glen Tilt is situated in the narrow part of the glen, close by the side of the river; to the east of it rises, almost perpendicularly, a part of Benygloe, green as far as the eye can see; on the west, stupendous stony mountains, fragments of which are strewed over the glen, with innumerable springs issuing at every ten yards. About a quarter of a mile above the lodge is a small simple bridge, of one arch, over the Tilt, and a fall of river under it, very pretty indeed. I was informed, that towards the head of the Glen the scenes become still more romantic, wild and sublime, with a number of falls of water, particularly one of the Tarf Water running to the Tilt. The head of the Glen Tilt is but an inconsiderable distance from the head of the river Dee, which rises in the

great mountains that close up the head of Glen Tilt. I was told there would, some time or other, be a very good road from Blair, by Lude, across the hills to Glen Shee and Glen Beg, which lead to Castletown in Braemar.

The drive from Atholl-house to the Forest Lodge is beautiful; the Tilt is for ever noisy throughout its rough course; its banks are highly ornamented with trees, broken precipices, and furrows in the mountains, pouring down their ample tribute to the rapid Tilt.

I was regaled at the Forest Lodge with what that district is famous for, namely, Atholl Broze, made of Whisky, eggs, and honey. To a lover of whisky it is a delicious treat, and much prized by the people of Atholl, having good reason, I suppose, for doing so. One instance of its efficacy I will mention: the daughter of an inhabitant of Atholl, having been placed at one of the first boarding schools in Edinburgh, was seized with a violent fever; her father was sent for, as she was thought in great danger; and upon his arrival, being told his child was at the point of death, and that every thing the physicians could do for her had been done, without effect; he earnestly exclaimed, "but has she had any Atholl broze?" "No." He then had a good doze of it instantly prepared, and making her swallow it, she soon recovered.

I only saw a very small part of Glen Bruar, namely, its fall of water out of the Glen, which is reckoned very fine; and though the sides are very bare, it certainly is so. The great number and variety of smaller falls, extending all the way down from the high fall to the houses in the town of Bruar, are very pretty; and one in particular is extremely curious, the water having perforated the rock, and made itself an arch, through which it tumbles in a very picturesque style. I first went on the east side of the water, in a small carriage, to see the high fall; but the lesser falls are to be seen on the west side; and a fine scrambling walk it is, over fragments of rocks, stone dykes, (walls,) and ground full of springs, but the beauty of the scene repays the fatigue of following it up to the summit of the high fall. Since I saw the falls of Bruar, the Duke of Atholl has had an arch thrown over the high fall from rock to rock, and the banks planted: these plantations, when grown up, will render the falls completely beautiful.

I got out of the carriage somewhat to the west of the town of Bruar (in the Highlands every thing is a town, if it consists only of a cluster of huts), and walked to the bridge leading to the kirk town of Strowan. The small falls of the Garrie, at that bridge and above it, are very pretty; and there are two below it, fine, with high rocky banks, covered with wood; and they are beautiful to look at on both sides of the river. I believe they are salmon leaps, and it is astonishing to what height that fish will leap, and what an amazing body of water they are able to resist. I saw one at Fascalie; but unfortunately it did not succeed, and fell back into the pond. When I was at Fascalie, at the fall there was a great bag, made of net-work, fastened to a roundish hoop of iron, and hung like the pockets at the corners of billiard tables, from a long pole; this bag is usually either fastened horizontally upon some rock, or held by a fisherman just under the fall, to catch the fish, if they do not succeed in their leap. The fishermen, at such great falls as those of the Tumel, are themselves securely fastened to the shore, otherwise they might fall off the rocks on which they sit, and be lost in the torrent; for, it is said, the noise of it has the effect of making them fall fast asleep.

The Duke of Atholl possesses, about Blair, an extensive tract of forest, where he often takes the amusement of deer hunting; but those animals being extremely shy, they give the hunters very great trouble and fatigue. Whole days are sometimes spent, from the dawn to the setting sun, in shooting one of them; much dexterity too is required to accomplish it. The Duke is one of the best shots in Britain; but notwithstanding, his Grace is often obliged to be scrambling about the crags for eight or ten hours before he succeeds. The venison of the wild deer is delicious, sometimes fat, and runs to a great size. During the time I had the honour of spending at Blair, I lived upon red deer venison and moor-foul. The red deer so abound, that they are often seen in Atholl forest in herds of many hundreds.

The drive from Blair to Dalnacardoch inn, is close by the river Garrie, amongst wild mountains: but to me, even after the village of Bruar, and the kirk-town of Strowan, there was all the way something delightful about the banks of that river to its source, the lake Garrie; having innumerable little picturesque cascades, mountain torrents, and rocky banks, here and there adorned with birch, alder, mountain ash, and an infinity of bushes and creeping shrubs diversifying the charming scene. The view of Loch Garrie from a simple bridge over a torrent, facing the lake, is beautiful. The rising hill from that bridge leads to the source of the Truim water, and the neat solitary inn of Dalwhinie, close to its edge. A person accustomed only to the scenes in the vicinity of London, or the greatest part of England, would be dismayed at the sight of this lonely habitation, the only one for miles around where not a tree or a shrub is to be seen; only desolate crags, and a boggy heath of great extent on every side; nothing cheering, but the babbling Truim water running to the Spey river. Dalwhinie pleased me; and though the evening was chill, and a mist coming on, I walked to the head of Loch Ericht, about three quarters of a mile over the boggy heath. The high bare crags on each side of Loch Ericht sweep precipitately to the loch's edge, with now and then patches of wood creeping up their lofty sides.

From Dalwhinie to Pitmain inn the face of the country is much the same, till I drew near the river Spey. On crossing the Truim water from the west to the east side of it, is an extremely pretty simple bridge, and a fall of water through the arch, which is truly picturesque, with a salmon leap; and the banks and surrounding rocks (not very gigantic) are sweetly ornamented with birch, alder, small oak, etc. I got out of the chaise to admire this simple sweet scent; and then proceeded towards Spey bridge, till I came within sight of gigantic mountains indeed, particularly those to the left, from amongst which the Spey issues, to receive the tributary water of Truim. I never saw more bare black, black, tremendous mountains in any part of Scotland, than those near the junction of the Truim water with the Spey.

Spey bridge is a noble arch of grey stone; and the face of the country around it becomes more smiling than the other part of Badenoch I had passed through. After crossing Spey bridge, the road winds round some noble mountains, and soon ascends to the neat inn at Pitmain, from whence is a fine view of a small lake formed by the river Spey, called Loch Inch: the vale it is in is tolerably well sprinkled with trees, besides a pretty extensive wood, through which the road advances, still catching the banks of the lovely Spey, until it sweeps round a beautiful craggy mountain, and is lost to the traveller for a few miles. I was sorry to lose sight of this charming river; but I was made some amends by the scene around two small lakes, with the noble crags of Tor Alvie, and the mountains to the right, where I lost the Spey. About half a mile further, by a zig-zag amongst crags and wood, the road sweeps beautifully through a very fine birch wood, down to the very edge of Spey; opening to my view a very lovely scene indeed of the widening vale, rich and well ornamented with wood, and sheltered by mountains not to be described: here I entered Murrayshire. On the opposite side of the river I saw the district of Rothemurchus beautifully situated, bounded by the Cairngorm mountains, whose hollow clefts are filled with never melting snow. The cap of the winter upon these mountains was a contrast to the luxuriant smiling summer below, which I had never before beheld, and I was delighted with it. Aviemore inn was within sight when I came down to the side of the Spey; and my heart jumped at the idea of passing the night in a spot so grateful to my sensations, because nature there shines in its natural garb, and in high beauty: but no sooner had I put my foot within the walls of that horrible house, than my heart sunk; and I was glad to escape from its filth and smoke very early next morning. The sun, however, was sufficiently high to gild the mountains and the lovely scenes around Rothemurchus; and for many a mile my eyes were feasted by the white patched hollow sides of Cairngorm. It was impossible to breakfast at Aviemore inn, I therefore stopped at a small house, eight miles further on the new road to Dulsie bridge, and I got a comfortable meal in the chaise, having provided tea, sugar, bread and butter, tea-pot, etc., so that I wanted only boiling water and milk, which I got, extremely good, from the cottage. After breakfast I entered upon a wild moor, the road itself admirable; but for twelve miles, nothing but bare hills and blooming heath were to be seen, except a small lake at some distance, called Lochindorb, with a castle in it; even this extensive wild pleased me, and gave scope to boundless reflection. The beautiful bloom of the heath, its variety and fragrance, its novelty, and the *tout ensemble* of the scenery, engaged my attention; till on a sudden I descended from this naked moor to the bridge of Dulsie. My senses were there lost to every thing but admiration of rocks, wood, and water tumbling furiously round, and over huge blocks of redish stone, some of them hanging over, others choking up the arch of the bridge, which rests on projecting masses of rock. The bridge itself is not so well looking as most bridges in Scotland, and is of an irregular structure, occasioned by the situation of the rocks on which it rests. The inn is on a high bank on the north side of the bridge, under an extensive thick wood, mostly of large birch trees, larch, and fir. Very soon after the Findhorn river has forced its way through Dulsie bridge, it is lost to sight by high banks and thick woods, and runs its course to the Murray Firth, into which it empties itself by a large bay near Forres. A short way above the brig of Dulsie the river takes a turn round very high points of rocks, and forms several handsome falls between the turn and the bridge. A beautiful landscape of this place might be made, taken from below the bridge; including that and the rough bed of the foaming river, dashing against the huge blocks of smooth redish tinted rocks, lying heaped one upon another, and every where impeding the stream; also chasms, excavated by the water being violently driven out of its course against the rocky bank; with a vast variety of projecting rocks, bushes, and trees; fern, moss and large aquatic plants sprouting from every crevice, and clinging to every stone which is seen through the arch of the bridge, and in front of it. On the left side of the bridge, on a very high rocky bank, are tall ash trees, birch, beech, abele trees, and mountain ash; some carelessly spreading over the side of the bridge, branching down to the arch; others from the shelves of the rocks; with huge trunks, and flowing branches rising from their bare fibrous roots, shooting an incredible distance, from crevice to crevice, in search of nutriment, where the human eye sees no soil: likewise the hazel, the alder, and the crooked maple, with all sorts of shrubs feathering down the rough bank to the water's edge; and to complete the beauty of the bank, a broken cascade tumbles heedless of the havock it incessantly makes of the shrubs and plants over which it dashes. The fore-ground of the landscape might be the right bank, which is broken ground, with some pieces of rock and small shrubs hanging about it.

I was grieved to quit such a charming spot as Dulsie bridge;

but I had sixteen miles to travel to Fort George, and the horses had already brought me twenty miles, which, on the whole, would be a great day's work. On leaving the brig of Dulsie, I penetrated the wood behind the inn, and beyond that wood and found little that interested me, till I came within sight of the mouth of Cromarty Firth, and the wide expanse of sea to the east. The sun was shining with great lustre upon the lofty rocks on the north side of the entrance into the Firth, and I never saw rocks look finer or more grand than they did. The town of Cromarty was hid from me by the point of land south of it; this town lies at the north-east end of the peninsula, formed by the Murray and Cromarty Firths, which run almost parallel to each other from south-west to north-east. Just within the Cromarty Firth is a ferry from the town of Cromarty, to a corner of Ross-shire, and a road from the ferry to Tain.

At about seven miles from Fort George I came to Castle Calder, and by a new made road passed close to its old walls. It is more like a very ancient house than a castle; but it has small round towers at its corners on the uppermost story, which descend no lower, with narrow slips in the walls to admit light and air, and I suppose sufficiently wide to peep at an enemy without. In all very ancient buildings belonging to the chiefs there are very few windows, and those extremely small, with walls immoderately thick. There is one internal wall now at Blair above seven feet thick. As I did not know when I passed Castle Calder that I could see the inside of it, I did not stop there: and by that means lost the opportunity of seeing King Duncan's bed on which he was murdered by Macbeth, in Inverness castle. There is a large thorn tree growing through the middle of the house of Calder, older (I was told) than the fabric itself, the house being originally built round the tree, leaving it standing. The whole place is at present a deserted ruin, imbosomed in, and over-run by rude neglected trees, both forest and fruit. A multiplicity of what I took for *gyne* trees (a small sort of plumb), notwithstanding their being choked by high nettles, and other weeds and rubbish, were covered with ripe fruit as I passed this ancient ruin. The road from the castle winds round the orchard wall, and soon comes to a burn, which for width should be called a river, issuing from the matted trees of Calder, and guarding its eastern side. In approaching to this burn I found the road very rough and stony; but I was astonish-ed when I came to the burn's side to find no bridge, and the broad bed of the burn full of very large round stones, washed from the mountains. These stones lie very thick all over the bed, heaped one upon another, except just in the current. I called a council to determine if I could step from stone to stone. — No. There was that day too great a depth of water, where the current ran, even for the servant to wade it. I was therefore obliged to sit still, and the poor horses began to scramble amongst the stones, of which many, I am sure, were three feet above the bottom of the burn; where the poor animals found room to place their feet between them, or sufficient strength to drag the heavy carriage over them, I cannot imagine. It took a length of time, and I was not free from great fear, that some disaster would befall the chaise before it reached the shore; the stony bed being, I verily believe, twenty yards wide. I shall never forget the crossing of the burn of Calder, at Calder Castle, which in flood must be a furious rapid water. I passed by a small lake or two, and soon got a perfect view of Fort George, the Firth by it, and the bold shores of Ross shire in the background, with Inverness and its mountains on the left hand. At a distance Fort George looks like a large castle in the sea; for the flat sands to the east of the fort (the only dry approach to it) are, even at a moderate distance, confounded with the sea, which bounds it on every other side. Indeed the sea seems to have been robbed by damming up the oblong sand bank, whereon the fortification is erected.

Fort George is in complete repair, and fit for defence. As for Fort Augustus and Fort William, they are now only make-believe forts.

The entrance into Fort George struck me with awe; for as the carriage drove to the outer gate, "stop" was the word, with fierce centinels on every side, crying, "who goes there?" My name given, they slowly marched to the governor, or fort major, for permission to enter. After waiting a considerable time, the outer gate was thrown open, and the postillion bid to come on. Thump, thump, went the horses' feet over a draw bridge and through a covered way, with wood on the bottom, sounding like thunder; and when I was fairly in the fort, they closed the huge gates, grinding on their hinges, leaving me in the midst of red coats, cannon, musquets, and bayonets. I felt a little unusual on the occasion, something like being shut up in a prison, whence I might never escape. I am totally unqualified to give a proper description of fortifications; but so far I can say, that Fort George, within itself, is like a small town. The common parade is spacious; it is an oblong, with four angles, having handsome houses joining each other on every side, except an opening, about the middle of it, of a street leading each way; the one to the chapel, magazines, and work-shops; the other to the grand parade, where are the governor's and fort major's houses, with many other good houses, besides apartments belonging to the soldiers. The walk round the rampants is very pleasant in fine weather; but in winter it must be very bleak and cold, having no shelter of any kind. The sea must often run very high at Fort George, form the wide part of the Firth to the narrower, the fort being just at the strait between the two. I should not be very desirous of crossing the ferry from Fort George to Fortrose in Ross-shire, observing the vessels passing between those places

to be prodigiously buffeted by waves. The Beauley ferry is by far the shortest and safest between Inverness-shire and Ross-shire. Though I was entirely unknown at the fort, the lieutenant-governor, the Hon. Colonel Stuart, with the utmost politeness, sent an officer to conduct me over every part of the fortification, and to shew me every thing I was capable of noticing. It rained the chief part of the time I was inclosed in the fort, which was a great mortification to me, particularly in the afternoon, as it prevented the usual parade. The Lorns were at that time quartered at Fort George; a fine body of men; and to have seen them all drawn out and perform their exercise, would have pleased me very much; but such disappointments must often occur in a long tour.

CHAPTER TWO

The morning on which I repassed the sounding draw-bridge cleared up, and I had a fine drive by the Firth side to Inverness, towards which every step I took delighted me. Castle Stewart, Lord Moray's, is a fine old ruin, seven miles on the road; and the noble mountains running south-west, plainly pointed out the situation of the great lake, to the banks of which I was eagerly hastening. One mountain in particular fixed my attention, high towering above the rest, blue, and conical, the noon-sun shining brightly upon it; — I never saw anything more sublime than it appeared: I afterwards learnt it to be Meal-four-vounie, on the north side of Loch Ness, opposite to the Fall of Fyres. It is 3060 feet above the level of the sea; but in a near view it appears, as its Gaelic name denotes, a lump of cold moor, though the side of it down to Loch Ness is clothed with wood to the water's edge. There is a lake of fresh water extremely cold upon its summit, the depth of which cannot be fathomed; and the country people affirm, if anything be put into this lake at night, it is sure to be found in the morning, in the great lake below.

About two or three miles from Inverness, I saw, at a small distance from the road, the new house of Culloden; and on one side of it (but not very far), the ground on which the memorable battle was fought in 1746.

I was very pleased with the appearance of Inverness, and found it a neat town, charmingly situated: the fine river Ness runs close by it; and it is within a very short distance of the Murray Firth, where there is another ferry to Ross-shire. A very good bridge over the Ness leads to that ferry, and to Beauley, and the country of Aird; and by another road south-west, to the places that lie upon the north west side of Loch Ness, Glen Urquhart, etc. When I was at Inverness there was not a trace of its ancient castle; some person lately removed the small remains of its ruins to build offices, or some such thing,

for his own convenience:— what an Hottentot! There is at Inverness a provost, or mayor, and twenty-four magistrates. A judge visits that town twice a year, in his circuit. It was on a Thursday when I entered Inverness. The provost, with the rest of the magistrates, were going in procession through one of the principal streets to church; it being the Thursday preceding the sacrament Sunday. On those Sundays there is always great preaching, both in the church and in the adjacent field; and also on Saturday and Monday. On the preaching days all the shops are shut, and nothing can be bought during divine service. There is a decency in the appearance, manners, and deportment of the people of Inverness, and around it, that is extremely engaging; and the accent of their language is so soft, it charms the ear: it is not in the least like the accent of the Lowland, or any other part of the Highland English language that I heard; it being extremely insinuating, I could almost say bewitching: neither has it any resemblance to the Lowland Scotch in idiom, being very pure English, accompanied with a sort of foreign tone, which is very pleasing; in short, it is like broken English, proceeding from the soft voice of a beautiful female foreigner, taught English purely and grammatically. I did not remain long in the town of Inverness, as I was on my way to Dochfour; but all I saw of it pleased me excessively. The inn I stopped at was very neat, and tolerably large; and I was told the other inn was equally good, if not superior.

As soon as I crossed the bridge over the Ness, and quitted the suburbs of the town, I turned my face towards Dochfour, and with delight enjoyed the scene before me, but I knew not what to admire most; the river flowing on my left, bordered on each side by wood and rich land, with mountains upon mountains, in every form; fine trees in the narrow flat, and wood creeping up on every crag's side; the mountains increasing to a vast size and height as I advanced towards Loch Ness, buried in the bosom of two ranges of mountains not easily described. Tom-ma-hureich to my right, one mile from Inverness, must not be forgotten, though its form is more curious than beautiful; being like the keel of a ship turned topsy-turvy; and planted to the top with firs, so thick; that it looks like a fir wood of that shape.

I was four days under the hospitable roof of Alexander Baillie, Esq. He, his half-brother, his amiable nieces, Miss Frazer of Belladrum, and Miss Chisholm, in short, all who belonged to that friendly worthy man, vied with each other who should pay me most attention, or afford me most pleasure, by shewing me every thing that was to be seen in that quarter; and those pleasures are above description, because every spot about that lovely and sublime situation is a never ceasing source of contemplation to an observing mind. The weather, alas! was not

A neat town, charmingly situated.

favourable. One day we went to the east border of the country of Aird, in which is Belladrum; and much did I lament that our time did not allow us to reach that place. We drove from Dochfour to Inverness: we did not go into the town, but continued on to the edge of the Firth; then turned towards Beauley. The town of that name, on the west side of the river, makes no inconsiderable figure in the view, greatly ornamenting the head of the Beauley firth. The houses being chiefly white, the town is seen at a great distance, backed by hills of all heights and shapes, some covered with wood; and trees in abundance on all sides.

In the country of Aird the soil is very productive, in corn, as well as grass; and I was told, that both there, and in other parts around Inverness, some lands let from three to five pounds an acre. On the east side of the Ness, between the bridge and the Kessack ferry, are large thread and cotton works erected; which disfigure the town, but doubtless add to its riches. Inverness is the port that supplies all the inland parts of Inverness-shire, south of the Murray Firth, which necessaries and luxuries, not produced in the country, particularly coals, grocery, etc. These articles are conveyed by water with great conveniency, from the Bona ferry, at the foot of Loch Ness, to Fort Augustus, the Glens Urquhart and Morrison, and other places.

I have already mentioned the *present* amiable manners of the people of Inverness, and the adjacent country; and I must also add, that they are now perfectly secure in their property, as well as polished in their behaviour (which is not always the case in the south), retaining the honest simplicity and hospitality of the patriarchal age, which the rub of refinement has not impaired. Indeed, not only in Inverness, but in most parts of the Highlands, the manners of the people are pleasant to a degree; and the poorest of the poor will vie with each other which can most assist, or gratify a stranger, provided it be not a Sunday. On that day, if a carriage breaks down in the Highlands, there it must lie, for no hand will be found to mend it; not for want of good will, but for conscience sake. In the Lowlands, in and about large towns, particularly where there are manufactories, or in sea ports, there are as many depraved folks as in England: but in the Highlands all is safety and security; — no fear of thieves by night or day. All the doors and windows are left unfastened: and I have seen sideboards, covered with plate of great value, stand open in parlours, night and day, without fear of its being touched.

One instance, however, will shew what they *were* in Inverness-shire, in former times, and what I found them, and described them to be *now*.

One of the McDonells of old, probably from Lochaber, coming down to visit Culloden, near Inverness, observed how numerous, and how very fine his cattle were. Culloden lamented, that in all probability he should not have sufficient pasture for them during the winter. McDonell eyed the cattle, and told his friend he could accommodate him in that matter, if he wished it; he having fine pasture in abundance. The bargain was made for so much a head, for a stated time; and McDonell promised to take the utmost care of the beasts, if Culloden would have them driven up to his lands; which was accordingly done. In about two months a man from McDonell came down with a long face, saying, "his chief was in great trouble and dismay, at Culloden's cattle having been all stolen away." Culloden, who perfectly well understood the meaning of all this, without expressing either anger or concern, ordered his head servant to take great care of this messenger, and ply him well with meat and drink. After a day or two, the man signified he must return. Culloden, before he departed, called him before him, and without saying a syllable of the cattle, asked him if he had been treated to his heart's content; gave him money and dismissed him. The messenger returned to McDonell, and said to him dryly, "the man must have his cattle back again." This peremptory speech astonished the Highland chief, who remonstrated; but the other insisted, and swore if he did not comply, he would blaze abroad his roguery, and oblige him to it by force. McDonell knew his man, and the consequences if he continued obstinate. He therefore quietly submitted; and in a short time sent the same person again to Culloden to acquaint him, that he was very happy in having overtaken, and rescued his cattle from the thieves who had driven them back.

To return to Dochfour. One day I walked through the beautiful woods of Dochfour to a burn, running precipitately from one of the large mountains to the north of the house; forming in its way a number of beautiful falls. I only saw the last of them; which for beauty and concealment, might tempt Diana's self, and favourite nymphs, to cool themselves in it. The access to it is difficult, as it is deeply imbosomed, and almost excluded from light by rocky banks, thick bushes, and trees of fir, oak, birch, maple, mountain ash, etc., many of which recline over the limpid stream, that like a mirror, reflects and doubles their beauties. As I stept from stone to stone, a passage in the Gentle Shepherd came to my recollection, where Jenny says,

> "Gae farer up the burn, to Habbie's How,
> Where a'the sweets of spring and summer grow,
> Between twa birks, out o'er a little lin,
> The water fa's and maks a singand din,
> A pool, breast-deep, beneath as clear as glass,
> Kisses wi' easy whirls the bord'ring grass.
> We'll end our washing while the morning's cool;
> And when the day grows het, we'll to the pool,
> There wash oursells. — It's healtfu' now in May,
> And sweetly cauler on sae warm a day."

This pool is sometime made use of as a cold bath, by the lovely lasses who frequent Dochfour.

Another day I walked to the foot of the great lake, passing by some old monastic ruins, on a small peninsula between the great lake and the branch of it, opposite Dochfour house. Few scenes can be found more majestic than that, viewed from the foot of the lake, and under the Redhill mountain on the north side, and even all the way to the entrance into Glen Urquhart. The whole of Loch Ness is before you in front. Its length is twenty-four miles; its breadth, from two to two miles and a half; perfectly straight, running from south-west to north-east; completely filling the space between the sublime over-hanging mountains, with their summits in the clouds; some covered with wood, others rearing up, from a bold base, their craggy heads, frowning majestically over the wide glossy vista beneath them, and fading into the horizon, while the tops of the more distant mountains appear mellowed down to the softest shades, till all is lost in unison with the clouds, which sweep behind the nearer, and huge projecting sides of Meal-four-vounie, rising up between Glen Urquhart and Glen Morrison. From the foot of the great lake, I continued my walk some miles on the north side of it, at the bases of the grand sweeping mountains of Redhill, etc. The road is only the width of a cart, in some parts running close to the edge of the water, at others on a shelf blown out of the rocks, which are perpendicular, above and below; but wherever a bit of soil is to be found, there the alder, birch, mountain and common ash trees take root, some bending over the crags to the lake, others creeping up the rugged sides of the mountains; and here and there wide channels filled with round loose stones, brought down from the mountains by torrents and burns, in hard rains. The projecting shore on which the grand ruin of Castle Urquhart stands, forms a noble object in the view; and the bold rocks and wood of the southern bank complete this truly sublime scene. I was unable to walk as far as the beginning of Glen Urquhart; but I was told it was a perfect Eden. The fine ruin of the castle of Urquhart, erected by the Cummings, and demolished by King Edward, now belongs to Sir James Grant. I was told the inhabitants of Glen Urquhart are so wedded to it, that not one native has quitted it, nor one foreigner taken up an abode therein, for ninety years. There is also a curious well, of which women drink after child-birth, instead of being churched.

With great regret I turned my back on this grand scene; but my legs would carry me no further, I was therefore obliged to submit.

Let a frost be ever so hard, Loch Ness never has been known to freeze; it is therefore imagined, the whole bed of it is sulphur. The water of the Ness river, and I believe most of the water about Inverness, is strongly impregnated with it, which often disagrees with man and beast, particularly with strangers unaccustomed to it. In the spring, 1796, some military men were obliged to be removed from Inverness, many of them having died of the flux, in consequence of the water being so strongly impregnated with sulphur.

There is the finest salmon trout I ever saw or tasted, in the small lake, or rather a branch of Loch Ness, just below Mr. Baillie's house; and in such abundance, that whenever he had occasion for fish, he had nothing to do but to send his fisherman on the lake, and in half an hour, or less, he produced such trout as were quite a picture to look at, and a feast to taste.

It has been said, and I believe written too, that the Duke of Cumberland, on the memorable day of the battle of Culloden, suffered his resentment to extend beyond all bounds of humanity; that he had the wounded Highlandmen shut up, and shot in cold blood. The fact was really far otherwise. His orders were positive to succour, not to butcher: — Colonel Hobby, however, instead of obeying these orders, went into the field after the battle, and himself shot all the poor wounded creatures he found alive. He afterwards, at Edinburgh, declared he was the man who did it; and even glorified in his horrid inhumanity.

CHAPTER THREE

Unfortunately the day on which I took my leave of Dochfour became cloudy and unpromising; but having ordered my carriage to go from Inverness by the south road to meet me at the Bona ferry, where the river Ness issues from the lake, I was obliged to set out. Before I joined the great road it began to rain, and a thick mist soon covered the tops of the mountains: though every now and then it was sufficiently fair to give me an idea of the grand scene before me; a view of which I had taken a few days before from the other side of the lake. The road on the south side of the lake is a military road, made under the direction of General Wade, which must have cost his men infinite labour. From the foot of the lake to General's Hut (so called from Wade), the road runs through an almost uninterrupted wood of young oaks, birch, alders, mountain ash, etc., climbing from the water's edge to the very summits of the boldest rocks. Indeed the wood wants to be thinned, as it screens the beauties of the lake far too much. The road sometimes descends to the margin of the lake, and again rises to a high shelf, winding round and up very steep masses of projecting rock, blown up for the purpose of making the road, whose towering fragments, huge and solid, hang over the narrow way just the width of a carriage. At about ten miles from Inverness, I came within sight of the Black Rock, and it seemed as if it were impossible to pass by it; in truth, it does require courage and steady horses to venture upon a very narrow shelf blown out of the rocks; and to get upon it you ascend a road almost as steep as the ridge of a house, winding round a huge projecting mass, that looks as if it were ready to crush the bold adventurer who dares come under its brow: for it actually hangs over part of the carriage in passing it. Trees are branching, shrubs and bushes bending over and sprouting from every chink of the rocks, which tower almost to the sky; and on the right hand feathering down to the water, over a rocky precipice of perhaps eighty or a hundred feet perpendicular; and no security whatever, either in climbing to the shelf, or upon it, should the horses there take fright. The scene, however, made me amends for the little palpitation occasioned by the attainment of the awful eminence on which I was mounted. The long extent of the lake, Glen Urquhart, and the ruins of its castle, boldly projecting into the loch, were in sight. The noble mountains, on each side of the lake, covered with wood, through which peep masses of huge rocks, some descending perpendicularly to the lake's edge, others sweeping with bold variety into it, break the line without lessening the majesty of its straightness, which is its peculiar character; for in that respect no other great lake in Scotland is like it. About a mile further I came to a simple bridge, thrown from the rock

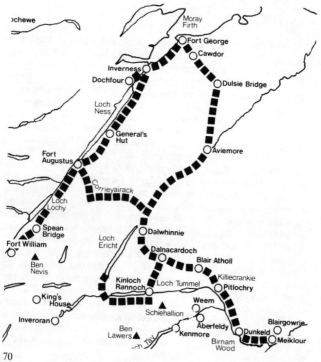

over a rapid river, issuing from a beautiful close cluster of wooded rocks and high hills. This river, swollen to a great height by the violent rains, came tumbling furiously through the arch; dashing afterwards unseen through thick wood, and down almost perpendicular rocks to the bosom of the lake below. The road takes a qick turn from this romantic bridge, and soon leads to the ruins of a kirk, once the only one of Strath Errick, on the other side of the mountains, and then to General's Hut, the only habitation, except a few hovels, that I saw on the south side of the lake from one end of it to the other.

The outside of General's Hut is repaired since an account of it was given by Henry Skrine, Esq. As to its interior, I am, from my own experience, no judge of it: the peep I had into it from the carriage was not very inviting; but had it been more so, I should not have quitted the chaise; being accustomed to have it drawn to the best points of view at every inn I came to, and there sat, whilst the horses rested, eating my dinner. Then drawing, or if there were nothing worthy of the pencil, I wrote or walked; but without meaning to affront any body by thus acting: though I learnt both the good folks at General's Hut, and at Letter Findlay inn, were displeased at my mode; attributing it, I suppose, to disdain or nicety, which was not entirely the case.

As I drove to the General's Hut, it was pouring with rain; I never saw harder. My only consolation in such a deluge was the idea of the perfection in which I should see the Fall of Fyres; but how to get at it was the question, without being drowned? As I sat in the chaise, I saw a gentleman wrapped in a plaid, with a guide, penetrating the wood through which the road leads to the fall. In about three quarters of an hour he came back dripping wet. In such sequestered regions ceremony sleeps, and the heart expands to anything and every thing like humanity; I therefore intreated the dripping stranger to take a comforting drop from my bottle of rum, to keep off the danger of his drenching. When he came near, I found he was one of the officers from Fort George, who had rode from thence to see this famous fall. I was happy in an opportunity, even though so trifling, to shew I was sensible of the civilities I met with at the fort: and I hope my spirits prevented the gentleman from getting cold, of which he ran great risk, as I saw him, immediately after I spoke to him, canter away without changing his Highland waistcoat. After waiting until the horses were ready to proceed, I walked to the fall, leaving the carriage to follow me. At that time the rain had ceased; but the ground was every where swimming, and the trees and torrents streaming.

Mr. Baillie had, with infinite consideration and kindness, sent with me a very clever intelligent Highlandman, to whose assistance I was indebted for a full and complete view of the Fall of Fyres from every spot that was possible for it to be seen. The road, about a quarter of a mile from the Hut, quits the lake, (on

whose steep banks there is no possibility of proceeding further,) and strikes up through the mountains towards Strath Errick. Within about half a mile of it, the thundering noise of the fall announces the approach to it. The first station I attained was on a promontory, at some distance below the fall, and about a hundred feet above the surface of the water rushing round the rock, on which I stood. I saw from the first point of view, the river issuing with violence from its confined channel above, and dashing in one shoot between broken rocks down to the pool; but a projecting slip of green bank, and other obstacles, screened from my sight the better half of the cataract. The rocks on each side of the fall are clad with hanging trees, chiefly of birch, mountain ash, and young oak, peeping through the expanded spray. The river, after running from the pool, has several other projections to compass, before it reaches the foot of the promontory on which I placed myself; I was in ecstacy with all around me; but to get to this station was a bold adventure (for a woman) when the ground is wet, being obliged to creep from one slippery bank to another, and to step from rock to rock, supported only by stumps and branches of birch, and in continual danger of tumbling headlong over pieces of rocks, and into bogs. But I was determined nothing should hinder me from seeing this grand object in all possible points of view. On my return from the promontory I met four travellers, males, not very active in body, who came tumbling and slipping down the banks, with fright and dismay, that made me smile. They stared at me, as much as to say how came you there! But bad as the first scramble was, it was nothing in comparison to the hazard (in slippery weather) of creeping to the green bank, close to, and in front of the fall. My postillion's curiosity had carried him thither before me: he met me at his return, to tell me it was impossible for me to venture to the green bank; and if I did, at least, I should be wet through in a few minutes. I could not be much worse in that respect than I was; for my shoes and stockings were by that time complete brown boots, so covered were they with dirt and slime. By the help of the Highlandman, and my own servant, I however slipped, and hung by trees, and clung to pieces of rock, until I got down on the desired bank, which is on the whole not more than two yards wide, and projects, perhaps, twenty or more feet in direct front of the fall. This bank, whether by art, or worn away by frequent visits, I cannot say, but it has on it a sunk path, in the middle of this slip of rock (in shape like a marrow-spoon), sufficiently wide to take in the legs of those who venture themselves in it: the bank rises on each side, and at the end of the path, forming a green earthen parapet, about knee high. I advanced to the furthest point, looking at the vast leap of the river, and tracing its course from the pool

The noise was beyond belief!

round the green bank on which I stood, two hundred feet below me, winding and dashing towards the promontory on which I had first gazed; and the top of the cataract was two hundred and seventy feet above me! The noise, as it was in flood, was beyond belief; it was impossible to hear any other sound; and the spray, in a great degree, deprived me of sight and breath; so that I was obliged to recline upon the green parapet, and every now and then, by gulping, and shutting my eyes for relief, I was by intervals enabled to look and breathe; to admire, and I might say, almost adore. The river, in its fall, diffused its spray in every direction to a vast distance, over my head, and far beyond my situation. The water bounded from the pool, rising like innumerable high fountains, and in the return fell with prodigious force and weight against, and partly upon, the green bank, by which, and the spray, I was in a few minutes pretty well drenched. The want of breath and sight obliged me to quit this grand work of nature, much sooner than I wished. If ever I am happy enough to see it again, it shall be in a drier season, when perhaps it may be more picturesque, though far less sublime and awful; besides, in such a season there can be neither danger nor difficulty in getting at it.

I believe the Highlanders to be stout men, both in body and mind; and I also know they will dare do many things for whisky: but I cannot well credit what was told me at Fort Augustus of one who, for the trifling wager of a bottle of that spirit, not only put himself into the river at the top of the Fall of Fyres, but voluntarily went down the cataract into the pool. from which he paddled away like a duck, and climbed up the rock side, safe and unhurt, saying, "that was nothing to the Fall of Niagara," down which he had precipitated himself many a time. Now the Fall of Fyres is four hundred and seventy feet perpendicular, over broken rocks to the pool, and that no one knows the depth of. I own I cannot swallow any part of the history; but I give it as I heard it.

As soon as I left the green bank, I walked to the bridge, not above a hundred yards higher up the river. This is a scene truly picturesque and very romantic, as well as beautiful. A simple arch, from rock to rock, is ready to receive the soft winding river above, and admit it to its rough and narrow approach to the cataract; but its labours begin just before the bridge, where the rough masses seem determined to impede its passage through the arch, lying heap upon heap to stop the way. The contest becomes extremely violent, and the whirl-pools boil up with fury, and then dash through the bridge from fall to fall, entering with loud groans into the narrow gulf of rocks, from which it leaps with boisterous force to the pool above described; and thence glides, babbling and laughing as it were, at its miraculous escape, to imbosom itself in the great lake. Near the bridge I entered several caves, large and dry; where I was told that many of the unfortunate rebels hid themselves, before and after the battle of Culloden.

When I had seen every thing about this magnificent cataract, I entered the carriage, which was standing in a winding part of the road by the river's side, shaded by fine trees, and surrounded by hills of various shapes and heights. Such was my dressing-room. I drew up the blinds of the chaise, and dressed myself entirely; took a glass of wine, and gave bumpers to the good Highlandman, the postillion, and my servants; and then proceeded with admiration of what I had seen, and what, at every step, I continued to see. After winding a little way on the margin of the river, the road crosses a burn, and suddenly turns up a steep hill, leading to a defile of mountains watered by burns; which are, at the beginning of the defile, bordered by a great variety of trees and bushes, creeping up and down the braes (sides of hills) and sloping banks of burns, till I again crossed the river by a bridge, and entered Strath Errick.

About four miles before I came to Fort Augustus, I wound round a lake of a conical shape, something like the present fashionable military cocked hat with two islands in it: this lake is called Loch Andmive: from one corner of it issues a stream that soon swells into a very rapid torrent, running deep and close below, under the shelf on which the road descends by a zig-zag of about a mile down to the river Doe, with which the lake torrent unites. As soon as I crossed the Doe, the road mounted another shelf hanging over the river, unseen, but heard; dashing through wood and over rocks, forcing its way by perpendicular shoots, down the mountains to Loch Ness, which it enters. It was a sad pull for the horses up the shelf over the Doe; but within a mile after that rise, I started from my seat at the view that unexpectedly opened to my sight. The head of Loch Ness, with a verdant flat around it of about a mile in diameter; watered by two large rivers in different directions, with bridges over them near the mouth of each. Fort Augustus itself, like a large ancient palace, whose white walls rise on the centre of the Loch's head; the rivers forming a rampart on each side of it, emptying themselves into the lake close by the walls of the fort. The town appears like offices attached to it, and a few trees filling up the vacancies unite the whole. The lake; its majestic sides of rocks, some bare, others dressed with wood, and enriched by every tint that nature paints, particularly a soft purplish red blended with yellow, gave such a rich softness to the rays of the sinking sun, lingering on the tops of the mountains, as cannot be described. From the lake and fort my eyes wandered to the rough points of hill, sharp and jagged (called in derision Glen-Garrys bowling green) continuing the chain which the small plain at Fort Augustus has somewhat interrupted, and bounding the river Oich and the lake of that name. These mountains, although jagged, are most of them green to their picked tops, and finely wooded to their bases, which extend to the margins of the river and the lake. In short, the first view of Fort Augustus from Strath Errick, in a fine day, is like a little paradise; hemmed in on every side, and to appearance, by obstacles impossible to surmount, leaving no means either to enter it or escape from it. — In that respect it resembles the happy valley described by Doctor Johnson in his Rasselas, or Prince of Abyssinia.

When I had feasted my eyes with this fascinating view, I began a descent of about a mile; in which, indeed, it seemed impossible for the poor horses either to keep upon their legs, or hold up the carriage behind them, though the wheels were dragged. Had I not had perfect confidence in Allen, and his steady beasts. I must have walked down the precipice, notwithstanding the wet and dirt from the rain in the morning. Fort Augustus is in a state of great neglect, and appears to be going very fast to decay. There were only a few old invalids in it when I was there; and the sight of these old firelocks, on the parade, rehearsing their exercises before the Governor's house in a morning, was quite a burlesque scene of soldiering. The same ceremony, however, was practised at Fort Augustus as at Fort George; and the creeping centinels hailed us with "who goes there?" — I had letters to the worthy Governor, which I sent in, and was admitted over the thundering drawbridge, and through the dark gateway, to the parade and the Governor's door; who, with his lady, received me with every mark of kindness and hospitality. Alas! since that period, that good man, Governor Trapaud, is gone from his earthly friends to reap the rewards of his numerous virtues!

The next morning I set off early, to follow the hollow from sea to sea. After crossing the bridge I left the river Oich to my right; and at the end of a mile, entered between hills that secluded it from my sight for two miles or more, when the foot of Loch Oich, and its river flowing from it, opened to the view, with a range of mountains on each side, verdant from their bases to their summits, excepting every now and then where rocks covered with wood break the line, and bare masses of rock too, peeping through, just to prove that the outsides of the mountains are fairer and smoother than their insides. The whole way I beheld fine pasture for sheep, both on the sides of the mountains, and in the tiny flats between the chain of lakes. A little before the road joins Loch Oich, a burn crosses the road, tearing away the soil, and leaving only a large bed of round stones. Trees of birch, alder, arch mountain ash, and other wood, ornamented the whole space: at times creeping to the mountain's top, and again hanging over the river and the lake; which, towards the middle, is contracted by the projecting land at Invergarry, where the river Garry issues from the glen, bold and broad, shaded by fine trees. The road I was upon is a shelf, hanging over Loch Oich, with lofty mountains, almost perpendicular, of broken and shivering rocks: which, notwithstanding their excessive roughness, are mostly covered with thick Alpine wood; through which rush torrents from their very high summits. One of the boldest of these falls is in full sight of Glen-Garry's house; and a fine object it must be to it.

From the Chalder water, whose flood I before mentioned, as having torn away and overwhelmed the road with stones, to High Bridge, a distance of about seventeen miles, I counted at least a hundred mountain torrents, and above thirty of them fine ones. These torrents require some sort of bridges to cross them, and art and constant labour are requisite to keep them in passable repair; but it is impossible, without seeing such scenes, to understand or conceive their beauties from description. I was the whole way in constant exclamation; — here is another; oh, how fine! how beautiful! how dashing! — hopping and rushing sometimes down mountains perpendicular to the road, so that I was continually obliged to draw up the glasses of the carriage to prevent the spouts coming upon me. Again, on the opposite side of the lakes, where the mountains are equally high and woody with those on my side, I saw white stripes of foaming torrents, as numerous as those I was passing: but all this happens only on a rainy day; as most of these falls suddenly flow with fume and violence, and as quickly subside, when it is fair; leaving nothing but a rough channel to shew where they had been, and would be again the first hard shower.

When I went to Fort William it was a fine day, consequently the greater number of these torrents were quiet. It was the next day, on my return, when it rained hard, that I was so delighted with these beautiful dashers. Having two days of different weather between Fort Augustus and Fort William, I saw on one day that charming defile, sublime, bright, soft, and smiling; on the other, terrific, gloomy, and dripping. Mr. McDonnell's house at Invergarry is sweetly situated, fronting Loch Oich, and close on the side of the river Garry, issuing from a lovely glen, amongst mountains pointed and jagged, with their bases richly clad with wood. A few acres of verdure are seen adjacent to the house, ornamented, as far as I could see, by fine trees, in a picturesque, natural style; and not far from the house, on a bold projecting rock, is the ruin of a castle; whose broken walls, turrets, and fragments, are seen imperfectly through beautiful trees, shrubs, twining ivy, and coarse grass. In front of the ruin is the soft reflecting lake, and at its back the lofty range of mountains called Glen Garry's Bowling-green; whose tops are grey crags, and from their bases creep wood, intermixed with patches of verdure, wherever they can embrace these rough majestic sovereigns. I determined to take a sketch of this place on my return, as I should then face the most beautiful landscape; but I forget the old true adage, that delays are dangerous. The same determination prevailed when I came in sight of Loch Lochy; but behold! the next day both these delightful picturesque places were darkened, and mostly concealed by rain and mist, to my great mortification. The road continues hanging over Loch Oich to its head (whence the water runs towards the North sea), and then it descends to a marshy flat, and soon reaches the head of Loch Lochy; where the water runs the contrary way, to seek, towards the south-west, the Atlantic ocean.

At the head of Loch Lochy is a charming landscape; the lake almost filling the space between the mountains on each side of it. The Loch itself is a fine vista; reflecting the shores in the softest tints, fading away to a beautiful conical hill, which closes the centre in the distant horizon. The road again mounts a shelf hanging over the lake, and at about the midway of it I found Letter Findlay inn, close on the edge of the lake, screened at the back by high mountains, and very much shaded by wood. At the door of the inn is a small green patch, bordered by birch and alders; rushes, bushes, and shrubs creeping down to the water. On this fairy green I had the chaise turned that I might face the grand scenery of the lake, wood, and mountains, on the north side of the Loch; whose bold sides, with precipitate projections, drive back the encroaching waters. Two solitary huts I saw under these mountains, nodding, as it were, at Letter Findlay; but how they were got at, I could not imagine. A patch of coarse verdure adorns these habitations; all around besides is wood and rocks, arising from them and the lake nearly perpendicular. Had I not afterwards been told to the contrary, I should have imagined that ravens must feed the beings, if they were, dwelling there, as in appearance nought but what drops from the clouds can reach them; by being informed there was a ferry to them from Letter Findlay, I was better satisfied with their fate: besides, I was told they were shepherds, and that they and their flocks made as little of all those crags and mountains, as I do of stairs, in seeking my dinner from a high room to a low one.

After eating my meal, and sketching what was within my view, I proceeded on the side of the lake, in the same style of scenery, till I came within a mile of Low Bridge, when I was surprised with a variety of beauty that delighted me. It is an opening from Loch Arkeig, with a river sweetly winding amongst little and great hills (verdant and woody), seeking repose in the bosom of Loch Lochy, I do not remember seeing any habitation in that romantic Eden. The banks of Loch Arkeig, however, and its neighbouring glens, are tolerably well inhabited; but the cluster of hills near Loch Lochy, so close up the glen, that it is impossible, from the side of the lake where I was, to look into it.

It was in the neighbourhood of Loch Arkeig, that Prince Charles Stuart (the Pretender) fled after the battle of Culloden, where he met with great friendship from Loch-Eil, and others. He again visited that part of the country when he returned from the Isle of Skye, where he had been safely (though with infinite risk) conducted by Miss Flora Macdonald, from the island of South Uist. After leaving the Isle of Skye, Charles entered Loch Nevish, which is not a great distance (to the west) from the head of Loch Arkeig. Whilst he was skulking in that district, four hundred men, under General Campbell, arrived on one side of him, and five hundred more, under Captain Scott, on the other. These officers gaining some intelligence of him, began to form a circle round him, not above two miles distant. In this dilemma he sent to Donald Cameron of Glenpean, who, in the night, conducted him through the guards who were in the pass they were obliged to take; and at one time they were forced to creep upon all fours, so close to the tents, that they heard the soldiers talking to each other, and saw them walking between themselves and the fires. This was only a prelude to their dangers and difficulties, as they still had to pass through the line of little camps, twenty-seven in number, called the chain. The night was very dark, and Charles's faithful guide, Donald Cameron, passed alone through the chain, by way of experiment. He returned safe, and with success conducted the Pretender through it. Before Donald began this hazardous expedition, he said to Charles, "Oh! Sir, my nose is yuiking (itching), which is a sign to me that we have great risks and dangers to go through."

After having passed the guards without being discovered, Charles accosted his friend, and pleasantly said, "Well, Donald, how does your nose now?" "It is better now," said he; "but it still yuiks a little!"

Many were the hardships this suffering patient young man afterwards underwent in Glen Morrison, Lochaber, and in the mountains hanging over Loch Ericht, which became his hiding-place, till he made his escape to France, in September, 1746.

Somewhat before I came in sight of Low Bridge, the road turns from Loch Lochy, and is cut through steep rocks, high and beautiful to look at, covered with wood and bursting torrents; but in a wet slippery day, not very desirable to pass in a carriage. Low Bridge is of one noble high arch, thrown over a water running from a glen behind the range of mountains, screening Letter Findlay inn, and is called Low, because it was unnecessary to be built so high as that over the Spean river, about three miles from Low Bridge, to which I came by a road round, and up very steep sides of mountains. At High Bridge, I got a more extensive view over the district both before and behind me: it is very wild, but not totally devoid of beauty. High Bridge is a great work, constructed under General Wade's direction; and is next in wonder to that going by the name of Wade's Bridge, or Tay Bridge, in Appneydow, eight miles from

Taymouth, and close by the small town of Aberfeldie. The road at the top of the hill approaching to High Bridge, winds round on a shelf, hanging over the deep and close, bare, rocky (but in some parts verdant), banks of the Spean; which, as if glad of its escape through the arches of the bridge, was dashing with rapid bounds from one bed of rock to another; eager to finish the remainder of its tortured passage to the foot of Loch Lochy, deep below.

The day was decling and getting overcast, I therefore did not dare venture to stop to sketch the bridge; which I much wished to do, as a curiosity of art and nature. As I stood on the ground higher than the bridge, it appeared to be a region of the utmost wildness; bare craggy mountains, one above another, on every side, and a dreary rough moor before me. The Spean, though violent just above and below the bridge, came quietly, and tolerably level, from amongst the stupendous mountains towards Badenoch. But this river, at times, rises to an immoderate height, particularly at the melting of snow; as it is fed, not only by five lakes (two of them tolerably large), but by innumerable torrents from Ben Nevis, and other far more distant high mountains, south-east and north, from the place where I was admiring it. Some of the feeding streams rise from the mountains farther north than Loch Spey, and near it; others as far east as the ridge hanging over the west side of Loch Ericht, near Rannoch; consequently, at the breaking up of a frost, or in a season of great floods, the Spean river must be filled with huge pieces of ice, accompanied by a weight of water sufficient to carry off and devastate every thing in its way, with a violence not to be imagined or understood by Lowlanders, unaccustomed to the ravages of rivers in Highland countries.

Through the vast moor before me, there was nothing but the road to be seen except a few scattered huts; some of them in such bogs, that it seemed impossible for any thing human to exist in such places. Peat-moss, rushes, coarse grass, and now and then a patch of heath, are the whole produce of this up and down waste. The eight miles from High Bridge to Fort William, is the most dreary, though not the ugliest, space I travelled in Scotland. It is very thinly inhabited; but notwithstanding its non-productive appearance, I never drank finer milk than I did there, from cows I found milking on the road's side; and what was still more extraordinary, though I gave but a trifle more than the value of what was drunk, the honest creatures thought it *too much*, although they *seemed* the poorest of the poor in Scotland. The huts on this moor are very small and low, are soon erected, and must very soon fall down. They consist of four stakes of birch, forked at the top, driven into the ground; on these they lay four other birch poles, and then form a gavel at each end by putting up more birch sticks, and crossing them sufficiently to support the clods with which they plaster this skeleton of a hut all over, except a small hole in the side for a window, a small door to creep in and out at, and a hole in the roof, stuck round with sticks, patched up with turf, for a vent, as they call a chimney. The covering of these huts is turf, cut about five or six inches thick, and put on as soon as taken from the moor; therefore it seldom loses its vegetation, as I hardly saw any difference between the huts and the moor; for what heath there was on either, was equally in bloom. In these huts they make a fire upon the ground, and the smoke issues in columns at every hole, so that if an inhabitant within be induced to take a peep at any travellers, they are seen in a cloud of smoke; notwithstanding which, the curshes (caps of Highland women) were as white as snow, and the faces of the children mostly fair and blooming. At night they rake out the fire, and put their beds of heath and blankets (which they have in abundance) on the ground, where the fire had been, and thus keep themselves warm during the night. The chief of their furniture is an iron pot, a few bowls, and spoons of wood, and pails to put their milk in.

A person accustomed to the comforts and luxuries of life, cannot conceive how it is possible for human beings to exist, in a state so near that of the brute creation.

It is curious to examine the interior of an habitation called a house, in a cluster of houses, termed in Scotland a town. It consists of a butt, a benn, and a byar; that is, a kitchen, an inner room, and a place in which to put cattle. In the centre of the gavel end of the butt, is heaped dirt and stones, in which are fixed small iron bars; leaving a hollow by way of grate, with a hob on each side: there is also a sort of crank that moves any way, to which is hooked the meikle pot. There is no resemblance of a chimney, but the hole at the top; so that the whole side of the gavel is covered with soot from the fire to the vent. The dirt floor is full of holes, retaining whatever wet or dirt may be thrown upon it; consequently it is always a mire. In one corner is a box nailed to the partition, between the butt and the benn. This box opens with a door in front, in which is a heath, or other bed, with a great number of blankets. Into this box creep as many as it can hold; and thus they sleep, boxed up on every side, except the small door in front. In the house I was in, close to the box bed, stood another box similar in size, containing provisions of milk, oat cakes, broth, etc., and eating utensils. If the family be large, the benn too has a similar bed or beds; between which and the byar, there is generally only a very partial partition. A small farmer will say, he delights to sleep thus close to the byar, that he may lie and see, and hear, his beasts eat. Another pretty fashion among them (and it is universal), their dunghill is close to the door of the house, or hut; let the spot about it be ever so lovely, to them their sweet midden is their choicest, their chief object. Next the dunghill stand their peat stacks; whilst, perhaps, on the back part of their house, where they seldom never go, all is neatness. What a perverse inclination for nastiness!

In most of the sequestered parts of the Highlands, the substitute for tallow candles, are the stumps of birch and fir trees, which the Highlandmen dig out of the peat mosses when they cut that fuel. These stumps appear to have lain buried in the bogs for a vast time; and when prepared for candles, they really give a charming light, but of short duration. After drying these stumps thoroughly, they cut them in slips like long matches, which are burned singly, or in a bundle, according to the light required. It falls to the lot of whatever useless being there is in a hut (old folks or children), to hold the torch, and renew it; for it burns out very fast. It is a pleasant sight to see an old woman of seventy or eighty, dressed in her snow-white cursche, sitting by a cozy (snug) fire, holding this clear taper for her daughter and grand children, while they are, some spinning, others singing and dancing, and a group of youngsters playing on the ground with each other, and their faithful sheep dog.

I had observed no beggars in the Highlands, till I came upon the moor between High Bridge and Fort William; but there, at the sound of the carriage, came bounding like fauns, through the dub and the lare (mire and bog), swarms of half naked boys and girls, muttering Gaelic. Having no half-pence, I shook my head, and made every sign I could think of to make them understand I had nothing for them; but notwithstanding, one fly of a girl kept skimming over every thing in her way, by the side of the carriage, for at least two miles; I screaming, "to-morrow I will give you something." Whether she became weary, or conceived what I meant, I cannot say; but at length she took a different direction, and bounded away through bog and heath, to a hut on a dismal looking swamp, at some distance. On the morrow, the rattle of the wheels again brought forth a swarm, and my skipping lass amongst them; I had not forgotten her; but all Maryburgh could not furnish me with six-penny worth of half-pence. The girl bounded before me smiling; and seemed to express, by her countenance, that to-morrow was come, and that she claimed my promise. On a steep rise she came close to the window of the chaise; she did not speak, but she looked in my face so expressively, that out came a silver six-pence from my purse, and I threw it before her. She stooped to pick it up, expecting, I suppose, a half-penny: but no sooner did her eye catch the white metal, but she jumped a full yard from the ground, uttering such a scream of joy and surprize as startled me, and might have been heard at a great distance. She then quickly turned to her companion beggars, shewed the six-pence to them, and, with a smile of delight, bounded away towards the huts with an incredible swiftness. I never gave a six-pence with so much pleasure in my life; nor do I suppose one ever was received with more ecstasy.

As I advanced towards Fort William, at a distance, amongst the ridge of stupendous mountains on my left, over the tops of which the clouds and mist were every instant varying, I perceived the hollow parts and clefts of one of them filled with snow; and when I came opposite to it, I was all admiration and astonishment at its noble crescent of crags; the regularity, the sublimity, and seemingly perfect architecture of which, with the bold massy towers of rocks on each side, convinced me, (though impenetrable clouds concealed its major part) that this mountain could be no other than the Scotch Atlas, Ben Nevis. As I returned the next day, I was, with respect to a view of this gigantic mountain, in high good luck. Its cap of cloud is very seldom off; but the morning was bright, and the mist fast creeping up every side of the mountain. I anxiously watched the humour of the sovereign, and with joy perceived, in his majesty, a strong inclination to uncover. I set off, and by the time I came under the shadow of his wing, his cap disappeared, and I had a fine view of every part that is possible to be seen from the road. In its shape there is beauty, mixed with the sublime and terrific. In front of a soft verdant sloping hill; behind which is an hollow, and a lofty crescent rising from it, with its high pointed horns; joining to one of which are towers of huge rocks, furrowed by continual torrents; with hollows and chasms filled with snow, forming a rare contrast in summer, with the black and grey rocks of the crescent, and other huge masses adjoining. The whole, to an eye below, appears to be capped with soft verdure, except where the never-melting patches of snow keep possession. The summit, however, of Ben Nevis, I am told, is a bed of white pebbles, some of them beautiful. There are but few who attain so high a station, it being a very laborious journey to climb that mountain to the top.

I learnt, in those parts, another instance of the great love a Highland man has for whisky. A lady of fashion, having conquered that ascent, before she quitted it, left on purpose a bottle of whisky on the summit: when she returned to the fort, she laughingly mentioned that circumstance before some Highland men, as a piece of carelessness; one of whom slipped away, and mounted to the pinnacle of 4370 feet above the level of the fort, to gain the prize of the bottle of whisky, and brought it down in triumph.

Loch Eil, a salt water lake, is in shape something like a compass half opened; running from west to east as far as the angle, and then south-west, to enter into Linnhe Loch, an arm of the sea. A traveller from Fort William, whether he proposes to return south, either by the Appin road, or through Glen Coe to Tyndrum, must keep close by the side of Loch Eil, to the ferry at Ballachelish, at the mouth of Loch Leven, where that lake also empties itself into Loch Linnhe. The Appin road from that ferry continues south west close to the sea; the new road towards Tyndrum runs nearly by the south bank of Loch Leven, until it enters Glen Coe. This glen runs nearly east to King's house in the Black Mount. The road by the devil's staircase is at the head of Loch Leven, but now never travelled: it is, however, the continuation of the military road from the Black Mount to Fort William. Even so late as in General Wade's time, they knew not the art of road making so well as they do now; for his military roads generally go up and down mountains, never dreaming that he could wind round the bases of them.

CHAPTER FOUR

The day, after I returned to my friends at Fort Augustus, was very bad; I therefore did not dare face a storm over Corryarraick, but remained quietly at the fort. A fortunate day's rest for the poor horses, who had been sadly off at Fort William, and dreadfully fatigued by the rough road from thence, after a sleepless night; there being at Fort William scarcely any thing for the poor beasts to eat, and nothing to lie down upon. The fare for man, at either of the inns there, is not much better than for horses; but as I had my own bedding, and some food and wine with me, I was very independant of their accommodations.

As we were sitting at breakfast with the good Governor at Fort Augustus, an Oxonian sent in his name, begging leave to see the fort. He had permission, and was invited to breakfast: he was a very genteel young man, and gave us some account of his tour, which had not been quite so fortunate as mine. He left England, one of a large party; their new coach had broken down several times before they got to Glasgow, where it was sold for a song; and two chaises taken instead, which had also broken down; and I think overturned: at last, however, they all arrived safe at Dalwhinie, an inn I have before mentioned, where were collected, from the different branches of the roads, travellers to the amount of near thirty. Every room in that little inn was stuffed brim-full, with standing beds, boxed beds, and shake downs. A shake-down is a bed upon the floor or carpet, and there prepared to sleep upon. At Dalwhinie, the road to Fort Augustus over Corryarraick, branches from the great Inverness road. None of this young gentleman's party dared to encounter that road, except himself and servant, on horseback; the rest went on to Inverness by the great road. The day he crossed Corryarraick was a continued violent rain and storm of wind, which gave it the appearance of wild desolation, beyond any thing he could describe; and the whole of the road itself, he said, was rough, dangerous, and dreadful, even for a horse. The steep and black mountains, and the roaring torrents, rendered every step his horse took, frightful; and when he attained the summit of the zig-zag up Corryarraick, he thought the horses, himself, man and all would be carried away, he knew not whither; so strong was the blast, so hard the rain, and so very thick the mist: and as for cold, it stupefied him. He thought it almost a miracle to escape unhurt from such horrid wastes, roaring torrents, unwholesome vapour, and frightful fogs; drenched from top to toe, frozen with cold, and half dead with fatigue. He said he had heard people had gone that pass in a carriage, but he was sure it was impossible. The governor's family assured him it was done frequently; and turning to me, said, "here is one who means to do so to-morrow, in a chaise." — The gentleman stared, and added, "then I must alter my journal, for I thought it impossible." A young lady present said, she had crossed the mountain on horseback in winter, when snow was on the ground; but it was hazardous. Many, by imprudence, have there lost their lives in winter; and some indeed from fatigue and cold; particularly one poor woman, attending on a marching troop, carrying an infant in her arms. At the top of the mountain she sunk, and would not be persuaded to be removed, nor suffer the child to be taken from her. She fell asleep, and the people who were sent the next morning from the fort to seek for her, found her sitting against a stone, nearly covered with snow. The woman was quite dead; but the infant at her breast, being entirely covered with snow, was not absolutely lifeless. It was carried to the fort, where the governor's lady (from whom I had the sad tale) restored it to life; but it did not recover the perfect use of its limbs for many weeks, so much were they frozen. Soldiers too, in their march, have often perished there, by imprudently drinking quantities of spirits at the inn on the Moor, thinking thereby to keep out the cold; but alas! it was the sure way to destruction.

All these accounts did not deter me from going over the pass: I wished to see it, and I had come back from Fort William on purpose. My postillion had been over the pass in May; he said, though the road was bad and rough, he could drive me over it with safety; and if I could get a pair of horses to put to those I had to help to draw us up the hill, it would be of far more use than the assistance of all the invalids in the fort. I followed his advice. The smith carefully examined the carriage, put all right that was wrong, and the morning looking tolerable, at eight o'clock I took leave of my good friends in the fort, and drove to the inn, where they had added two plough horses, harnessed with ropes, to mine. The road over Corryarraick, quits the Fort William road about a mile and a half from the inn; and immediately begins to wind amongst, and up the district of mountains to the south east of Fort Augustus. Not a foot of level ground was to be seen for nine long miles; nothing but ups and downs till I reached the summit of Corryarraick. My head was continually out of the chaise window, gazing at the scene I was leaving below; a scene not to be described. Nothing but the eye can convey to the mind an adequate idea of it. When I entered into the bosom of the mountains, which would perhaps for ever hide that view from my bodily eyes, I really felt my spirits sink; the road became rough, but not in the least alarming: all the pain I felt was for my poor horses, on whom it bore hard, notwithstanding the pair before them. The first seven miles of ascent are not positively on the sides of Corryarraick; but of other mountains nearly equal in height. It is not till after crossing the bridge over the river Tarff, at the hollow, called in Gaelic Laga na-viene, the hollow of milk, that the base of Corryarraick begins. All these mountains afford fine pasture for sheep farms; though formerly both black cattle and sheep were raised on them. There being some wood hanging about the broken banks of the Tarff, the descent to the bridge is very pretty; but in crossing it, and mounting the narrow steep road on the opposite side, I preferred the safety of my own legs to a reliance on the horses. At about four miles of the ascent from Fort Augustus, the ploughman-driver informed us, that five Edinburgh gentlemen had that morning gone up so far that road, in order to cross Corryarraick; but they became so terrified with what they saw before them, and what they dreaded to meet with, from the account of the young Oxonian, that they fairly, from fear, turned about and took the road to Fort William. This however, did not alarm me. I saw nothing to hurt any body but the horses; and they being assisted, I trusted all would go well. — From the base of Corryarraick to its summit, the road lies on a broad side of it. The ascent is to be sure very long and steep, but not excessively so; nor does the hill sweep from the road very precipitately to a stream below, which is at a considerable distance from it. The mountain on the left rises high; and on each side of the passing track, is a stony rough pasture, mixed with rushes, and a black boggy-looking heath down to the stream; on the other side of which, the mountains have the same hue as that I was ascending. Not a shrub, or bush to be seen, nor trace of a house, except two or three huts at Laga-na-viene; so that the scene at all times, and in all weathers, must be black and dreary. Long poles are driven into the ground, by the edge of the road, at stated distances, all the way up the ascent; and also down the zig-zag on the other side, in order to mark the track, in the season of snow. Just at the winding to attain the summit, there is a degree of precipice, but neither perpendicular nor very dangerous, unless for a phaeton in a high wind; as one was actually blown from thence, and turned over and over, down the mountain, the year before I saw Corryarraick. Having arrived at the top, where there is a small plain, of perhaps half a mile, I got out of the chaise, that I might be the judge of the climate there. It was certainly cold enough for my great coat; but I became neither torpid or frozen. I discharged my plough horses, and began to examine the surprising scene all around me. I had been before on many high mountains, whence I had seen lakes, plains, and far distant objects;

but the view from Corryarraick is totally different. No lakes, no glens, no plains; all is a boundless space of a rough ocean of mountains; whose tops seem to wave one beyond the other, to the distant sea in the west; and on every other side, as far as the eye can reach. Fortunately, when I was thus high, the day was tolerably clear, but not being bright, the whole scene was cold and dismal; — it was uncommon; — it was astonishing, but not at all terrific. My mind was raised to a state of awe and seriousness, that led to the great Creator of all; and I almost forgot I belonged to this world, till the postillion reminded me it was time to re-enter the carriage. When I came to the beginning of the zig-zag, the sun began to shine; and to the south-west, above the rest of the mountain ocean's waves, I saw Ben Nevis, which I distinguished from the other mountains; it being rendered conspicuous by the sun shining upon its white patches of snow. At the commencement of the zig-zag I got out of the carriage, and walked down at my leisure: amusing myself by picking up stones and pebbles in the channels made by the torrents, which cross the road at every five or ten yards. Round the base of the mountain, at some distance from the zig-zag, is a stream, into which the other torrents dash; leaving behind them, broad channels of smooth round stones, washed from the higher parts. The road is so cut up by these violent torrents, from the top of the zig-zag to the entrance on the plain, that for four or five miles, scarcely ten yards can be found free of them; which is, indeed, sufficient to pull a slight carriage to pieces. — Allen led the horse, and the wheels being dragged, he came quietly and safely to the bottom of that extraordinary pass. I will do my best to describe its appearance, from the approach to it from Garvimore. I will take my station upon a narrow shelf, cut on the side of a mountain, rising high on the right, of grey stone, partially covered with very coarse verdure. To the left is a precipice of no great depth, or danger, down to a small rough space of heath, bog, and rushes; scattered over with stones, and reaching to the stream coming from the base of Corryarraick: on the other side of that stream, rise mountains of dark hue, bare, and wildly jumbled together. In front stands the broad side of Corryarraick, sweeping almost perpendicularly to the right and left; every where rough and bare, except patches of rushes and coarse grass, growing about the springs. At the summit a zig-zag road begins, about twelve feet broad; and from one angle of the zig-zag to another, about thrice the length of a carriage and pair of horses; the guide poles continuing to point out the track, should the road be by any means rendered invisible or obscured.

On each side the zig-zag are innumerable springs and marshy places, with thickly scattered loose stones, and fragments of rocks, brought from the heights by violent rushing waters in hard rains. I can easily conceive this to be a frightful pass in a flood; when torrents at every step must threaten destruction to the traveller, and the natural desolation of the place is rendered terrific by the additional gloom of rain, hurricanes of wind, and the frightful night of such mists as frequently obscure, and hide Alpine districts. I had none of these alarming difficulties to encounter; the day was sufficiently dry for walking, and the mountain torrents were all hushed, by a cessation of rain for twenty-four hours. I had heard and read so much of the horrors of this pass that, I confess, I was disappointed at its tameness. At the same time I made great allowance for the difference of appearance in a very bad day, and a tolerable one. I had read, that the Spey river, at Corryarraick, spreads horrid devastation, tearing away every thing before it, and also thence takes its source, which is not quite correct; for the torrents which issue from Corryarraick, are only trifling tributaries to the noble Spey river, which has its beginning in Loch Spey, far to the south-west of Corryarraick, in that part of Badenoch leading to Fort William, from Garvimore; and when I reached the plain, I met it quietly gliding through the vale, and issuing smoothly from the opening between the vast ranges of hills leading to Loch Spey. Whatever *fury* the river Spey acquires before it finishes its course, it does not shew it till many a mile below Garvimore: for when I left its banks, eight miles below the inn on that Moor, it was gliding away towards the huge mountains near the bridge of Spey, just as quietly as at the first moment I saw it. The *tearing* waters about Corryarraick, are in fact, no more than copious springs, incessantly flowing from that mountain; and in great rains, swelling to furious cataracts, carry every thing before them, to the stream which conveys them to the Spey valley.

At the foot of the zig-zag, I looked up the mountain of Corry-arraick with astonishment, to think, that by a distance of only a mile and a half, I had descended an eminence that was full nine miles to climb on the other side. I longed, but I longed in vain, for the effect of a moving zig-zag, such as was described by my friend Major Barry. One part of the 24th regiment, in which he served in the year 1746, was, on a fine sun shining day, marching from Fort Augustus over Corryarraick. The officers, to add to the uncommon-ness of the scene, ordered the men to walk one by one down the zig-zag; and the baggage and women to bring up the rear on horseback. What an extraordinary appearance in such a desert! To see a military moving zig-zag of almost two miles; their arms glittering in the summer sun beams, shining full upon them, and their officers at the bottom admiring the sight. I had not the pleasure of seeing a living being there except the men and horses with the chaise, slowly creeping down the curious ridge: but in my mind's eye, I saw the Major's troops; I beheld their arms glitter; the women mounted, bringing up the rear; and he himself by my side, in raptures at the effect of their plan.

The whole of the way from Garvimore to Dalwhinie is particularly wild; but to my taste, far from ugly, as long as the road keeps by Spey side; and when it turns from that sweet river, nothing is seen but bare mountains, and walls of stone for enclosures; yet as I amused; my mind finding always something, to contemplate; those bare mountains, of granite, gneiss, and micaceous shistus, appeared to me full of metallic substance, as when the sun-beams gilded their huge sides, they sparkled like gems; and from the walls on the road side, when I walked up the steep places, I picked numberless pieces of stones, filled (to an ignorant eye) with gold, silver, etc. The stones were so pretty I could not throw them away, though I knew they were neither uncommon, nor, to a mineralogist, worth a straw. The sun was set before I left this secluded Alpine scenery, and nearly dark when I came within sight of Dalwhinie inn.

From Dalwhinie I retraced my steps to Dalnacardoch; it was the 18th of August, a fine bright day. The attendants, and horses of sportsmen, who were come to the Highlands to shoot, enlivened the scene at Dalnacardoch: and as I sat in the carriage writing, the carters as they passed, regaled me with soft, sweet, Gaelic ditties, that delighted my ear. Nothing can exceed the melody of the Gaelic tunes, sung by a tolerable voice. The murmuring of the river Garrie also added to the harmony; so that the hour and a half the horses required to rest, seemed to be very short. I was not a little amused with the expressions of the comers and goers, but one of Allen's was quite new to me. A chaise coming from the road I was going; driven by a Perth lad; — Allen hailed him, by saying, "What like is that road?" the answer, "Dreadfully hilly!" Which I afterwards found very true. The day was hot, and the sun tinged the distant mountains most beautifully, particularly those of Atholl Forest, and the towering tops of Benygloe. All around me was a world of mountains, with craggy tops, and sides of sheep pasture; mixed with peat, moss and heath.

When I arrived at the highest point on Mount Alexander, the scene that opened to the west and the east surprised and delighted me. I got upon a wall to take in the greatest extent of it: the sun shone finely upon Glen Tumel, stretching below me far to the east; the only part of Loch Tumel was in sight, with the river winding towards it; and beautiful mountains hanging over it to the north and south: wood also enriching the glen, and creeping up every sweeping mountain's side, almost to the top. My eye then turned to the west. Rannoch presented itself: a space of about twenty miles in length, nearly straight, and about two and a half in breadth. The lake nearly fills fifteen miles of the space; and its shores are beautifully indented by sweeps of mountains, and wooded points of land, running far into the water: some islands also add much to its beauty. The mountains on the north-side are very high; and their steep sides, wherever the crags will permit it, are cultivated; producing barley, oats, and grass, with wood creeping up the rocks where cultivation is denied. On the south side of the lake is another ridge of mountains; some of them little inferior to the proud Schichallion: these mountains are finely covered by extensive woods of firs and birch; even some of the highest crags are thus beautifully clothed. As I advanced towards the town of Kinloch, at the foot of the lake, I passed on a narrow high shelf, hanging over a precipice to the river Tumel, deep below. The road is but just sufficiently wide for a carriage, and no fence whatever on the precipice side of it. On the other hand are lofty mountains shivering from their tops, with huge detached pieces of rocks lying from the summits to the bases, ready at the least shock to crush the passenger beneath them. To be in that pass was frightful, and I was glad when I got beyond the threatening danger.

Close to Kinloch is a very curious torrent, which in hard rains must have a very uncommon appearance. It falls between two bare mountains, in an irregular channel, narrow at the tip, but spreads, as it descends, on large flat stages of reddish smooth stones. I never beheld so singular a cataract; but I did not see it in perfection, there being but little water in it when I walked up its side. Some brush-wood, and a few shrubs and rushes hang about the broken pieces of rocks, forming irregular weirs, between the broad stages that come, step by step, from the top of the high mountain to the bottom, over which the water, in dry weather, slides in the oddest shapes imaginable; and in a flood, by the violent bounds, from one flat stage to another, the water forms a chain of semicircular spouts all the way down the channel.

At Kinloch, I crossed the Tumel just after it quits Loch Rannoch, over a very good bridge, and then wound round the foot of the lake, and proceeded on its southern margin, by a road truly beautiful; and were it not so rough, it would be a drive of fifteen miles that few can equal. There are two tolerable houses, and several hamlets on the way. One of the houses is a shooting box, belonging to Baron Norton; the other is called Garrie. For the whole distance, there is but a small flat between the ridge of the mountains and the lake, sometimes not broader than the road. The great variety in the woods and groves through which the road winds, renders every step picturesque. The Black Wood is an extensive tract of fine firs growing up the sides of the mountains, and covering every crag; and the bases, tracts of charming elms, mountain ash, oak, ash, birch, and many other sorts of trees intermixed; and by the lake's edge, an abundance of alder, hazel, mountain ash, young oaks, and a great variety of shrubs and small branching wood, all in its true natural state. The shavers and dressers have never laid their frightful hands on that lovely district; it being, to this day, in Nature's sweetest style. The extent of the Black Wood may be imagined, when I say, from a late survey of it, in order to ascertain the number of trees fit for use, it was found that there were in it five hundred thousand, from six inches and a half, to three feet in diameter. What a pity it is there is no water carriage from Rannoch; for were that the case, this fir wood would be a vast treasure to the owner of it. Had I not been in some fear for the carriage, from the roughness of the road, I should have enjoyed the drive through Rannoch exceedingly. By and by I came to the bed of a large burn, another Calder burn with respect to its bed of stones, and the entrance into it even worse. Perceiving higher up the burn, a plank laid from bank to bank, I got out of the chaise, and made the best of my way to it. I found it in a very tottering state; but it was better than being in the carriage, for which I trembled, fearing it would be shaken to pieces every jolt it received, in going up and down over the stones in the burn's bed. That burn, in hard rains, rises suddenly to a prodigious height; and when I meant to return to it, it shut me up for a day, as there was no possibility of getting through it. As I approached the head of the lake, the district of Rannoch appeared to be entirely excluded from the whole world besides, by mountain upon mountain all around, and no means of escape; which indeed is nearly the case, except for Highland men and birds. It is true, there is an outlet to a flat towards Glen Coe, nearly west, by the river Avon-gaur, that winds round some mountains from Loch Lydoch, to empty itself into Loch Rannoch; but this plain is full of bogs and roughness, which none but highland men can master: it is even dangerous for a shelty (a Highland poney) to go over it. From the west end of Loch Rannoch to King's House in the Black Mount, near Glen Coe, it is only nine Scotch miles; but it was impossible for me to get to the district called the Black Mount, that way, for the reasons above mentioned; I could only look at it from a mountain top, and afterwards went no less than eighty miles round to get thither. At the head of Loch Rannoch, or as is generally called the west end, there is on the north side a shooting box belonging to Sir John Menzies. On the south side is a cluster of huts, called George's Town; and near it the remains of a barrack, but now a shooting box belonging to the chief of the Robertsons. There is an inn too, but it is only fit for drovers to put up at; also a farm-house, and a cluster of huts, by the side of a pretty mountain cataract. One day I ascended the hill at the back of the farm (not a very easy scramble); but when I had attained the eminence, the distant mountains formed a grand prospect, though all between them and me was a dismal waste of flat moor, several small lakes, and the winding Gauer flowing from one of them: but beyond the waste, as far as my eye could reach, mountain beside mountain lofty and jagged, gratified my

never satisfied sight for such objects. To the north-west Ben Nevis is seen, with its towering head above the rest of the Bens. Due west, at the end of the Moor, the tremendous mountains in Glen Coe, and about King's House, rise in every sort of form, thence sweeping away to join the ridge on the south-west side of the Black Mount, having their tops lost in the sky; and those tops, what could be seen of them (from the motion of the clouds), varied in shape every instant. The sovereigns of Glen Orchy, with the sharp pointed tops of Cruchan Ben, hanging over Loch Awe, shut up the view to the south-west; and near the Rannoch mountains bound the sight on the south; the soft round top of Schichallion looks down on its neighbours to the east; and the glittering bare crags hanging over Loch Ericht, close the scene to the north.

As I looked at the head of Loch Ericht, when at Dalwhinie, I was desirous of seeing the southern end of it, near Rannoch. Eight miles was the distance named; but I am sure it is fourteen at least. I was placed upon a shelty, which was led through the Gauer river by a Highlandman, hip deep; but he cared far less for that, than I did for the splashing of my petticoats. As soon as I left the side of the Loch, to mount the river Ericht's side, I could no longer take care of myself; therefore the good High-landman became my friendly leader. I stuck as fast to the pummel of the saddle as I could, and thus mounted, I descended such places as were sufficient to scare a lowland female out of her wits. At the end of a mile or two we quitted the bank of the river, and every track that had been gone before us, entering on the roughest and most uneven boggy, rocky, watery, black mountain moor, that human being ever explored. It was with the utmost difficulty that the poor little beast could keep upon his legs, though born and bred on such wastes; but there is a sagacity in the shelties not easily credited: if they be left to themselves, they will pick out their way in these horrid places with as much caution and wisdom as a man can. I afterwards met with three German gentlemen who were on their road from the island of Staffa. To get to that island, they had crossed the Isle of Mull upon these little animals. There were four men in that party, and they could procure only one saddle and bridle; the lucky he, to whom this luxury was allotted, soon resigned the use of the bridle; trusting like the rest of his companions, to the better knowledge and experience of his shelty. They all declared to me, that when left to themselves, those sagacious little beasts, on the most difficult and dangerous moors, would pat a suspicious place with their forefeet, and try a slippery piece of rock, before they would venture to step upon it; and were continually looking to the right and the left to discover which was the soundest spot; and after a mature examination,

Such a solitary waste I never before beheld!

would turn this way or that, or take a circuitous route to gain the safest footing. The little shelty that carried me to Loch Ericht was not quite so sagacious; but, on the whole, he did tolerably well, and I last arrived at the lake; but such a solitary waste I never before beheld. The lake looks like a broad river, with tremendous, and most of them bare craggy mountains, rising perpendicularly from it; except here and then alpine wood creeping up their sides, till the shivering stones debar vegetation. On the east bank of this lake, at the south end of it where I embarked, is a prodigiously high, rough, bare mountain, in the hollows of which, as I have before mentioned, poor Charles Stuart concealed himself. On the west side of the lake, opposite to this mountain, is a patch of verdure by a little burn's side, backed by the mountains of Lochaber, and the stony crags of Ben Aulder forest, hanging over the western side of Loch Ericht. On this green plat stands a solitary sheel (or shepherds hut), in which lives a shepherd, whose employer, at stated times, conveys meal and other provisions to him, by means of the lake; but he and his family never quit this sequestered spot, except to preserve and follow the sheep entrusted to their care. The wind rose too high to permit me to land, otherwise I should have been pleased to have seen such aborigines. The boatman assured me, there was not a more healthy, or more *bonny* family in the Highlands than this shepherd's; and what is extraordinary, they can neither speak nor understand Gaelic; a strong proof of their solitude, and that they have no communication with their neighbours in Rannoch. I think there cannot, in nature, be a more forlorn or desolate place than that about Loch Ericht; but I am glad I saw it; and as I returned from it, and came down towards Rannoch, that district appeared, in comparison, a perfect Paradise. There are between the lakes a great many excessively pretty falls of the river Ericht, which I should have enjoyed, had the road been less dangerous, or I on foot instead of on horseback.

The greatest part of the district of Rannoch, (which I describe more particularly than most others, because it is less known, yet well worth seeing) has been for ages in the possession of the chiefs of the Robertsons. In the last rebellion, Robertson of Strowan, the poet, was their chief; a man, at that time, near eighty years of age, his body hale and strong, and his mind in vigour. He was at the battle of Preston Pans; and for his share of booty was allotted the carriage of Sir John Cope, there defeated. Strowan drove it in triumph, as far as he could, towards his district; and when the roads became impassable, he summoned his vassals to carry it into Rannoch. Amongst the other contents of Sir John's chaise, were a number of rolls of brownish stuff, which were concluded to be very valuable specifics for wounds, particularly as they were safely packed in a soldier's carriage, to be ready, as it was thought, in case of accidents. These precious rolls were cried in the streets of Perth, "Wha'll buy Jonny

Cope's salve.'' They were rolls of chocolate.

Not half a mile below Alexander, is the famous fall of the Tumel river; its noise is heard at a great distance; and it is a stop to the salmon, it being far too high for them to leap. It must be full forty feet high. It is not, to be sure, so lofty as many other falls in Scotland; but few equal it in majestic grandeur, at the time of a great flood; not only on account of the rose of the river, and the prodigious body of water in it, but chiefly for the wild appearance it exhibits, when dashing furiously, in all the different forms that can be imagined, over the huge and irregular rocks at the cataract.

There is a very singular well at Mount Alexander, called the Silver Well, from the bright sand in it; and which is inexhaustible; for the well has frequently been cleared to a considerable depth; notwithstanding which it filled, and rose to the usual height, in a short time. Between Mount Alexander and the bridge of Rynachan, on the south side of the river Tumel, are vestiges of a temporary habitation, which, from its Gaelic name, must have been built for King Robert Bruce, when his affairs being at the lowest ebb, he was received in Rannoch by Duncan of Atholl, ancestor to the Robertsons of Strowan.

The common language spoken in Rannoch, and throughout the Highlands, is the Gaelic, or Erse; though most of the inhabitants speak some English: for, except at the small town of Trinefour, between Dalnacardoch and Rannoch, I never, during the course of my peregrination in the Highlands, found any difficulty in getting myself understood. — The iron hook which keeps down the pole of the carriage having been forgotten, Allen did not mention it till we were near Trinefour; we concluded, however, the smith there would set us to rights; but behold, the smith was not at home, and his wife could not understand what *we* wanted, nor we what *she* said. I could ask her in Gaelic where her husband was, but alas! I could not understand her answer. After bawling to each other a considerable time, and making signs to no effect, until we were tired, we both burst out with laughing; and then went on as well as we could, without the iron hook.

With much pain I turned my back upon the district of Rannoch: particularly as I reflected, that it most probably would be the last, as well as the first time, I should ever visit these parts. It would be a very desirable place to live in, were it not for its great distance from any medical assistance; there being none good nearer than Perth; forty miles from Mount Alexander: and when I was at the west end of the lake, wheat-bread and post letters were sent for from Aberfeldie, which is thirty miles.

Part Three

CHAPTER ONE

I did not quit Rannoch by the road I entered it, except the length of the lake; for at the east end of it I left the shivering rocks on the north side of the Tumel, taking the road to the south side of that river; till I arrived at Cross Mount, at the base of Schichallion, where I ascended a very steep hill, and turned my face towards the south, still winding at the foot of Schichallion; rising high on the right above the clouds.

It was on a shoulder of this mountain that Doctor Maskelyne, a few years since, erected a temporary habitation for his observations. All the country gentlemen thought it their duty to pay the philosopher every civility in their power, particularly by frequent visits; which, probably, the Doctor would gladly have excused, as he must thereby be continually interrupted in his pursuit. The lower class of people believed, and declared, he came thither to look for a lost star.

In a short time after I quitted the base of Schichallion, which is 3564 feet above the level of the sea, I entered the high road from Tumel Bridge to Crieff, at about seven miles from Weem. Around the junction of the roads, nothing can be more desolate and dreary; but soon after I came to a steep declivity, leading to a plain, the richest and most beautiful in Scotland; and taking in the tout ensemble, it is equal to any thing in that country; its wood and mountains, at the declivity, were the only parts that began to open to the sight. The wheels of the carriage were dragged, and I went slowly down the winding steep hill, with a torrent, and the ruin of Garth on my right. The ruin is surrounded by a variety of ground and wood. At length I came down close by the burn side, just above Cushaville, where it falls in a very beautiful manner, and extremely picturesque; bursting from a dark-looking cave, forming a sort of arch; partly concealed by a profusion of beautiful wood, of birch, ash, nut, crooked oak, and mountain ash, hanging over the cataract, and creeping to the top of the rocks and banks; branching and twining in the sweetest style. The very great variety of the trees and bushes, at the fall at Cushaville, afford such a mixture of lovely tints, that I was charmed with every part of it that I could get within my view. The owner of it would do well, if he would clear a passage to the bottom of the fall, and cut openings for it to be seen more perfectly from the small field near it, on the road side; for it certainly is a very pretty fall. This burn rises in Schichallion, called the burn of Haltnie, running to the Lyon

River; to which I soon descended, and met it issuing from its glen. A very handsome stone bridge is over it, less than half a mile before its junction with the Tay. On the road leading to Kenmore, near to the bridge of Lyon, and hanging over it, are charming trees; amongst which is a ruin of an old castle. I did not, at that time, go to Kenmore, consequently turned to the east; and the scene before me was every thing to delight the sight. It was in the midst of harvest, a fine afternoon, and the inhabitants in the fields, busy with their corn. The west end of this valley, called Appneydow, is bounded by high lofty mountains, and the extensive and luxuriant woods of Taymouth. Appneydow may be about a mile in breadth, of an uniform flat; with the Tay, joined by the Lyon, winding through the middle of it; stretching nearly eastward as far as the eye can see, to join the Tumel at Logie-rait. The vista is bounded by a gradation of mountains on each side of it, beautifully blending in the distant horizon. The ranges of mountains, both on the north, and the south of this valley, rise steep and sudden; some craggy, but mostly covered with wood. Tay Bridge, or Wade's Bridge, that noble structure, presents itself with its obelisks, in the middle of the vale; there teeming with plenty of corn of every sort, and grazing ground; all richly ornamented with wood and water. The southern ridge of mountains are finely clad with trees, and their bases enlivened by gentlemen's houses, and the town of Aberfeldie; over which hang the heights of Moness, covered with timber, and beautiful woods, which continue towards the east as far as I could see. Under the northern craggy range of hills, is the kirk of Dull, Castle Menzies, and the inn at Weem; besides other houses and huts, dotted amongst crags and trees. the trees close to the Castle and the wood creeping to the tops of the highest crags both behind it, and extending as far as I could see to the east, form one of the finest views of the sort that I think can be seen. Castle Menzies is a large antique-looking building, with frightful short round turrets, the whole whitened with lime; but it being much concealed by the hanging woods on the crags behind, and the fine trees that surround it, neither its white glare, nor its clumsy turrets, offend the eye. The view from it must make ample amends for every imperfection of its shell: and after all, I question whether it does not suit the scene it stands in, far better than a modern house would do. The enclosures about Castle Menzies, and at Taymouth, pleased me prodigiously, being in character with the style of the country. They consist of short round pillars of rough stones, with conical tops placed at certain distances, and wooden bars or chains running through them, to prevent cattle from leaping over or creeping under; trees growing carelessly here and there amongst these pillars, which had been whitened, but by the weather were softened to the mellow tints of grey, brown, green, and yellow, mixed; coarse grass and weeds also sticking about them, giving them less the appearance of a fence than any thing I ever saw; they are also lighter, and far less formal.

The small inn at Weem, when I was there, was not a good house, but a new one was building: what the house wanted, however, the landlord, Menzies, made up by civility and attention. I arrived at Weem to dinner; and in the evening drove over Wade's Bridge to Aberfeldie, and to the top of the brae, near the house of Moness: no farther could I go in the carriage. From thence to the falls, is about three quarters of a mile. I entered the wood accompanied by my servant, and a guide, a boy about twelve years of age; and I walked on, delighted with the scene before me, on the bank of a burn, so shaded with wood and rocks, that, as I advanced between them, daylight became twilight. There is a very good path winding amongst the rocks, and leading to the falls, which I began to hear, though I could not see them. By way of something to say to my little guide, I asked him who had made the walks, which were so convenient, and executed with so much judgment; "ah!" said the lad, who spoke good English, naming the late proprietor, "he is a fine man, and did a great deal of good, and took much pleasure in all these places; he planned all these walks himself, worked at them, and helped to blow up the rocks; planting and improving the place all his life." — I asked, "is he dead?" "No; he lives the other side of the river!" — "Why did he leave Moness, which he was so fond of?" — "What makes many leave what they like; the want of money!" — I began to look upon my diminutive guide as a very sharp wight; which, ere long, I was thoroughly convinced of. The evening was towards the close, and I was amusing myself with my guide's remarks, till I entered the windings of the darker recesses of the woods and rocks, hanging over the water; when on a short turn, we perceived before us, a stout man, whose aspect was by no means promising. The lad came near me, and whispered, "he is a thief." — A hatchet was on the man's shoulder; it struck me (particularly as I was in the Highlands), that that instrument aimed at wood, not at me; so I advanced without fear, and passed the man; who, however, looked very conscious of executed, or meditated mischief. The lad and he turned the point of a rock, and began talking Gaelic pretty loud: still I advanced, thinking more of what I saw before me (for just then I came to the beginning of the Moness Falls), than of what they were chattering about. Soon after, the lad came running after me, and laughing, said, "I have sent him off over the hills as hard as he can run." — "How have you done that?" "I told him you were Mrs. Campbell, my Lord's mother, and that you would send him to Botany Bay for stealing the wood." — Moness now belongs to Lord Breadalbane. I could not help laughing at the quick invention of the boy, who certainly had an amazing capacity for his age. The falls of Moness are far superior to any falls in that part of Scotland: they extend nearly half a mile in length, and are very numerous; not only of the burn itself, but of a continued chain of torrents dashing in every direction from the rocky banks; some hopping from rock to rock, others, from vast heights, slipping down grassy beds, winding round the stumps and stems of trees, and through dark thick copse. The explorer now begins to walk from rock to rock, in the bed of the burn, or creeping over places blown out of the rocks hanging over the falls and whirlpools, which, when full of water, that walk cannot be attempted. The broken rocks on each side rise perpendicularly to a great height, inclining to a junction at the top; and are entirely covered with trees of all sorts, which branch wide, and feather down to the edge of the burn; and by their embraces at the top, form a beautiful canopy over the whole. The masses of pointed and flaky rocks, constantly washed over, look brown and dark; others are covered with green slime, moss, fern, and rushes, which joined by the never-ceasing roar of the numerous falls, give a darkness and solemnity to this scene not to be described. At length, after creeping over slippery stages of flaky rock, and clambering up and down steps on the rocks, from one huge mass to another, the pools whirling beneath me, and the water dashing, white and foaming around me, with the mirky canopy above, for a quarter of a mile, I arrived at the highest, and first fall. It is a termination like the concave head of a cavern, open at top, though almost darkened to night by the high over hanging rocks and trees, which no axe has ever reached; no track of any sort, but the channel made by the water, that from a very great height gushes with prodigious violence round a pointed rock, from a black confined passage, arched over by rocks, considerably above it, and covered with impenetrable wood. The water then spreads, and forms one of the most beautiful cataracts in Nature; I say in nature, for at the falls of Moness that goddess reigns in triumph, there not appearing the least trace of man, or his interference; it is even beyond the art of man to copy them, it having been often tried without success; and I am persuaded, that no pencil can truly delineate the beauties of the falls of Moness.

The next day I turned my face towards Taymouth. Every step was beautiful; but the house I could not see, by reason of the intervening hills and woods, until I came to the lodge gate, to which the road winds down a sharp descent, through a fine and extensive wood. The large front of the house faces the lodge at this entrance. The extended centre of this noble mansion is in a very old style of building, with short round turrets stuck on from the top of each corner, downwards, for only one story, something like those at Castle Menzies. Two large flights of steps lead to the doors, and, like Castle Menzies too, the fabrick is whitened with lime. There are also two extensive wings, in a more modern style, and joined by covered colonnades to the old

centre. All around the house, except immediately in front of it, there are as fine trees as any I ever saw, with the Tay unseen winding at the back of it. Permission is given to drive through the park, which is but a small plain, surrounded on every side but one (towards the lake), by high mountains planted to their summits; and those plantations are flourishing luxuriantly. Clumps and single trees of very fine timber grow handsomely in every part of the park. There is no view from the house, it being built upon the lowest ground about Loch Tay, and on a dead flat. To the east it has the castle-like small hills that I observed generally blocked the entrance of almost every great lake I saw. Those to Loch Tay being covered by very thick trees, the castle-shapes are confounded by a general outline of wood; but when I walked over the pleasure ground, I perceived Loch Tay has its natural castle guards, as well as Loch Catherine, Loch Earn, &c. At the western gate of the park is the almost new and neat town of Kenmore, built close by the foot of the lake. The view from Kenmore is mostly similar to that which is seen from Maxwell's Temple, in his lordship's pleasure ground. The church of Kenmore stands upon ground rather higher than the town, from which (though not joining) a row of houses, on each side, form a broad street towards Lord Breadalbane's gate. The inn and its appendages take up the chief of the northern row, between which and the church-yard a road winds down to the bridge; a beautiful one of five arches over the Tay, as it issues from the lake. The church and church-yard are on the very brink of the lake; but not a tree immediately about them. On my arrival at the inn, as it was a fine day, I directly got a conductor, and proceeded to see the beauties of Taymouth. My search was not for what is to be seen in the interior of fine houses; for when one has seen half a dozen, they are in a manner all seen; I therefore refused to run over the house at Taymouth, determining, all the time I had to spare, should be dedicated to the out-of-door beauties. Very soon after I entered the pleasure ground, nearest the inn, I arrived by a verdant bank at Maxwell's Temple; a very neat room, with a green platform before it; on other sides nearly surrounded and covered by trees and shrubs. In it was a large prospect glass, with a black-ground on a moveable stand; which (like all other glasses of the kind) diminishes, and sharpens every part of the landscape, and at the same time mellows down every object to the softest tone. I turned my back upon the Temple, and advanced to the edge of the grassplat; before me, to the west, was a view which must be a feast to every eye that delights in the noble productions of Nature. The immediate fore-ground is an uneven lawn, and shrubberies leading down to the town of Kenmore, and the river; then the town, the church, the bridge, and the wide expanse of the lake beyond them, extending to a great distance, with bold projecting prom-

Every step was beautiful.

ontories, and fertile tracts of land running far into it; also a chain of woody mountains bordering it on the south; and on the north a still higher range, broken by small glens, and sloping fields of corn descending to the lake's edge. The part of the road to Killin, on the north side of Loch Tay, near to Kenmore, makes no inconsiderable figure in the landscape, as from the bridge it winds up an almost perpendicular crag, chiefly covered with firs. This brown-looking road. and its wall of defence, indicate that the crag may be ascended by man and beast; otherwise it would seem that none but winged animals could soar thus high. Beyond that cragsweep away to the west mountain upon mountain (Ben Lawers occupying the middle of the gradation high above its neighbours), till all is lost behind the towering points of Benmore, in the centre of the utmost distance, The mountains on the south and on the north of the lake, are chiefly clothed with wood; even the corn and grass-fields partake of a copious share of trees. In short, the view is a complete landscape of lake and alpine scenery, mixed with the haunts and habitations of man, and all in style; no eye-sore; no red tiles or bricks; all is harmony and in tune. I must not forget a small island, not far from the bridge, towards the north shore of the loch, covered with trees, through which peeps a ruin, adding to the beauty of the rest of the scenery. I was almost rivetted to the spot, though I did not, the first day, see it in perfection. The sun had gotten too forward to the west, but the next morning made me amends, by that luminary shining gloriously in the east upon the opening to Killin, and beyond it. Benmore too was uncovered.

When I left Maxwell's Temple, I entered a beautiful walk close to the Tay, and an avenue of lime trees, more noble than I can describe, which leads round the back of the house. After crossing the Tay, I came to an elevated broad terrace, called the Beech Walk, or Drive, hanging over the river. I was told it continued many miles, bordered by fine beech trees. Through a wood, and by a pleasant walk, I afterwards ascended a high hill, opposite the house, where is a sham fort; from it are lovely views both to the east and west. Having tired my legs, and greatly feasted my eyes, I returned from the beech walk, through some pleasant corn fields, to the stone bridge over the Tay, and Kenmore.

I had heard and read of the great yew tree at Fortingal, in Glen Lyon; I therefore, in the afternoon, took the north road on the river Tay, under a towering woody crag, and arrived at the bridge over the river Lyon. The view, over Appneydow at the turn of the road from Kenmore towards that bridge, is charming. I then came to the picturesque cluster of trees about the old ruin, near Lyon bridge, which I crossed, and retraced the steps I took from Cushaville, until I came to the entrance of Glen Lyon; a narrow, but beautiful district, flanked by high mountains;

some well wooded, others bare; and the space between them tolerably fertile in corn and grass. The fine river Lyon winds through the glen, shaded by continued wood, and very fine trees hanging over it, which mostly meeting each other, partially conceal, and greatly ornament the water, as it roughly rolls along. Its banks are dotted with tolerable houses on each side, and many small clusters of Highland habitations and farm houses. In short, Glen Lyon is a beautiful, though a confined district. At length I arrived at the kirk of Fortingal; and in that kirk yard is the ruin of the famous yew tree, which, when in vigour, measured fifty-two feet in girth. The sound of the carriage at the kirk gate, brought out the clergyman from his manse adjoining. No set of beings can surpass the inhabitants of the Highlands (of every description), in hospitality and attention to strangers; but at the same time they are extremely curious, and must know every thing, of every body who comes in their way; who they are, what they are, whence they come, and whither going. They in an instant combine circumstances, and are au fait in a moment. They put me in mind of what Doctor Franklin mentions of the Americans. That their curiosity about strangers and travellers, took place of every other consideration; that they would not stir an inch till that curiosity was satisfied. He, therefore, when he travelled through the country, in order to save time and trouble, made it a custom, the moment he went into an inn, to accost the landlord with "I am Benjamin Franklin; I am a printer; I live at Philadelphia; I am going to Boston, or — ; I have with me a servant and two horses; now pray tell me what I can have for supper?"

Perhaps this sort of curiosity may be common to all thinly inhabited, and seldom visited, countries, where the novel sight of strangers leads to a desire of knowing every thing concerning them; particularly as in such an uniform round of life, where their minds are less employed and filled, than in cities and places of commerce and trade, their mental powers are open, and quickly alive to every adventitious incident.

The worthy Mr. Macara accompanied me to the fence of the yew tree, which is surrounded by a high wall, to secure it from being diminished by depredations for ornamental boxes, &c. The door leading to the tree was nailed up, and I found the wall too high for me to scale. The black wild mountains in the closer and higher parts of Glen Lyon now caught my eye; at the same time saying to my reverend conductor, "these are wild indeed; but not more so than in the region of Rannoch." "Have you been in Rannoch, madam?" "Yes." "At Carrie, perhaps?" "No, but at the west end of the lake." "Oh! madam, you are Mrs. Murray; I heard you were there." (Glen Lyon and Rannoch, over the hills, are not at a great distance; but the carriage road is near 40 miles.) At this part of the conversation Mrs. Macara appeared; and with infinite kindness pressed me to

enter their habitation, where tea, she said, was made, and I must partake of it. I could not resist the hospitable manner in which I was invited; my name was announced to her, and I was soon acknowledged by her as a relative by marriage. An abundance of every good thing was then produced; the horses were fed, my servants treated, and I was in an instant looked upon as one of their family. Two young men entered; the one Mr. Macara's son, and the other, a son of the gentleman who owns the yew tree. I was introduced to them, and before I quitted the house, the door to the yew tree was forced open, and the way cleared for me to enter the enclosure. In short, had I been a queen, I could not have been treated with greater attention; and what was still more pleasing to me, with the affection of relations; I learnt too that Mr. Macara had been the instructor of my husband's two brothers in their early youth. In short, all conspired to make me feel myself at home, and as easy as if we had been friends of a long standing. I left them with regret; and proceeded, by their direction, to a bridge over the Lyon, somewhat above Fortingal, and turned from the river to the left, which was soon lost to me in the tremendous mountains of the glen, which I also there quitted, to join Loch Tay; which in a mile or two opened beautifully to my view, and I soon entered the north road from Killin to Kenmore, and came down by that hanging steep piece of road already described, seen from Maxwell's Temple.

CHAPTER TWO

From Kenmore to Killin, it is sixteen miles. The south road is somewhat more than the north; both are hilly, and include a great variety of scenery, and rich too throughout. About the midway of the lake, the huge Ben Lawers raises its craggy head, with verdant sides; and Benmore, with its two pointed tops, high above its neighbours, is seen in the utmost distance.

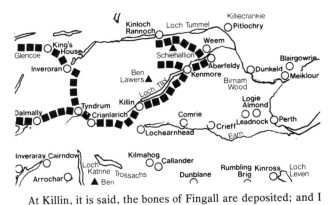

At Killin, it is said, the bones of Fingall are deposited; and I was told also, that Lord Breadalbane had had the ground, about the supposed grave, thoroughly examined without success, for finding the bones. The space about the grave looks as if it had been enclosed for a burying ground, and the old kirk of Killin stood near it. The present church seems by no means of modern erection; the church-yard is in a very romantic situation near the river Lochy, there joining the Tay, and both entering the lake within sight. The Lochy river issues from a glen of that name; which, about Killin, is finely wooded, and through that wood, under a crag, peeps a picturesque ruin of a large castle, once inhabited by the Breadalbanes. Both the rivers Lyon and Lochy, take their source from some small lakes, and the high mountains, which tower to the north of Tyndrum, and near it, on the right of the road from thence to Fort William. I had on a former visit to Killin seen some part of it, but Glen Lochy I had not entered. I ascended, by the Manse, a very steep hill, hanging over the winding road from Killin to the bridge over the Lochy, leading to Taymouth; and as I had heard there is a tolerable fall of the Lochy above, at no great distance, I descended the precipitate side of the mountain, very near the bridge, where I found a Highland town, and all hands busy at housing hay; which they were carrying from every quarter of that verdant, smiling district. The crops of hay seemed abundant; but this must be a backward climate, as it was then the 9th of September; much later than at Appneydow (only twenty miles distant to the east of Killin), where, a few days before, they were busy in corn-harvest. As I was creeping down the crag side, the children and women came to the doors to gaze at a fearless female stranger, scrambling alone amongst the crags. Comerie hache (how do you do), and la-mah-chuie (good day to you), were nearly the only Gaelic words I could say to them; but here, as well as in all the other sequestered Highland glens, English is in some degree spoken. As I have a great passion for water falls, I wished to reach that of the Lochy, but knowing distances in

Scotland to be often misrepresented, I much doubted the accomplishment of my desire. The Scotch wee bit is nearly equal to their mile, and a mile with them is almost double the distance of an English measured mile. However, I enquired at the village, and was told it was not so much as one mile; nearly which I walked, and met a man with a cart loaded with hay; the driver told me he believed it might be a mile and a wee bit; another Highlandman soon came in my way. "How far is to the fall of the Lochy?" "I ca'nae say, but it maun be twa miles or mair." I still advanced, not from any further idea of reaching the fall, but to take a nearer view of a house prettily situated before me. The evening was closing fast, when meeting a woman, I had the curiosity to question her about the distance to the fall. She could scarcely understand me; but by words and signs, she, as I suppose, at last comprehended I meant the fall of the river; for she shook her head and said, "mony miles; it maun be pick mirk ere ye'se gate at the fa'!" I then totally abandoned my project, and turned about; but I could hold no converse to signify with the gude wife, who soon left me to my own thoughts, which naturally turned to the impossibility of getting at facts, such as they really are. It was dark when I re-entered the inn, where my servants began to wonder what was become of me; but seeing me go towards the Manse, they fancied I had therein found another good clergyman, like Mr. Macara, of Glen Lyon, who, in like manner, might be regaling me with the wonders of Killin.

The Lin at Killin is very striking, and uncommon. The Tay advances to it from Glen Dochart, and widens to a very considerable breadth as it approaches Killin; which is a row of small houses, facing the Lin; the road only between it and the houses. The broad bed of the river is there choaked up by large masses of rock lying one upon another, in every kind of form and direction. These fragments of rocks have been most of them, at least, washed thither by floods, and in a course of years have collected soil sufficient to unite many of them together, so as to form rough islands, covered with beautiful bushes, and trees of no great size; but sprouting from every crevice, branching and weeping over the rocks, in a style that delights the eye. Two small bridges, from rock to rock (but not in a line), lead from the south to the north side of the river. Just at the bridges the river is divided by the head of a small rocky high banked island. This nook is the terra firma between the bridges; against which, and the rocks before it, and at the arches of the bridges, the water dashes, foams, and roars to such a degree, at the time of a flood, that it is scarcely possible to hear the sound of a human voice, even close at the ear. I wonder the inhabitants of Killin are not all deaf (like those who are employed in iron and copper works), from the thundering noise of the rushing waters. Standing on either of the romantic bridges, the scene around is prodigiously grand, awful, and striking. To the west, is the river winding from a narrow opening between green mountains and crags, rising almost perpendicularly from the margin of it. The observer is in the midst of the Lin, at least fifty yards in breadth, surrounded by its flat, and very irregular bed of rocks, partially covered with weeping trees, and branching underwood, with loud white reeking cascades and torrents, dashing in every direction; altogether forming a picture, not to be imagined, unseen. To the east, in front, is the abovementioned island; to which is a communication from the rocks forming the piles on which the bridges rest, and this communication is a narrow slip of rock, covered with grass; the entrance to the island is closed by a gate, kept fastened by the owner of it. Round the rocky base of this island the Tay dashes furiously, both on the north and south sides of it, until it is again united at the end of the island. There are, besides the row abovementioned, clusters of houses on the south and north shores, with a road before each, leading to Taymouth. The opening from the bridges to the lake, is concealed from the eye by the church, the inn, the winding towering mountains on the sides, and the thick wood at the bases, filling the whole space, and hiding the courses of the rivers towards the soft bosom of the lake.

I had a strong desire to go upon the forbidden island, but bars and locks denied me entrance. It is entirely covered with fir trees, whose dark hue casts a solemn shade over a burying place erected in the middle of the island, and railed round with iron. It belongs to a Highland chief hard by, who once, on laying his pretensions and possessions at the feet of a fair lady, whom he courted for his bride, told her, as an irrestible charm, that he had the most beautiful burying-ground in the world. Whether the lady preferred beauties she could enjoy in life, to those offered her after death, I cannot say, but the chief was not accepted; nor has he ever worn the chains of matrimony, though he has added to his family thirty-two children.

After quitting Killin, the road continues for a mile or two close by the Tay, and then turns up a very steep hill to join the road from Loch Earn Head towards Fort William. All roads, in such mountainous regions, are continually torn away by violent torrents, and require constant repair. The road between Killin and Tyndrum was, in 1796, getting a very thorough repair; and at the unsound parts of the moors, they were turning it; forming arches in some places, and levelling others, so that by this time, that drive of eighteen miles may be as fine a road as any in the Highlands.

Glen Dochart is a region of mountains, moor, and water, till near, and at the head of it, though all the way the banks of the Tay, at the bases of the mountains, are mostly ornamented with wood, and now and then gentlemen's houses; but the forms of the smaller hills, hanging over Loch Dochart, the verdure, and in short, the whole is enchanting. On the south bank of the lake, the huge sides of Benmore give great majesty and solemnity to the scene. The islands in the lake are extremely picturesque, particularly the one that is formed by a large rock, covered with wood, through which a ruin is seen. All the surrounding objects conspire to make Loch Dochart, a view of the sublime and beautiful united. Towards Tyndrum, as Glen Fillan opens, the general scene changes to an appearance of higher mountains (except Benmore), and to a bare wilderness, in comparison of the head of Loch Dochart. The district to the west of Loch Dochart, takes the name of Strath Fillan; the river also, which flows through the Strath there, bears the name Fillan. As we were baiting our horses at the small inn of Suie at the foot of Benmore, a curiosity of considerable antiquity was presented to us. It is a crook, which is believed to have been at the head of Saint Fillan's staff. It is hollow, large, and of wrought silver. It had been gilt, but the gilding is mostly worn off. At the smallest end of the crook is a red stone set in the silver; it is in colour like a ruby, on which is engraven the head of the saint.

It is said that a man named Doire was in the service of the holy bishop, (probably his crosier bearer,) and that this wonder-working relic had been carefully preserved from father to son in the Doire family, from the time of Saint Fillan to this day; and that it has been a continual source of emolument to them, which, probably, they were in danger of losing when they had the royal grant of their sole right to this relic registered in Edinburgh.

The relic is said to cure cattle of very disease by springling them with water in which it has been immersed. The inhabitants of Suie Fuelan, the seat of Saint Fillan, believe that he used to preach on a hilloc at that place. Mr. Doire, who keeps the inn at Suie, (which is a tolerably good one,) favoured me with an anecdote of his uncle's relic, which I had not heard before.

When king Robert Bruce was going to the battle of Bannock Burn, he sent a message to Doire to carry the relic thither. Doire was apprehensive the king might retain the relic when in his power; he therefore left it at home, and carried only the box in which it was usually kept. This box, on the morning of the battle, was, by the order of Robert Bruce, placed in the midst of the army, and the sacrament was administered around it. In the middle of the service, the lid of the box opened of itself, and presented the relic to view, and then instantly re-closed, to the astonishment of the whole army, but still more to the amazement of Doire, who knew he had left the relic behind him.

At Tyndrum inn the road branches in a triangle. To the east, is the road I came, towards Taymouth and Loch Earn Head; to the west, towards Dalmally, Oban, and Inveraray; to the north, up an excessive narrow opening, overhung by prodigious crags, is the road to Fort William. The inn at Tyndrum is reckoned to be on one of the highest spots on which any house stands in Scotland. All things go by comparison; for when I looked at the mountains around me, the spot whereon the inn is built, appeared to me in a hollow. Innumerable torrents and springs rise in every direction at Tyndrum; and within half a mile of the house, the two branches forming the river Tay, have their source. The one rises in the mountains facing the inn, the other in those to the north, at the back of the inn, and rolls round two sides of it, almost close to the door, and is called the Fillan water; over which is a pretty simple bridge leading to the west and north roads. Within sight of the house, in the side of a very lofty mountain, is a very fine lead mine, and the ore extremely pure. The mountains in which the Fillan rises must have a great quantity of sulphur in them, as that water turns the stones over which it falls, of a green colour. There is little to be seen or to admire ar Tyndrum; the landlord, however, wished me to see a holy well near Strath Fillan kirk, whose water, he told me, cured every disease but that of the purse. My head was more full of the virtues of the well, than the wit of the innkeeper; and concluding, as he pronounced the words, that the disease of the purse was a Gaelic name for some malady, I simply asked what it meant in English? "Money, madam; it will not cure the want of that." The water of Fillan holy well must needs be a radical cure for madness, in the way it is there administered for that disease. The poor creature thus afflicted is dipped in the well, afterwards tied (I believe naked) in the kirk hard by, and there left alone all night. If the saint comes and unties the poor object, and in the morning he or she be found loose, they are pronounced cured. I should imagine death, and no saint, in most instances, must break the cords of life, and thus release those unhappy sufferers. The inn at Tyndrum is a tolerable one for so desolate a place; when I was there, I was very fortunate in having arrived early in the afternoon, before a most violent stormy rainy night came on, and such a crowd entered, that at last every corner in the house, and outhouses too, was crammed. There is one large room with two beds in it, shut up in cupboards; but as they rolled out, I took possession of one of them, and had it drawn to the middle of the room, reserving the other for my maid. It happened that Falkirk fair was just over; many of the sellers of black cattle and sheep were on their return to the Western Highlands, and islands, and began to fill the inn. The rain and wind were excessive, and the night so dark, that it was impossible to see. In this dreadful weather, nothing but rap, rap, at the door. "Who comes?" was the frequent question; "Drovers, madam." This continued till the house was in a perfect uproar; my servants could not get a place to put their heads in. My man took his sleep in the carriage; and the poor horses were almost crushed to death in the stables. about eleven o'clock at night, in this dreadful storm, two chaises had found their way to the door; the horses were knocked up, starved with hunger, and half drowned. The ladies and gentlemen in the carriages had been misinformed; they had come from Loch Earn Head, and concluded they should find entertainments and rest for themselves and horses at one of the huts, or inns, as they are called, on the Moor, at the base of Benmore; but when they came there, to their sorrow they could get nothing for themselves or horses, and were obliged to creep on to Tyndrum, which made them so late. At first, they were told at Tyndrum, that neither they nor their horses could have the least room; but as the beasts could not stir a step further, and the night was so dark, the drovers crowded together, and gave up a very small bed room. When I learnt the situation of these travellers, I sent the landlady to inform the ladies that they should be welcome to one of the beds in my room; but they had settled the gentlemen amongst the drovers, and had kept the small room for themselves. I mention this circumstance, to caution travellers never to depend upon the two dreadful huts on the Moor in Glen Dochart.

I much wished to see the Glen, which was the scene of the cruel massacre in King William's time, and for which that monarch has been severely censured; but in all probability he knew nothing of the matter, as throughout, it has the resemblance of private pique, cloaked in public punishment. One would think the name of the district was prophetic, for Coe signifies lamentaton.

The Earl of Breadalbane having been grievously thwarted in a favorite scheme, by Macdonald of Glen Coe; he was determined to wreak his vengeance on him the first opportunity that offered. To be sure, Macdonald's motive for frustrating the earl's intentions arose from a private circumstance, which ought not to have been confounded with matters wherein the public weal was concerned.

King William had, by proclamation, offered an indemnity to all those who had been in arms against him, provided they submitted and took the oaths by a certain day; with a denunciation of military execution against those who should hold out after the end of December. Macdonald went to Fort William the last day of that month, and desired that the oaths might be tendered to him; but the governor of that fortress, being no civil magistrate, refused to administer them, and Macdonald immediately set out for Inveraray, though the ground was covered with snow, and the weather intensely cold. He travelled with such diligence, that the term prescribed by the proclamation was but one day elapsed when he reached the place. Sir Colin Campbell, sheriff of the county, in consideration of Macdonald's disappointment at Fort William, administered the oaths to him and his adherents; then they returned to Glen Coe, in full confidence of being protected by the government to which they had submitted.

Breadalbane had grievously misrepresented Macdonald as an incorrigible rebel and ruffian, and declared he had paid no attention to the proclamation. In consequence of such representations, an order was signed to extirpate Macdonald, with his family and dependants; and particular directions were sent to put all the inhabitants of Glen Coe to the sword; and to take no prisoners, that the scene might be the more exemplary. In February, Campbell of Glen Lyon, marched into the valley of Glen Coe, with a company of soldiers, on pretence of levying the arrears of the land tax and hearth money. Macdonald asked if they were come as friends or enemies? as friends, was the answer; and the commander promised upon his honor, that neither he nor his people should in the least be injured. In consequence of this declaration, Campbell and his men were received with the utmost kindness and hospitality; and lived fifteen days with the people in the valley, seemingly in perfect friendship. At length the fatal hour arrived; Campbell and Macdonald having passed the day together, parted about seven in the evening, with mutual professions of affection. The younger Macdonalds perceiving the guards doubled, suspected treachery; but the old man would not entertain a doubt of Campbell's sincerity. The young men went forth to make further observations; they overheard the common soldiers say, they liked not the work; that though they would willingly fight the Macdonalds of the Glen fairly in the field, they held it base to murder them in cool blood, but that their officers were answerable for the treachery. At the return of the young Macdonalds to their father's house, it was in flames; and the old man was shot dead in his wife's arms. A guest in the house, of another district, who had a protection in his pocket, was also murdered without queston. It is said a boy, of eight years old, fell down at Campbell's feet, imploring mercy, and offered to serve him for life. Some say a subaltern officer stabbed the boy; others, that Campbell himself took him by the feet and dashed out his brains. The design was to murder all the men under seventy in the valley, amounting to about 200; but as the passes were not sufficiently secured, 160 escaped. After Campbell had finished his murderous deed, he ordered all the houses to be burnt, made a prey of the cattle and all the effects that were found in the vale; and left the women and children without food or shelter, in the midst of the snow that covered the whole face of the country, at a distance of six Scotch miles from any inhabited place. Most of them from grief, cold, fright, and apprehension of immediate death, perished in the waste before they could receive comfort or assistance.

In order to satisfy my curiosity with respect to Glen Coe, I turned out of my way to go thither from Tyndrum; particularly as by going that road, I must pass over the Black Mount (a district so called), and near the Devil's Staircase, to get to that

Glen. Accordingly I set forwards early in the morning towards King's House. For three or four miles there is nothing between prodigious high bare mountains, but the width of the road, and the Fillan water, which roars down its steep rocky bed, forming in its way several very beautiful falls; not a tree to be seen, but some birch and other branching wood hanging over the precipices to the torrent. The road is very rough and bad, till after the crossing of a bridge over the river Orchy. At the top of the hill from Tyndrum, I arrived at the source of another torrent, taking a different direction from the Fillan; and then I came within sight of Auch, belonging to Mr. Campbell, one of the Glenfallach family. I was struck with its situation; from the top of the hill I looked down upon the house, built upon a very small plain of grass land, with tremendous hills on every side. The road I was pursuing towards Auch, is on a shelf of vast height above a stream, and that shelf only the width of the carriage, but broken into deep channels by the torrents from the high mountains on the right; which also bring down quantities of huge stones into the road; and no fence or prop, whatever, to support the loose ground of the precipice (to the water), which shook at every jolt the carriage made. This is a dangerous as well as an unpleasant pass for a chaise; but a glorious scene soon diverted my attention from every thing that was disagreeable; the morning was misty, the vapours were floating up the mountain's sides, and successively covering and uncovering the summits; but just as I came opposite the house of Auch, the sun was shining, and a conical crag of micaceous shistus glittered above the clouds, like a cap of diamonds set in a huge socket of the softest grey. Not a breath of mist eclipsed its radiant front, under which the white clouds rolled rapidly along. I had not seen any thing like it, and I was quite in raptures. As I crossed the torrent under its base by a simple bridge, I peeped amongst the high towering and closely jumbled mountains, amongst which the Lyon and the Lochy rivers take their source. Soon after I crossed the torrent at Auch, forming the Kinglash river, rolling to the Orchy, I came in sight of the mill, and the bridge over the Orchy river; and a dreadful looking zig-zag road over a high brown mountain. This track is the old military road; but the new one, which is easy, winds round the base of it to Loch Tollie, and the inn at Inverouron, close on a river's bank. From Loch Tollie, the river Orchy winds its way to the lower part of the Glen of that name, and empties itself into Loch Awe. From Inverouron, the mountains of the Black Mount rise wonderfully high, black, pointed, and jagged. The new road winds up their sides, far easier that General Wade's over the tops of them, and will be a very fine piece of alpine road, when it is completed as far as King's House. The inn of King's House, as I approached it, looked like a dot in the midst of a barren wilderness; surrounded, except to the east, by the most craggy, bare, stupendous mountains that the mind can form an idea of; and the opening at their bases stretching to the east, and to Rannoch, is nothing but a dreary, black, boggy moor, the loose soil of which is quite black, broken by pools and small lakes, and very thinly covered, where the water does not remain, with the coarsest brown heath, rushes, and bogs; but there is a crag to the west of the inn of a stupendous height, in some degree conical, of grey rock over rock, which as the sun shone upon it, assumed a most beautiful tint, contrasted with the dark russet of everything beneath it. Few beings, but drovers, take up their quarters at this house; not wholly because of its desolate situation, but because it is very dirty. It is one of the houses government provides; therefore, as those who keep it have it rent free, it ought to be made more comfortable for travellers.

My mind was bent upon a fascinating pursuit, consequently trifles neither deterred nor disgusted me. Although I had travelled but eighteen miles, the horses were tired; it was nine or ten miles more to the place I had set my mind upon visiting, and the road bad; so I determined on an eighteen mile's drive in a peat cart, across which was fastened a board by way of seat. As soon as I had taken my short meal, and secured my pighole to sleep in, I left my maid to take care of every thing, and mounted the cart; my servant did the same, and away we went. I crossed the small bridge by King's House door, over a stream, which joining other torrents, helps to form the Etive water, falling afterwards into the lake of that name, which in that country is called Etie. I then turned my face to the west, towards the stupendous mountains which close up the head of Glen Coe; I never saw such mountains! even the inhabitants of Fort Augustus think nothing of their own mountains, in comparison of the height and wildness of those in Glen Coe, and they have reason for so doing. As I advanced, every succeeding hill seemed more tremendous than those I had passed, and I very soon got into a labyrinth of them. At the foot of the Devil's Staircase begins a dreadfully steep zig-zag, up the front of a mountain, ten times more terrific than the zig-zag on Corryarraick; but as this wicked named pass, made by General Wade, is superseded by a somewhat easier one, through Glen Coe, I only took a peep at it. Indeed I cannot conceive how any sort of wheel-carriage could ever go up and down it, or even the shelties keep upon their legs. A breed of mules, such as pass the heights about the Andes, should have been procured at the time the Devil's Staircase was in use. Those mules, I have read, sit down on their haunches and curl themselves up in such a manner as to slip all the way down the dangerous heights, with safety to themselves and to those upon them. The Highlandman assured me, the descent on the other side of the mountain, called the Devil's Staircase, is beyond comparison more steep, rough, and dangerous, than what I was looking at. About six miles from

King's House I came to the torrent forming the head of the small water of Coe, where it falls from the mountains in a very fine cataract, into a dark, deep, narrow passage, dashing over and amongst steep rough rocks for at least a mile, till it gets to the small plain in the middle of Glen Coe, where it gently empties itself into a little lake. Just at the cataract at the south-side of the glen, under which the water dashes after its fall, are huge towers upon towers of solid rock, forming a multitude of stages to the greatest height, and all in a drizzling state; which in some degree looked like thousands of icicles, dropping from innumerable points of rocks upon every stage; and forming, from the top to the bottom, one of the most curious sights I ever beheld. In violent rains a cascade must there be formed, so grand and majestic, that I cannot conceive any thing equal to it; except a sudden frost should congeal this grand cascade when tolerably full, and in that state having the sun-shine upon it. These tower-like crags may, perhaps, have lakes in the hollows on their summits; for springs without number must be every where about them, or they could not weep without ceasing. The constant dripping has rendered them of a very black and dark green hue, consequently very gloomy. Adjoining this extra-ordinary weeping mass, is a continued range, of a mile in descent, of other crags equally perpendicular and high; in most of which appear caves and arched passages, with pillars, like the communication from one aile to another, high up in the sides of Gothic cathedrals; also small Gothic-like windows and doors. The whole mass, to an eye below, appears like an immense and inaccessible fine ruin, mouldered, defaced, and become uneven by a vast lapse of time, and inclemency of weather, which has variegated its native grey, by ten thousand soft tints, that nothing but time and weather can produce. In a few of the very high hollows I perceived considerable protuberances of some-thing white, like crystals, (and the Highlandman told me they were such) which, when the sun shone upon them, glistened like diamonds. It is under this grand range of crags, that the Coe dashes loud, though unseen; at the edge of which birch, alder, mountain ash, nut, and many other small branching trees growing out of the crevices of the rocks, give a degree of soft-ness to this solemn, sublime, gloomy, steep pass. Probably the weeping of the rocks, and the groans of the water under them, was the original cause of its name, Coe; the signification of which, as I have before mentioned, is lamentation.

The mountains on the north of the Coe are amazingly high; but shivering, and rounder than the opposite range of rocks, and have some verdure about them. There is no space between the south rocks, and the north mountains, but the road down to the flat of the glen, twisting and turning round and between projections of the mountains on the right, and the river Coe, under the rocks, on the left.

As I was advancing through this steep narrow pass, I perceived a cavalcade and a small chaise meeting me; such a sight, in such a place, is an event; and to those I was meeting, I and my rustic equipage, must have been a matter of mirth and curiosity, especially to the chief, for it was the lord of the beautiful burying-ground at Killin, accompanied by several of his family; they were making the best of their way towards King's House. I thought it lucky my maid had taken possession of one of the best sties; at the instant, that was the subject of my cogitations. What the chief and his party thought of me, and my expedition, I cannot say. He reported, however, from the distance he met me from King's House, that he was sure I could not return thither that night; but he was mistaken.

When I was in Glen Coe, I heartily wished I had been provided to go on to Ballachelish, where I was told is a striking view of mountain and lake; but it was then out of my power to do so, and I continued my route in Glen Coe, as far as the time before dark would permit. The plain of the glen may be about four miles, with a lake in the middle of it; it now consists of two sheep farms, and there are not more than three or four mean habitations in the glen; and its population is much under thirty persons. As I passed by the spot where old Macdonald and the greatest part of his clan were massacred, I could not help paying the tribute of a sigh for their melancholy fate. To be in friendship one hour, and butchered indiscriminately the next by those whom they had feasted and caressed, is a tale to shudder at. The spot on which the bloody deed was perpetrated is about the midway of the plain.

When I had walked and carted for about nine miles from King's House, I was with regret obliged, out of compassion for the Highlandman and shelty, to turn about and retrace my steps; but I did not enter King's House till after dark, and in the rain, which came on soon after I quitted Glen Coe. King's House was full of people, and I made my way to my sty through columns of smoke. This sty was a square room, of about eight feet, with one window and a chimney in it, and a small bedstead nailed in the angle behind the door. Throughout Scotland you will not see a casement, such as are in cottages in England; but the houses have universally sash windows; be upon your guard when you approach a window in that country, or you may get your hand mashed, or a finger taken off, by the sudden fall of the sash, to which there are no pullies or lines. I speak feelingly on this matter, for at King's House the window was to me very troublesome. The usual prop in such habitations, for the sash, is a poker, or hearth broom.

My maid, for her bed, had a shake down upon chairs; as for me, my eighteen miles carting had made me quite ready for repose. I soon ate my bit of supper, half choked with smoke, and in danger of getting cold by an open window, the damp from the rain pouring in, and my petticoats tucked to my knees for fear of the dirt, which was half an inch thick on the floor; but notwithstanding all these obstacles I had no sooner laid my head upon my pillow, than I fell asleep, and did not awake till morning. Thanks, however, were due to my little maid for such a comfort, for she was all attention. I was also indebted to my independance in point of linen, blanket, quilt and pillows; perhaps the cart ought not to be forgotten; its exercise certainly had no small share in making me sleep soundly. The next day I retraced my steps to Tyndrum, to pick up my trunk; and as Allen was of opinion we could reach Dalmally that day, I stayed at Tyndrum as short a time as possible, and entered Glen Lochy.

CHAPTER THREE

Glen Lochy is a very narrow tract; and near its entrance is a small lake, with a quiet river running through the middle of the whole glen; and a range of lofty green mountains on each side, from which flow innumerable torrents, feeding the lake and river. This glen is eight miles long, and almost uniformly wide, but winding; and produces nothing but sheep pasture; nor did I see any sign of human habitation, except a sheelin or two. In a bad day Glen Lochy must appear very dreary; though in sunshine very pleasant. Unluckily for me it began to overcast, and a degree of mist to rise, by the time I drew towards the end of this glen; but nothwithstanding the mist, when I came to the spot where I looked down on the beautiful and grand view of Glen Orchy, I exclaimed, oh! what a Paradise is there. You who read, imagine yourselves just at the end of a drive, of eight miles, between uniform green mountains up to the sky, and then emerging at once from this narrow defile, upon a precipice hanging over a very extensive vale, watered by a fine river, and enriched by an abundance of luxuriant wood, and fields of corn and grass, with houses, ruins, and kirks, scattered thickly throughout the glen, which is bounded by mountains of every form and hue; and in the distant front is Loch Awe, thirty miles long, with Cruchan Ben, rising above the clouds in terrific majesty of towering crags, volcanic concaves and points; also other mountains, with verdant tops and woody sides, but not equal either in height or sublimity to Cruchan Ben, whose northern aspect is as terrific, as are its east and southern, sublime and beautiful.

As I advanced to Dalmally, every step delighted me; but, alas! the clouds gathered thick, and a deluge of rain succeeded, which continued with unceasing violence the whole night and the next day.

The view, from the window of the inn at Dalmally, of Ben Cruchan, and the island on which Dr. McIntyre's manse and church stand, is very fine. I have a beautiful drawing of it.

When I left Dalmally inn, I crossed two bridges over the Orchy river, and advanced, winding round a side of a mountain, till I came within sight of the remains of Killchurn Castle in Loch Awe. This is a fine point of view of that ruin. At about two miles from Dalmally I came to a Highland bridge, and then turned to the base of Ben Cruchan. For several miles the road hangs over the lake, amidst a beautiful thick wood of forest trees, chiefly of oak. Loch Awe is a charming lake; and the number of islands in it, most of them woody, render a general view of it almost, if not equal to that of Loch Lomond.

In the summer of 1800 I determined to visit various of the Inner Hebride islands and, as that short tour fits well as a pleasant detour from the main journey, I shall here insert a description of where I went and what I saw.

After travelling five or six miles in the enchanting scenery on the north-west bank of Loch Awe, I turned almost due west, leaving the islands and the broadest part of the lake to pursue a good road blown through the rocks, just sufficient for a carriage to pass safely. The first time I saw that track before me, I trembled a little; for to look at it coolly, it is somewhat tremendous; but the imagination in an instant becomes so intoxicated with the beauty, the variety, the sublimity of the scene, that fear is lost in admiration. To add to the deception, the precipices are so concealed by fine trees and brush-wood, that, unless fear sharpens the eye, it cannot easily discern how very near the carriage runs to the perpendicular precipices hanging over the lake.

As I drew nearer to that part of the lake where the river Awe begins, the road enters a thick wood, which on one hand climbs the perpendicular lofty sides of Cruchan; on the other hand are perpendicular precipices to the water, so thickly covered with wood, that it is difficult to get a glimpse of the lake; for safety and ease to a traveller's mind, there is a parapet wall for three or four miles on this piece of road. Near the entrance into the almost impenetrable wood, the view following the river Awe is very striking; Cruchan, thickly clothed with wood, on the north side of the river. On the south side of it, tremendous crags crumbling and sweeping precipitately to the edge of the water, with streams dashing down every hollow; no track of living beings to be seen amongst them, except sheep paths; many of those little animals were with the utmost caution following each other slowly across the crumbling sides of the rock, at about twenty yards above the surface of the water.

At about half way through the wood, I came to a beautiful bridge. Above, below, and under it, dashed in every direction a river, forming the most picturesque cascades as far as I could view them for trees, which in that spot grow most luxuriantly. The road through the whole of this enchanting wood, is up and

down precipices. At the end of the wood, the road descends to the level of the river, and the width of the pass is there reduced only to what the river occupies, and a narrow winding track just sufficient for a carriage to creep round the rough points of Cruchan, who there quits his rich green mantle for his rugged, rusty brown coat of mail.

In about a mile after I had descended to the level of the river, I perceived, high mounted on a point of the steep rocks on the opposite side of the water, with his legs hanging carelessly over the roaring stream far beneath him, a herdsman, who was gazing at what, as I turned round a pointed rock, astonished me, a cataract bursting from the summit of Cruchan, and rattling down its rough sides. I looked with envy at the shepherd's temporary situation; perhaps he envied me mine.

I have a very pretty copy of verses in my possession, written by the Rev. Dr. John Leyden of Denholm, whom I met once by Loch Catherine's side. It is a lamentation on a misfortune he met with on that lofty eminence. With much labour and some difficulty he climbed, in a hot summer's day, the long rough ascent. When his difficulties were conquered, and he had reached the goal, he perched himself on the highest peak, and in rapture looked on all beneath him. He was seated on a rock, and with infinite glee drew from his pocket a bottle of cyder; he triumphantly raised the hand in which he grasped the bottle, loudly crying huzza; but alas! in the very act of the flourish, he struck the bottle against the point of a rock. The nector was spilt, the fragments of the bottle went click click down the rough rocks, and he was left dying with thirst, and almost petrified at his ill fated vehemence.

Beyond Tayneilt is the Connel cascade which I have seen three or four times; the first time I arrived at it, I went from erroneous information, at an improper state of the tide. I however saw a vessel shoot the narrow passage at the cascade, which astonished me by the velocity with which it came down the stream, and continues so for a considerable distance below the cascade. I cannot say I should very much like being in a vessel at such times, for it must be exactly like flying on the surface of the sea. Another time I had a long and troublesome walk of five miles in a high wind, from Oban to Connel, in order to see the cascade in perfection; which I should have done, as it blew a brisk gale from the west, had I been at Connel at half ebb tide, but alas! having been told at Oban that it would be high tide at Connel at two o'clock, I lost time by the way in sketching Dunstaffnage castle, concluding if I were at Connel a little after high tide, I should be in time for the best of the fall at half ebb tide, whereas to my great disappointment, when I arrived at Connel, although only a little after two o'clock, it was nearly low

I sketched Dunstaffnage Castle.

water.

I am informed that the agitated whirls near this cascade, will sometimes turn a ferry boat quite round, half round, and zig-zag three or four times in its passage across, and yet it will be in perfect safety. I should be sorry to trust myself in it at such times.

From Dunstaffnage Castle, Connel cascade often exhibits an awful and magnificent scene; forming a sublime fore ground to a beautiful landscape, in which the peaks of Cruchan in the back ground are conspicuously grand.

After I had the pleasure of passing a night in the ancient castle of Dunstaffnage, I was fortunate in the weather on the following day, for there could not be a finer. I went upon the battlements as the sun rose behind Cruchan; never shall I forget the glorious effect of that luminary rising and shining on the grand panorama below me. Nothing but the eye can convey to the mind, an adequate idea of such scenes.

The Campbells of Dunstaffnage have for years been noted for their great hospitality to strangers, my suffrage in testimony of it, is thankfully added to the numbers who have gone to Dunstaffnage before me. The castle is far gone to decay, having only the shell of the main wall, and one large tower of the ancient fabric standing. In the spacious and roofless area within the wall, is built a small modern house in which the family resided. In the tower there are two or three bed rooms for strangers, and a very good dining room. The steps of the stone staircase are so narrow and winding, that I could but just squeeze myself up them. I had the honour of sleeping in my lord's room, and my maid in the dice room, from which title it appears that gaming was in fashion formerly in secluded regions as well as in cities. Near to the castle is a chapel in ruins, and near the chapel is a range of inconsiderable rocks. At those rocks is a curious echo. When a person standing by them in a particular spot, speaks with a trumpet or loud voice, the sound seems to come from the burying vault within the walls of the chapel. Many tricks have been played with this deceptive echo, and amongst the rest, upon a farmer who was selling his grain at exorbitant prices. He came to Dunstaffnage, (for what purpose I forget,) and having never heard of the echo, the inhabitants of the castle agreed to frighten him, and, if possible, for the public good, make him lower his unconscionable demands for his grain. A walk was proposed, when one of the family slyly hid the trumpet under his coat, and without being observed, took the proper station at the rocks. The rest of the party were careful to prevent the farmer from approaching the place where the trumpeter was to perform his part. The farmer was admiring the sculpture over the door of the chapel, and others were explaining to him the meaning of the devices, when a sonerous voice issued from the burying ground in the chapel.

"Donald, within a fortnight thou shalt die; sell thy grain cheap in expiation of thy sins!" The man ran about in the ruins of the chapel like a madman, but nothing human could he see or find, but those who stood near him, when he heard his dreadful doom. Three times did the voice from the tombs of the dead sound in his ear, "Donald, within a fortnight thou shalt die; sell thy corn cheap in expiation of thy sins!" The farmer's corn was disposed of to the poor at a low price, but I did not hear he died the sooner.

CHAPTER FOUR

The drive from Connel to Oban is a pleasant one, although very little wood is to be seen; but the mountains and hillocs are so thickly and singularly disposed, that it is an unique scene. In going down to the town of Oban, the huge motley rocks on the righthand, seem as if they had very lately been singed, and in some parts appear absolutely to be burnt to cinders.

I am very much attached to the little town of Oban and its inhabitants, particularly the families of the Stevensons. There is a simplicity of manners, a strength of mind and judgment, and a friendly hospitality innate, I believe, in their dispositions, which is rarely met with in any station. They have been the founders of the town of Oban, and they have my good wishes that the town may ultimately be the making of their families.

To Mr. John Stevenson and his family I shall ever think myself indebted, for receiving me as a friend into their house, when I was too ill to bear the bustle of the inn; and this public testimony of my thanks is due to their kindness to me, not only on that occasion, but on many others since.

On this occasion, my mind was bent on visiting the famous island of Staffa, and as many of the western islands as I should find pleasant, as far as my courage might be sufficient to buffet the inconveniences of sea trips.

That I might be at full liberty, I determined to go quite alone. I procured letters of introduction to a few gentlemen's families in Mull, and prepared such baggage as I conceived would be conducive to my comfort, and some tobacco for the pleasure of others. The lower class of people in the highlands are extremely fond of tobacco, and it is amazing how many hours they exist without food, if they have a bit of it in their mouths.

It is very amusing to remain a short time at Oban in summer, to observe the different modes of proceeding, and the various ideas of parties who arrive at that little town on their way to Staffa. Some are in such a hurry to get away, that they run to and fro like maniacs, hearing every one's tale of the voyage, and subsequent route, without fixing on any, unless they have had the good luck of bringing a letter of introduction to either of the

Messrs. Stevensons. One party of young men from England, had brought from thence, choicely preserved, a fine piece of roasted beef; but behold, so great was their haste to embark for Staffa, that John Bull's roasted beef was left at the inn at Oban.

A young man the same year came to Oban, whose eagerness to get over to Mull was astonishing. He wanted a boat immediately to himself. It so happened that all the boats were engaged. Some hours afterwards he perceived a gentleman walking to the beach, and imagining that he had a boat going over to Mull, he ran with all speed after him. As he reached the pier the gentleman's boat was heaving off which made the impatient traveller cry aloud, for God's sake to be taken into it and conveyed to Mull. The gentleman complied with his request, and the boat put back and carried the stranger to Ach-na-craig. The gentleman found during the voyage, that the young traveller had nothing with him but what he had on his back, for so great was his haste, and desire to set sail, that he forgot every thing. Not a second shirt, nor shoes, nor stockings, had he with him; not even his night cap.

My difficulty was to discover the best route for me, to Torloisk on the west side of Mull, and what at last determined me upon going to Aros by sea, was an offer from Sir John Murray to convey me thither in the Oban excise cutter, engaged to carry him and his son on a tour of the isles.

On the 23rd of July 1800, I entered the Oban cutter, and set sail about noon with a tolerable breeze. In sailing out of Oban harbour, a most beautiful landscape presented itself. Dunolly, its picturesque ruin, and its fine woods, and rocks on one hand, and the north end of the island of Kerrera on the other. In front, Mull and the island of Lismore, with the bold hills of Morven behind it. A wide expanse of sea to the right and left, flowing from the south-west to the north-east towards Lochaber, and to the north into the Sound of Mull, with islands of various dimensions where ever the eye turned.

At the south end of the island of Lismore we sailed near a small rocky isle, over which the sea rolls at high tides; at other times it raises its rough head somewhat above the surface of the water. It is called the Lady's Rock, for the following reason.

In former times one of the McLeans of Duart, whose castle (now in ruins) stands on a promontory in Mull, in nearly an opposite direction to the Lady's Rock, married a sister of Argyle. The lady was handsome and amiable, but unhappily she was barren. In those days it was a high crime in the eyes of a husband, when his wife bore him no children. Duart hated his hapless lady for that cause, and determined on her descruction. To accomplish it with ease, and as he imagined, safe from detection, he ordered ruffians to convey her secretly to the bare

I am very much attached to the little town of Oban.

rock near Lismore, and there leave her to perish at high tide. The deed was executed to Duart's wish, and the lady left on the rock, watching the rolling tide rising to overwhelm her. When she had given herself up for a lost being, and expected in a very short time to be washed from the rock by the waves, she fortunately perceived a vessel sailing down the Sound of Mull, in the direction of the rock on which she was sitting. Every effort in her power was exerted, and every signal in her possession was displayed to attract the notice of the people in the vessel. At length they perceived her and drew near the rock. She made herself known. and related that it was by the order of her barbarous husband she was left on the rock, and thus reduced to the wretched state in which they found her. The mariners, ever a generous race, took compassion on her, received her on board their vessel, and conveyed her safely to her brother in Inveraray.

McLean Duart made a grand mock funeral for his much loved, much lamented lady, who he announced to have died suddenly. He wrote disconsolate letters to her relations, particularly to Argyle, and after a decent time went to Inveraray in deep mourning, where with the greatest shew of grief, he lamented to his brother-in-law the irreparable loss he had sustained. Argyle said little, but sent for his sister, whose unexpected appearance in life and health, proved an electric shock to her tender husband. Argyle was a mild and amiable man, and took no other revenge of McLean but commanding him to depart instantly, at the same time advising him to be cautious not to meet his brother Donald, who would certainly take away his life for having intended to destroy that of his sister. Sir Donald Campbell did meet him many years afterwards in a street at Edinburgh, and there stabbed him for his crime towards his sister, when McLean was eighty years of age.

Before we entered the Sound of Mull, although it was a fine day and nearly a calm, the agitation of the sea off Duart castle was considerably felt, even in so large a vessel as the cutter; what then must it be with a brisk gale, and in a small boat?

The entrance of the Sound of Mull is beautiful, Morven on one hand, the island of Mull on the other, Duart castle forming a fine object on the shore of the latter, and the old castle of Ardtorinish, with its bold cliffs on the former.

We advanced slowly, as it every moment became calmer and calmer, so that at times the cutter hardly moved. The weather was hot and the mists were floating, sometimes along the sides of the majestic mountains, at others covering their summits, and again rolling through the vallies below, in a style I never had seen before; it was like Ossian's ''Shadowy breeze that poured its dark wave over the grass.'' It was a perpetual change of light and shade, on majestic scenery that was beyond description glorious and enchanting.

When we left Oban, our plan was, that after the cutter had conveyed Sir John Murray to Ardtorinish, it should then carry me on to Aros, but for want of wind, it was six o'clock before we drew near to Ardtorinish, and it being at that time almost a dead calm, Sir John very politely offered to introduce me to his friends at Ardtorinish, saying it would be impossible for me to reach Aros that night. I thankfully accepted of the friendly offer, and we put into the bay close to Ardtorinish house. This bay is nearly surrounded by tremendous high cliffs, and in times of hard rain, innumerable streams from the mountains behind, reach the summit of them, and there form a grand cascade, falling in one semicircular sheet from the top of the cliffs to the sea. I should have been well pleased to have seen the cliffs of Ardtorinish in a streaming state, the wind blowing strongly from the west; for then I should have had the gratification of beholding the phaenomenon of the wind on the cascade, the water in which at such times is whirled back over the mountains in spray, by the violence of the west wind, so that not a drop reaches the sea.

The approach of the cutter was observed by the family on shore, and Mr. Grigerson and three of his fine boys came aboard. In order to hear the fine echo in the bay, a cannon was fired twice or thrice; it is impossible to describe the effect it had; it was like loud thunder rolling from hill to hill for an incredible length of time. The bay at Ardtorinish is nicely sheltered by the cliffs, and the cutter's crew found it a comfortable berth, for there came on such an amazing thick fog, that all the navigators in the sound were, throughout the night, in great distress. Many fishing boats, bound for a cluster of small islands not far from Ardtorinish bay, were heard by the sailors in the cutter, rowing to and fro, and their crews shouting the whole of the night, without being able to gain their station. Like blind folks walking, they were rowing every way but the right.

The night I passed at Ardtorinish house, was one of the hottest and closest I ever felt, and I seriously began to think I should be suffocated, and that my bones would have the honour to be laid in the dust of those of the great McDonalds, lords of the isles, the ruins of whose ancient castle stood hard by; but happily I escaped with no other bad effect than apprehension of what might happen. In the morning the whole family assembled in the hall of shells, and to carry on the analogy, the shell went round before breakfast. It is not however the custom, I believe, of the Ardtorinish family or any other, known to me, of these days, to do the like, but I was a stranger in Fingal's land; and, to do honour to it, did as Fingal and his heroes were wont to do, drank whiskey from a clam-shell. (scallop shell).

After breakfast we walked to the ruin of the castle, which must have been a prodigiously strong one. It was, as I have said before, the habitation of the McDonalds, lords of the isles. A fragment of an interior wall was measured; it was found to be fourteen feet thick.

Within a few years, I forget how many, workmen were digging near the ruin and found an enormous key; the length of which was at least a yard, and the breadth of the wards more than a foot. In short it was a wonderfully large key, and so heavy that one man could but just carry it. This surely must have been the master key of the castle, buried under ground for ages. The key was carried to the house, but unfortunately at that time Mr. Grigerson was from home. His lady saw it, and concluded the workman would deposit it safely till her husband returned. Alas! he did not so, but he carried it directly to the smith's shop and had it melted. When the key was called for, the workman answered, he thought it a great pity such fine iron should remain useless, he therefore had made tools of it. What a Goth, to melt down such a curiosity! I wonder Mr. Grigerson did not spit the man, upon his new pure iron forks.

July 24th, about nine o'clock in the morning, the thick fog dispersed, and the day became very hot and so clear, that not a breath of mist was to be seen any where. The cutter was ordered to proceed with me to Aros, Sir John being determined to remain all day at Ardtorinish, that he might have a conference with the Rev. Mr. McNicol, the minister of Lismore, on the subject of Ossian's Poems.

I was with great attention conducted by the gentlemen to the small boat waiting for me near the ruins of the castle, and with four oars soon reached the cutter, and therein seated myself, but not one inch could the cutter stir, for it was a dead calm. A council was held, and the head boatman's opinion was, that as the sea was as smooth as glass, the Sound would be safe even in a cockle shell; therefore if I would trust myself in the small boat, the four seamen could, and would row me to Aros in less than two hours; whereas the cutter might not get up so far in twelve hours. I took the boatman's advice, and replaced myself in the small boat, and a finer voyage no mortal ever had.

I arrived at Aros exactly in the given time. The sea was a mirror, the mountains brilliantly clear, and not a sound to be heard but the dashing of the oars. I was for a time quite lost in admiration, and to complete the magic-like scene, I requested the seamen to sing Gaelic songs, which they did the greatest part of the voyage. It is astonishing how much their songs animated them, particularly a chorus, that made them pull away with such velocity, that it was like flying more than rowing on the surface of the water.

From afar the boat I was in was observed by the good family at Aros, to whom I was totally unknown, but I carried in my pocket a letter of introduction, and I was received with infinite kindness and hospitality by Mr. and Mrs. Maxwell. The day was wonderfully bright, the scenery every where consequently wore a gay garb; but notwithstanding I was somewhat surprised to see on the shore, near the landing rocks, smart beaux and belles, red coats, and elegant snow drop dresses. It was a gala dinner given by Mr. Maxwell to his friends, and the officer who had arrived in Mull, on a tour of inspection of the volunteers of the isles.

As I was sitting at Mr. Maxwell's table, I could scarcely fancy myself any where but in a capital town, so nicely was the entertainment conducted; but what crowned the feast was the hearty welcome expressed in the countenances of the host and hostess.

I am such a fortunate woman, that I was once told, if I were thrown from the peak of Cruchan, I should without doubt light safely on my feet at the bottom of it.

Part Four

CHAPTER ONE

The morning after my arrival at Aros, was as fine as the preceding day. Mr. Maxwell advised me to lose no time, but proceed as fast as possible in order to reach Staffa before the weather changed. He lent me two horses, one to carry myself, the other for my baggage, and engaged two Highlandmen to accompany me. At nine o'clock the horses were at the door.

The picture of the outset.

A very good house facing the Sound of Mull; near it a ruin of what was once a castle, by which runs a river romantically enough. Mrs. Murray appears, accompanied by gentlemen and ladies, dressed in a red leather cap trimmed with brown fur, and a habit of Tartan such as is worn by the 42d regiment of Highlanders. She mounts a white horse, with a Fingalian stick in her hand, cut out of the woods in Morven. Her horse led by an honest Highlander. Then comes a sheltie with creels (paniers) on his back, containing the baggage, on which sat a Highland lad.

Thus moved Mrs. Murray's first cavalry expedition in the island of Mull, and laughable enough it was.

I was so pleased the preceding day with the Gaelic songs the boatmen regaled me with, that I soon requested an Erse air of my guides. One of them did not understand a word of English, and the other was no great proficient in the language. The oldest man could not sing and the youngest was shy, and said he must pass by all the huts before he could begin to sing; he kept his word, and we walked the horses on for three miles, in a very rough uneven track, till we came within sight of Loch-na-keall, and the huge mountain near it called Benmore of Mull; and a fine view it forms.

By land along the margin of Loch-na-keall, I found the road exceedingly rough, but where ever a piece of plain ground appeared, I found growing on it as fine barley and oats as any I ever saw in south Britain. At nearly half way down the lake, I came to what my guide had told me would be a very bad step; but I might remain, he said, on my saddle for he would answer for my safety. The step is a rise on a pointed rock hanging over the lake, and the shelf on which horses tread, is thickly strewed with huge stones standing and lying in every direction. These stones have fallen, and are every day falling, from the perpendicular huge mass rising to a vast height on one side of the shelf. The horse in going up and down this rocky broken shelf went cautiously, and slowly, as well he might, for the poor beast was obliged to put one leg as much as two feet deep amongst the stones and there let it remain till he could drag another leg from an equal depth; and so on, dragging his legs out and safely replacing them amongst the broken rocks. In ascending I was obliged to lie on the horse's neck, and in descending almost on his tail, but for all that, though with trembling, I could not help gazing at the huge masses of rock piled like folio books one upon another, all the way up the mountain, hanging over my head. Innumerable huge fragments too have from time to time separated from the mountain, and from obstacles in their way, have lodged at different distances down the face of the rocky precipice, others have fallen and lodged upon them, some very irregularly, others almost as even as volumes of books heaped on each other in haste. Many of these huge masses appeared to me in size and shape similar to those of Stone-henge, and like one of the stones lying across another at Stone-henge, seemed to be upon the balance, so that in appearance the least touch from a falling stone would send a shower of them into the sea beneath.

What adds beauty to this terrific pass, is the brushwood surrounding it, and even hanging from every chink of the broken crags from the summit of the mountain down to the edge of the lake.

Soon after I had conquered the difficulties of this pass, I arrived at a small village, and got off my horse to rest myself and eat a biscuit.

A woman thus alone in a strange country, was no small matter of curiosity even to poor folks, lounging at doors of huts, who rarely see a stranger. Their dress, their huts, and their mode of sitting, (that is the women,) at the doors of their habitations, were matters of as much curiosity to me as I was to them; but they had a great advantage on their side. They spoke the same language as did my guides, I could not. By the answer of one of my conductors, I however found the good folks had inquired of what country I was. "She is Sassenach." (English.)

I sat upon a low wall to eat my biscuit and drink my wine, near a hut from which was brought me a bason of fine milk, and presented by the master of the habitation. He did not speak, but he looked a kind welcome and I received his present thankfully.

As I advanced towards the head of Loch-na-keall, I came within sight of the island of Eorsa, Inch Kennith (island of Saint Kenneth), Ulva and many others, with the grand range of cliffs in Mull called Gribun, forming all together an exceedingly fine view. In short I was delighted with my whole ride from Aros to Torloisk, where I arrived about five o'clock rather fatigued, having been on horseback near eight hours. I travelled somewhat more than two miles an hour.

From the circumstance of the inspection of the volunteers, I was disappointed of the company of a gentleman who I expected would conduct me to Staffa; I was therefore under the necessity of venturing alone, having no time to lose for fear of a change of weather.

The 26 of July, the day after my arrival at Torloisk, proved a most delightful one. Mrs. McLean was accustomed to take a ride on horseback early in the morning, and at her return she advised me by all means to take advantage of the very favourable day, for in that climate the weather was extremely uncertain. She told me she had desired the boatmen to come up for my orders, and that whilst we breakfasted all would be ready for my departure. She also kindly provided us with something to eat and drink, and permitted a young man she could depend upon, to go with me as an interpreter; for neither of the seamen could speak English.

The boat was very small. The four rowers filled the body of it; the narrow head contained the provisions; and into the stern, equally narrow, I and my young interpreter squeezed ourselves. Thus equipped, I launched on the Atlantic ocean.

The tide was for us, and there was very little wind, whilst we were within the shelter of the isles of Ulva and Gometra. I admired the shores of those islands, particularly on the west side of them, where I perceived the rocks have all a tendency to the columnar form, and in many parts are pillars in various directions.

When we turned the north point of Gometra numbers of islands at different distances, came into view. The Tresinish isles and the Dutchman's Cap, were very conspicuous, also Colansa and Staffa. I-Columbkill and the narrow point of Ross in Mull, I saw at a great distance south west of me. I was eager to discover which of the islands was Staffa, but from my interpreter's not knowing it, and the seamen not understanding my questions, I never perfectly distinguished which isle before me was Staffa, till I came within half a mile of it. At that distance in the direction in which I was advancing, Staffa appeared a very common-looking rough island, or rather a huge rock with perpendicular cliffs to the summit, rising high above the ocean. I began to think I had ventured on the Atlantic for a curiosity much exaggerated by my adventurous predecessors, but as I drew nearer to the north point of the island, I soon saw what cannot be described, to be clearly understood by any but those who have had like me, the happiness of beholding Staffa.

In the highlands, local names are very expressive of shape or situation.

Why Staffa is thus called I cannot say, unless there is any word in the Danish language signifying staff, or pillar, from which the word Staffa can be derived. Its Gaelic name is Slothfuidh, literally expressing a surf beneath. It seems a mere stretch of the imagination in calling the wonderful cave at Staffa Fingal's cave.

The father of Ossian in the English translation of his poems, is styled Fingal; in Gaelic he is called Fhion, or the Fair.

When Fingal's cave is spoken of in the Erse language, it is called in the genitive case Uamh Bhinn, the melodious cave.

In the Gaelic alphabet there are eight letters less than in the English language. Mh sounds like v. Bh also sounds v, but not so nasal as mh. The vowel u is at all times pronounced as the Italians do that letter, and indeed almost every other letter in the Erse language is sounded as are the letters in Italian.

I am unable to point out the mineralogy of Staffa, the substance of its pillars, or the second causes of their form and regularity, but my eyes and mental faculties at the sight of this astonishing island, at once acknowledged the breath of omnipotence in its formation.

Light, earth, water, and animated nature, were created by the word of the Almighty; no second causes are known to have been requisite to complete them. Why then may not Staffa, the little island near it, and the giant's causeway in Ireland, have been produced at the creation, without the interference of either fire or water? But I am sensible I am out of my depth; I will therefore retreat to the level of my comprehension.

After we had doubled the point of Gometra the tide turned against us, and the wind in some degree got up, which occasioned waves and hard labour for the rowers; but when we came to Staffa not a breath of wind blew. The sea was as smooth as glass, which enabled the boat to get quite close to the shore, tacking continually amongst innumerable small rocks separate from Staffa, lying on the west side of it. Every length the boat made, new wonders came in view. On the north-west point, rises to a great height a small promontory almost perpendicular from the sea to its summit. The base of this promontory is rough and irregular for perhaps more than half its height, and where the uneven rock ends, the most beautiful perfect uniform pillars rest upon it, in a convex semi-circle; and were it not for their stupendous appearance, it might be thought that the finest statuary ever existing, had stretched his chisel powers beyond human art in forming them.

Advancing from this beautiful convex circle of pillars, I observed creeks and caves, and perpendicular rocks of great variety; but when I came within sight of the very regular pillars and elevated dome over the great caves, I was in an extasy.

Conceive, if you can, an infinity of small pillars thrown together in every direction at a very considerable height from the eye, bearing the resemblance of architecture, executed in the most masterly style, and highly beautified by various tints made by time, and weather, composing an irregular and continued facade to magnificent domes, from which descend

perpendicular, compact, smooth prismatic pillars, some resting, (particularly those at the boat cave, and on the west side of Fingal's cave,) on rough irregular sound masses of basaltes washed by the sea. Others morticed in the angles of stumps of pillars once entire, the uppermost joints of which have separated from the main mass of pillars forming the island.

It is said that the boat cave is much larger than Fingal's, but it is very little known, owing to ideal or real danger in going into it. The mouth of it is far from striking, or beautiful; its form somewhat resembling a barn door; but the dome or outside roof resting on the perpendicular prisms, with the symmetry of the pillars ranged in a compact form all along that part of Staffa, are beyond all description beautiful, even more so if possible, than the outward parts of Fingal's cave; but the striking coup-d'oeil of them is lost to all who approach Staffa by the south-east side of it; and it is not seen at all if the boatmen do not choose to be at the trouble of rowing to the west.

What is very uncommon and which gives a very singular beauty to the south part of Staffa, is, that from the commencement of its grand dome or crown, on the west side of it, till near the landing place for cattle on the east side, not a fallen or loose piece of rock or rubbish of any kind is seen.

I was almost overcome with astonishment and delight, on viewing the parts around the outside of the boat cave, and I remained in silent amazement at every succeeding object that met my eye, till I came to the entrance into Fingal's cave, which I did not perceive till I was nearly close to it, occasioned, (as we were rowing very near shore) by a round projection of most beautiful compact prisms descending from the magnificent crown or dome of small pillars in every direction, (beautified as before mentioned, by the softest mellowest tints that time and weather produce,) to a solid rough base of basaltes.

When I faced the mouth of the cave, what I could see of the inside, and what I gazed at on the outside, made my blood thrill through every vein; but when I got within it I forgot the world and every thing it contains. The omnipotence of the Deity filled my soul. I was lost in wonder, gratitude, and praise. My nerves were so wound up, that the smallest sound distracted me. Never shall I forget the sublime heaven-like sensations with which Fingal's cave inspired me.

From the grand works of nature my mind has often been raised in adoration to the Author of them, and they have been to me the best of sermons; but Staffa produced the highest pitch of solemn, pious, enthusiastic sensation I ever felt or ever can feel, in this my house of clay.

I was in an extasy!

133

CHAPTER TWO

There can be no doubt but Staffa is a huge bunch of prismatic pillars, nicely and closely fitting each other in every part, having its high summit covered with soil and grass. The pillars are jointed at unequal distances, and frequently the sections at the joints are concave on one side, and convex on the other. This may be plainly seen in the inside of Fingal's cave, by noticing the stumps forming the pavement, and their corresponding parts in the arched roof over them. From this circumstance some imagine the enlargement, if not the whole of this cave, to be formed, by the joints near the roof, having been loosened, the under parts sunk perpendicularly, to an irregular depth; but the most natural cause seems to be that time, or decomposition of the cement in the fissures of the angles, and between the joints of the pillars, having loosened their hold on the main mass or bunch, the violent surge has carried off the joints one after another, as the cement which held them together became weakened. Thus too, must have been formed the pavement on the outside of the cave; with this difference, that in the inside the summit, joints and angles have been strong enough to retain their union with their neighbouring pillars, and thereby have formed the roof of the cave. The summit on the outside, exposed to open air, has been too feeble to resist storms, consequently those pillars with the crown and soil summit, have been swept clearly away by the violence of the sea, when ever a decomposition of the cement has taken place.

It would seem that the sea was a preservative, because the joints of the pillars which are regularly covered by the tide, are to appearance firm as adamant, while their upper parts which were always exposed to the air, had fallen and been washed away, leaving their stumps to testify what once had stood upon them. As a proof of this, on my second visit to Staffa I was informed, and observed on the east side of Fingal's cave, that from 1800 to 1802, several perpendicular pillars had slipped out of their angles and been washed away, leaving their additional stumps in the pavement to prove their fall.

In all probability the pavement on the south side of Staffa will be continually enlarging, and possibly before the end of the world the whole of Staffa may exhibit nothing but stumps of pillars. Certainly the present pavement has been less than it now is. At the lowest ebb tide there is no finish to be seen of the pavement; nor do I suppose it has or can be ascertained how far out to sea the stumps extend.

I walked on the pavement as near to the head of the cave as I dared to do, and at the formidable narrow stump, viewed with delight the scene of solemn grandeur around me. The perpendicular compact prisms rising to the roof on each side of the sea in the cave, far below me, and the prospect of I-Ona's cathedral in perspective, through the arch of the cave at a great distance across the sea, greatly pleased me.

When the boatmen thought it time to leave the cave, I descended the steps of disjointed pillars to the boat, and wormed out of the cave as we had wormed into it. I was then landed on the broad pavement on the outside of the cave to the east, and from thence had a wonderfully fine view of the interior of it. This pavement is at all times bounded by the sea on one hand, and on the other by an irregular compact range of uniform, perpendicular prisms, rising solidly from the pavement to the continued dome or crown, of small pillars in various directions, to a height of about 120 feet from the pavement. The crown from the top of the pillars to the grass summit may be nearly one-third of that height.

Some visitors to Staffa have thought its crown, in appearance, too heavy for its supporters; so do the commonality of the isles; who allege that the weight of Staffa's head is too heavy for its legs, having bent them on the east side of Fingal's cave. The pillars there do most certainly bend outwards, probably from having their joints and hold in their angles weakened by the decay of the matter cementing them together, and not by the heavy load they carry.

After having walked on the pavement about 200 yards, I came to the narrow sound between Staffa and its herdsman or guard. In this sound in bad weather, by all accounts, the billows rise like mountains, covering not only Buochaile, but reaching to the summit of Staffa. It is at such times that the roof of Fingal's cave gains a fresh polish. When I was at the Buochaile's sound, it was so smooth that the boat might have passed through it. This little island is a mass entirely composed of prismatic pillars projecting from its solid body in every direction, and is so entirely covered with limpets, that the outside of it in colour, is that of the limpet shell. Indeed all the rocks, and most of the stumps of pillars at Staffa, are completely covered with limpets, and which stick so fast, that they seem to be incorporated with them.

The pillars on the Buochaile isle are not so large as those on Staffa.

I continued walking eastwards, having on my left hand thousands of stumps of pillars rising with great irregularity of height, forming terrible steps to the summit of the island.

When I came to what is called the Clam-shell cave, I was astonished by other pillars, more extraordinary, if possible, in point of natural production, than any I had seen before. They are the large bending pillars. I crossed the creek at the mouth of the cave, and sat down on huge convex prisms lying horizontally in a compact mass, and running a vast length into the sea. Opposite to where I sat, (across the little creek,) huge prisms curve in the arch of a circle down the side of the island, from the summit to the stumps near the mouth of the Clam-shell cave, forming a figure something resembling the ribbed inside of a scollop-shell, which I imagine has given the cave its name. These concave pillars exhibit at their angles, joints exactly similar to the perpendicular ones at Fingal's cave, and form a scene more sublime than I am able to describe.

Seated on the horizontal pillars I dined; never again shall I have such a dining-room, unless I have the happiness of revisiting Staffa. When I had finished my luxuriant feast, particularly of mind, I began my march over the horizontal pillars which lay like numerous keels of huge men of war, petrified in one mass, and jointed like masonry. By scrambling over some horizontal, some bending, and some upright pillars, I at length gained the plain at the summit of the island. This plain is about one mile by three quarters, having a thin strata of soil over the great caves, but on the north side of the island the pasture is admirable for feeding of cattle and sheep. It will graze from forty to fifty head of cattle from October to June, and heifers for the remainder of the year, giving the grass a months respite. I scarcely ever eat such fine mutton as what was fed on Staffa's pasture. That island when farmed, let for fourteen pounds a year. Staffa is part of the estate once belonging to Macquarrie, chief of the Macquarries, and when ever it has changed masters, it has sold with the island of Ulva. The present laird of these isles is Ranald McDonald Esq. of the house of Boisdale, whose mind and taste are fully capable of appreciating the jewel in his possession, the like of which, in all probability, cannot be found on the face of the terrestrial globe. What a pleasure then must it be, to be laird of Staffa?

The first time I was on Staffa I saw only a few sheep and three red deer; the latter on the summit followed our boat as we rowed at the base, and when we came to Fingal's cave, they stood to view us from the tremendous high dome over it.

As soon as I gained the top of the island, I made my way to the station occupied by the deer when I last saw them but being more fearful of turning giddy than they were, I laid myself flat on my breast, and thus crept forward till I got my head over the edge of the roof rising from the arch of the cave. The rocks at the mouth of the cave, which when I was at them were huge masses, seemed to be from this eminence like dots on the surface of the ocean.

Where the pillars have been broken off, or rather disjointed, the remaining stumps, at very irregular heights, exhibit a close mass of prisms of various angles; the most common and numerous are pentagonal and hexagonal. Their diameters also vary from one foot to four feet, yet all nicely fitting in each others angles.

If an uneven transverse slice of a honey comb were petrified, slightly polished, and of a brown colour, it would give a faint

idea of the appearance of the pavement within and without Fingal's cave.

On the south side of Staffa, there are no shelving rocks or ground. Smooth pillars, rough rocks, and stumps rise at once perpendicularly from deep water; so that there is no landing in that quarter but on the pavement, in the interior of Fingal's cave, or on that part of the stumps on the outside which the tide does not cover.

It was low water when I arrived at the cave, for which reason the entrance between the rocks and stumps into it, was narrower than at high tide. The day too was so very calm, there was not the least surf either near or in Fingal's cave, nor even in the sound between Staffa and the Buochaile isle, so that I had not the least difficulty in getting into the cave in the boat. I entered the narrow strait, having on my left hand rough rocks, forming a base, on which rise magnificent perpendicular pillars; on the other, irregular stumps of pillars, once equal in size and grandeur to their adjoining and opposite neighbours. Over my head a roof which is an arch formed by the remaining ends of pillars, so polished by the spray of the sea that they are beautiful.

The boat was not large, and the aperture it had at ebb tide to enter, is a trifle larger, so that we were obliged to worm in by little and little with a pole, continually pushing the boat from off one side to the other, until we got fairly into the cave, where the sea at all times widens considerably, particularly at high water. Whilst the boat was working through its narrow passage, I felt as if a huge monster had got the boat on his back, and was gently raising it, and again as gently letting it sink to its first level. As there was no surf, I could not conceive what occasioned that motion; but my alarm was soon quieted, by being told it was nothing but the swell of the sea.

When I got about half way in the cave, the boatmen advised me to step up the stumps of pillars, to the pavement of stumps on the east side of the cave, lest if they went further at low water in the boat, they might not easily get it back again. I did so, and when I found I had footing on solid stone, I was at my ease to admire, I may say, almost adore. I was told the sound of music in the cave would be enchanting. One of the boatmen was a player on the bagpipe, and had brought his pipes with him, and when I was walking on the pavement, struck up a tune. I could not bear the sound; nothing earthly at that moment could occupy my mind, my soul being absorbed in the wonderful works of omnipotence.

I do however suppose the sounds of soft good music in the cave must be charming, particularly vocal music.

Fortunately it remained a dead calm while I was in Fingal's cave, and being also low water, I had an opportunity of seeing more of the disjointed prisms on its sides, and the base on which the pillars rest at the head of it, than most of those who have been only once at Staffa. This base is at the extremity of the cave, and seemed to me of brilliant red granite (like the Egyptian) so smoothed and polished by the dashing sea, that it appeared at the distance I stood from it, like rubies, pearls, and other precious stones, intermixed. This appearance, however, of various colours, may be produced by the lodgments of sea weeds, shells, &c. in the cavities, and sticking on the rough parts of the basaltes.

From this jewel-looking curve rise smooth brown prisms, above 80 feet high, extending to the arched roof of remaining joints. This brilliant curve has been by some taken from the bottom of the cave. It may appear such when partially viewed through the medium of water, but I had the pleasure of seeing that part dry, and discovering that it is not the bottom of the cave, but the base of the pillars at the end of it. The bottom is a very fine white sand, quite free from rubbish of any sort.

The sea near the head of the cave is not so deep as at the mouth of it; the bottom may be six or eight feet below the surface of the water at the end, and at the mouth 16 or 18 feet.

Staffa rises perpendicular from the sea in every part except at one creek, running some way into the island, on the east side, where few visitors reach; it is there they land what cattle and sheep are grazed on the summit, and it is the most sheltered spot around the island.

From the summit of Fingal's cave, I walked on the west side as near the edge of the precipices as I possibly could, and crossed the hollow from the cattle landing place, and having gained the semicircular promontory I first mentioned, I sat down on the grass which covers the summit of those beautiful pillars. As that point is the highest ground in Staffa, I obtained (it being a clear day,) a panorama view of the surrounding islands and an expanse of the Atlantic towards America, as far as the eye could reach. A sudden change of weather did not enter my mind, nor luckily for me did any change take place, which not unfrequently happens at Staffa, otherwise I should have been in a woful state, totally unprotected and unsheltered, having for companions only four boatmen, to whose language I was a stranger, and a lad for my interpreter. Not a hut upon the island, nor a cave into which I dared to venture in a storm; I must therefore have submitted patiently, and like Lear address the elements, "Then let fall your horrible pleasure; here I stand your slave," an unprotected weak woman.

From the western promontory I proceeded on the summit to the northern parts of the island, where is a well of good water, also a small peat moss, necessaries provided by providence for the existence and comfort of man, if any were daring enough to take up their abode there. For a year or two a herdsman did so, and raised two huts; but he grew tired of the boisterous elements, quitted his station, and his cattle's shelter fell to ruins.

Many stories are related of the terrors this solitary herdsman endured, whilst he lived on the island, and amongst the rest, that his pot was often shaken while hanging over the fire, by the violent shocks the island received from the dashing sea.

After making the circuit of the summit of Staffa, I arrived at the cattle landing place, and descended by that hollow to the broken rocks on the sea shore north of it, where in the fragments of basaltes I procured many beautiful specimens (peculiar I was told to Staffa,) of a variety of crystals. I then reascended and came to the same steps by which I had at first gained the top of the island, and came down to the boat.

I a second time rowed slowly by Fingal's cave, and the west side of Staffa, and about nine o'clock at night landed safely at Torloisk. The boatmen declared they had gone a great many times to Staffa, but had never found at that island so calm, so safe a day, as that I was so fortunate to get. In the year 1800 I was the ninth female stranger who had ventured to Staffa; but none of them had gone valiantly alone as I did.

It has not been longer than twenty-eight or twenty-nine years since the island of Staffa has been noticed as an object of curiosity, for previous to the year 1770, it was avoided rather than sought after. It does not lie in the direct course, going through the sound of I-Colombkill, from the south to the north, nor indeed is it in the way from one island of the Hebrides to another, but stands in the middle of an extensive bay, formed by islands, in the Atlantic, and completely open on the southwest to that ocean; and from that point of the compass Staffa bears the storms and tempests from America; for not a foot of land lies directly between it and that continent. This may be the reason why such heavy seas are commonly around Staffa, and which cause it to be avoided by sea-faring people. Necessity never obliges any vessel to steer for Staffa; and as its curiosities were unknown, it was never visited, till within the last thirty years, by any but herdsmen, who probably ran their boats into the creek, where they landed their cattle, and then sailed off again as quickly as possible, without being at the trouble of going either to the south or west sides of the island; or if they did go thither, in all probability they only execrated the useless rocks, and the rough and dangerous sea around them, without conceiving that those billows surrounded the most wonderful production on the face of the earth, which they had neither sense to feel, nor understanding to comprehend.

Dr. Johnson had not the happiness of visiting Staffa. What a loss he sustained! The wonders of that island were very little known at the period he passed near it, in his way from Ulva to I-Ona.

Fingal's cave and Staffa's bending pillars might have been

doomed to waste their beauties in the desert ocean, had they not been brought to light by the account of Staffa published in Mr. Pennant's Tour. Mr. Pennant, like Dr. Johnson, did not go near Staffa, he only saw it at a distance, (as I was told,) and his draftsman took a view of its general appearance on the east side, where there is least to be seen.

The views in Mr. Pennant's Tour (I have been informed) of the Clam-shell and Fingal's cave, are engraven from drawings sent to him by Sir Joseph Banks, with the discoveries he had made at Staffa.

Sir Joseph acquired his first knowledge of Staffa from a speculative gentleman from Ireland. In Mull he went by the name of Leach, but it was thought it was not his real name. His speculation in the Hebrides was farming; and whether by accident or on a new speculation, no matter which, he landed on Staffa. He explored its wonderful caves, and had taste and judgment sufficient to comprehend the value of all he found on that astonishing island. Sir Joseph Banks met Mr. Leach at Dremin in Morven, from whom he learnt what a rare jewel stood unknown, and unnoticed, in the Atlantic; and offered to accompany him to it; an offer not to be refused by a philosophic mind, the philanthropy of which had carried him round the terrestrial globe.

It has been by a few imagined, that the summit of Staffa is supported by pillars, resembling a colonnade. A man, not long since, (I will not say of what nation,) arrived at Lagan Ulva, on purpose to see Staffa, with that imagination full in his mind. He ordered a boat to be ready the next morning to carry him to Staffa, but unfortunately for him he made all the enquiries he could concerning the pillars of that island, and when he was assured that he could neither sail nor row between the fine basaltic pillars, which he had been informed (he said) supported Staffa, he in a pet retraced his steps to Aros and Oban, without going thither; for he declared he would not give a straw to see that island, unless he could sail or row through it, under a colonnade of angular pillars.

I must end with mention of the Thunder cave; the reason of its being thus called is as follows: By some means or other a very large round stone incorporated in the mass of rock, supporting the pillars not far from the boat cave, became loose in its socket, and afterwards by continual friction, made itself a large aperture, in which it was in storms violently agitated. When driven with great force by the billows to the back of its socket, it rebounded with a noise like loud thunder, which was heard at a great distance. I had not a chance of hearing one clap, for not many years since, (I was told,) some Irishmen came to Staffa to view its wonders. They, on coming to the Thunder cave, and hearing of the miracle performed by the round stone, said amongst themselves, "By — let us carry it over to Ireland," and

they did so. A terrible noise, however, is still to be heard when the sea roars into the cavity the stone once filled.

CHAPTER THREE

On the 28th July, Mrs. McLean had the goodness to lend me her poney to carry me to Aros, and the young man, my interpreter, to lead it. She also provided me with another little horse and lad to convey my baggage. I returned by a different route from that I went by to Torloisk, chiefly over a high mountain and through moors.

The day after I returned to Aros proved bad weather, I therefore remained another twenty-four hours under the hospitable roof of Mr. Maxwell, and then set out on horse-back for Ach-na-craig.

The ride from Aros to Ach-na-craig, along the shore, is as beautiful as the voyage up the Sound. Mull does not abound with trees, but I passed by a farm called Scalesdale, nearly opposite to Ardtorinish castle, beautified by many; and I also went through a pretty extensive wood of different kinds of forest trees, prettily intermixed with birch, alder, mountain ash, and various shrubs, at a farm called Ard-na-craish; likewise as I wound round a hill not far from Ach-na-craig, I was surrounded by wood hanging and creeping about every rock, as well as growing vigorously on every bit of plain ground.

I was overtaken by a gentleman on foot and we readily fell into conversation on Staffa, and my journey thither. I told him I had a letter of introduction to a gentleman in Ross, but I should not avail myself of it, as I had determined not to visit I-Columb-kill. "Not visit I-Ona, Madam? you will have seen nothing if you do not see I, (I-Ona is thus called in the country,) for it is the greatest curiosity under the sun. Do let me persuade you to go to I-Ona; I know the gentleman and family for whom you have a letter, they are very happy to see strangers, and pay them attentions. I will deliver the letter to your friends, if you will please give it me, that they may be prepared to receive you. You can easily cross the country in one day, and you will find it a very pleasant ride."

I thought, if I did not go to Ross there would be no harm in sending the letter; I therefore gave it to the gentleman, and desired him to say, that if I should not be able to travel so far I should be sorry for it. Thus we parted; the good man took his way amongst the mountains, I continued mine towards Ach-na-craig.

In a glen coming from Torloisk, I met two Scotch gentlemen on Mull ponies, riding towards the west side of Mull; I concluded they were bound for Staffa, and so they were. They overtook me the day but one following, near to Ach-na-craig, and asked me if I were to cross to Oban that night; I did not intend to do so, because it was too late.

Young men, although ill mounted, easily out-stripped a woman in leading strings, (in the Highlands I have always had my horse led,) so they arrived at Ach-na-craig before me, but I was in time to hear from the window of a bed-room at the inn, their take leave conversation.

These young beaux had neglected to agree with the man, of whom they hired the ponies, for the sum they were to pay per day for them. The result was that an exhorbitant price was demanded, with which they did not choose to comply. When the gentlemen came without the door of the inn in order to depart, the owner of the ponies appeared to receive his reward. One of the young men offered him money, which the man refused to take. "Well then," said the other, "my name is — —, I live in Edinburgh, I am an advocate, and my uncle is a lord of Session, if you do not choose to take what I offer, you know where to find me." The poor man took the money, and retired groaning.

After I had taken refreshment at Ach-na-craig, I desired to see the master of the inn; the mistress of it received me at my first arrival; and on my asking her if she had a good bed to give me, she said, such as it is, Madam, you shall be heartily welcome to it.

I must premise that Mr. and Mrs. Maclachlan, who lived at Ach-na-craig in 1800 were people superior to those who generally keep inns. Mr. Dugall Maclachlan's conduct, not only to me, but to every one going to his house, was that of a gentleman; indeed he was such, although master of Ach-na-craig inn.

When Mr. Maclachlan came up stairs to me, I found him a sensible friendly good creature; I told him I wished to cross Mull to Ross, if I could procure safe horses to carry me thither; "Madam, I do not keep horses for hire myself, but there are labouring people who let ponies, such as you saw this afternoon, to travellers. Are you, Madam, the Mrs Murray who has written a book of the Beauties of Scotland?" "Yes." — "Then you shall be welcome to the best horse I have, and you may keep him as long as you please." See what an advantage it is to have written a book!

I accepted of Mr. Maclachlan's friendly offer, and requested him to find me a Highlander, to lead and take care of his horse, until I returned to him; also to procure me a pony and a lad to carry my baggage; adding, that I should be much obliged to him to make the bargains for me, and pay all charges, and I would with thanks re-imburse him at my return.

More friendly offices and attentions were paid to me by Mr. and Mrs. Maclachlan than I can describe. He not only made good bargains for me with others, but refused taking a farthing for the use of his horse, which I kept out sixteen days; nor would he suffer me to pay for any part of my entertainment at the several times I was under his roof, except for wine and porter. Mr. Maclachlan will never read this tribute of thanks on my part, for he is, I trust, in heaven; but I hope his surviving relatives will feel pleasure in this his due praise.

On the 31st of July I set off from Ach-na-craig for a ride of 40 miles, from one extremity of Mull to the other, through the heart of the island.

The cavalcade set forward exactly in the same style it left Aros for Torloisk, and I immediately began to mount a very steep hill, in a terrible rough track. Over the summit, and down its precipitous side to one of the heads of Loch Spelibh (sounded Spelive,) there is no track at all; and I was continually fancying I should be thrown over the head of the horse down a rocky high bank, bounding a roaring stony bedded burn, close over which the guide was leading me. Before me were lofty mountains, and deep glens between them; which attracted my notice; and my fears were lessened by my admiration of the sublime scenery towards one of those mountains, the name of which Dugall, my leader, told me was Ben Buy; and he continued in his broken English to relate the legendary history of other days, concerning that and its neighbouring hills.

Formerly, said Dugall, the mountains and glens you see, were inhabited by a race of giants, who thought nothing of stepping from the top of one mountain to another. They were constantly at war with each other, and many a brave giant fell in battle, but the most famous of all, was the giant of two heads, who being engaged in war with a neighbouring hero, consulted his bard, (who was the oracle as well as poet of the Highland chieftains,) what would be the result of the conflict.

The sage foretold, that if on the morning of the decisive battle he was obliged to ask for his breakfast, it would be an unfavourable omen; and if he on the same day should drink of a stream, and a trout should bite his lip, his life would be in danger. A third omen was named, (which Dugall could not explain in English,) which if it happened, would denote his total destruction.

When the morning of the battle arrived, the gallant chieftain arose and put on his armour. Alas! he had dis-obliged his wife, and put her out of temper to such a degree, that she gave him no breakfast until he asked for it. In the heat of the day he was thirsty, and put his mouth to a limpid stream. A trout bit his lip. The third bad omen was likewise fulfilled, and the chief was laid low in battle.

He fell, and had his head cut off; but by miracle, another head sprang upon his shoulders. He snatched up his own head, placed it under his arm, and then taking his three-legged horse by the bridle, vanished off the field of battle.

The spirit of the two-headed warrior, (continued Dugall,) has ever since, when a chief of Loch Buy is about to die, been heard walking around Moy, shaking the bridle of his three-legged steed.

When I arrived at the level of Loch Spelibh the ground was boggy, dreary, and wild, but the sides of that lake at a distance from me were covered with wood.

Loch Spelibh is a fine salt water loch. It empties itself into the sea on the east side of Mull. It has what may be called two heads, one of which almost joins a fresh-water lake between it and Loch Buy. Between the former lake and Loch Uisch, (water lake, for that is the literal interpretation of Uisch,) there is about a quarter of a mile of land, and three quarters of a mile between it and the latter.

On leaving Loch Spelibh, I followed a river running to it out of Glenmore, and soon entered that glen; and a wilder or more Alpine region cannot be imagined. Some hills are rough and rocky, others green to the very summits of them, particularly one, a higher hill than any in Mull, except Benmore, which stands insulated by narrow glens, and from the bottom to the top of it I never saw finer sheep pasture.

I journied on for many miles through this Alpine scenery, till I came to a diminutive plain, with three tracks from different glens leading to it. I was then riding on the brink of a river, and about two miles before us I observed a terrible steep zig-zag track, up an almost perpendicular face of a mountain. That, said Dugall, is our road; and when we came within half a mile of it, we steered our course over a boggy piece of moor, the remembrance of which almost makes me tremble.

When we arrived at the foot of the zig-zag ascent, I got off the horse; had I not done so, I verily believe I and the horse would have fallen back down the precipice, dragging Dugall the leader after us. It was one of the hottest days I ever felt, and the labour of scrambling up the steep road amongst loose stones for two miles was dreadful. Dugall said it was only one Mull mile, which is fully two measured miles. The people in Mull jocosely say of their miles, that they make up in measure for what their roads want in quality.

When I reached the summit of the hill, I looked around me, and to my sorrow perceived before me Benmore, in its fair day's glory, with its lofty top piercing the clouds, and at its base Loch-na-keall. I exclaimed, Dugall, we are wrong; how shall we get back again down the dreadful zig-zag? Dugall hung his head and confessed he had never gone the horse track through Glenmore, but he had often travelled (walked) over the hills to the west side of Mull.

We kept along the ridge of the hill for another Highland mile, and then descended to a glen in which is a small lake, and a hut or two at the end of it.

I was rejoiced at the sight of any human trace, and sent the boy to inquire if the track we were in, led to Penny Cross. It did, and we made what speed we could through the rugged glen. We were told by travellers, (walkers,) whom we soon after met, that if we did not travel hard, we should not reach Penny Cross by sun set. We had lost our way once, and were not very clear about that we were pursuing; therefore the intelligence received from the walkers was not very agreeable.

After going through beds of rivers, and in every imaginable uncouth track, we came within sight of a hut, at which Dugall said, eatables might sometimes be procured, but he did not think what we should there find would be worth seeking, particularly as it would delay us, it being somewhat off our road.

Other burns and rough passes were to be surmounted; at last we came to a spot from which two tracks branched; one I believe, leads to Moy at the head of Loch Buy, the other to the head of Loch Scridain. The pass to Moy being in shade, appeared tremendous amongst lofty black crags. Ours, although in sunshine, was terrific enough. It was along the side of a precipice, (which we had to climb and descend,) and it had no trees or shrubs to cover its coarse terrific nakedness.

I got off my horse for safety and rest, and sat down on a piece of rock projecting from a lofty range of broken cliffs above, and below me, at the foot of which is a wild plain with a river flowing towards Loch Scridain. I had but a short portion of provisions with me, not foreseeing that I should lose my way, nor knowing Glenmore to be a wilderness of considerable length, through which I was to wander.

On the pommel of my saddle hung a bag containing drawing implements, in which I had brought three or four biscuits from Aros. In a small mahogany case, containing hartshorn and lavender drops, and a cure for bruises, I had some wine, also a tumbler glass, spoon, knife, and fork. I produced my slender repast, which required none of the latter articles, and shared it with my guides. The poor beasts were left to nibble what they could find. Alas! they looked for grass, and found nothing but stones.

I walked down the terrific precipice and advanced, not without doubt whether we were in the right road or not. At length we came to a few huts, where women came out to gaze at us. I beseeched Dugall to inquire of every human form he met, if we were in the road to Penny Cross. When I heard something like the sound of pshe (it is,) in answer to Dougall's interrogatory, I was rejoiced, for I began to be very weary, and the sun was fast declining. Notwithstanding my fatigue, the scenery before me of Loch Scridain, and the bold mountains on the back ground of Kilfinechen, pleased me exceedingly.

In my wearied state, when I arrived at the head of Loch Scridain, how thankful should I have been to the Duke of Argyle, had his grace established an inn there!

The want of inns in Mull, may appear, to some people, of small, or no importance; on the contrary, inns would be of considerable benefit to the people of the country, and the comfort of them, if tolerably kept, to travellers of taste and curiosity, would be infinite. How is it possible, without inns, for any one less enthusiastic than I am, to get a view of the numberless curious spots in Mull? Gentlemen's houses in that island are mostly situated widely from each other; consequently strangers in travelling through Mull will meet with many difficulties, and the island by that means must remain a spot of insignificance and disgust.

All travellers whom I have met with, have execrated Mull as a barren, dreary, dreadful district; which is owing to their being unacquainted with the interior and southern parts of the island, where they may find scenery to astonish and delight them.

If there were an inn at the head of Loch Scridain, a traveller might scramble through Glenmore, which is a fine Alpine ride, in one day from Ach-na-craig thither, and then go on to Bunessain at the head of Loch Laich, which would be another very good station for an inn, where travellers might embark for Staffa and I-Ona; and they might also with more ease from Bunessain visit Inimore and Loch Buy, by sea, than by a terrible ride, (although much beauty and grandeur in the way,) over the mountains.

Much cannot be said of the inn at Aros, and yet that is one of the best situations for an inn, as most pilgrims to Staffa go thither, either from Oban by sea or by land from Ach-na-craig. Without a tolerable inn at Aros, the two hospitable gentlemen's families who live there must every year experience a heavier tax on their hospitality from an increase of travellers to the isles, with letters of introduction.

As I proceeded along the margin of Loch Scridain, the road became very rugged, or perhaps my extreme fatigue made me think it worse than it really was. About two miles before I came to Penny Cross, I rode through the channel of a burn, the bed of which was full of huge stones, brought by torrents from a lofty crag within sight, the hollow sides of which must in hard rains exhibit magnificent cascades, but they were not in beauty the day I passed near them, and it was well for me they were not, for had they been "grumbling And leaping and tumbling And hopping and skipping And foaming and dripping And struggling and toiling And bubbling and boiling And beating and jumping And bellowing and thumping," I should not have been able to have crossed the burn which rises to an enormous height after violent rains.

At last, on turning a promontory of rock, I saw my longwished for goal, Penny Cross house. I had no letter of introduction, nor was I known to the family, but I depended on the character of the inhabitants of the country, and rode up to the door of the mansion as boldly as my exhausted strength would permit. I inquired if Mrs. McLean was at home. She appeared, and I thus bespoke her charity. "Madam, my name is Murray, I am a stranger, and in my way to Mr. Campbell's, the minister, but I am so fatigued by a ride of ten hours through Glenmore, that I cannot proceed; will you have the goodness to give me shelter for this night?" "Madam, your being a stranger, is a sufficient reason for me to pay you every attention in my power; I beg you will come in." As soon as I was seated, I was asked what I could take by way of refreshment. I longed for a draught of porter, and expressed my wish. A bottle of porter was brought, and as it was a cordial to my drooping frame, Mrs. McLean smiling said, "Have no fears, drink it all, I will tell no tales." Mr. McLean Penny Cross was captain of the volunteers, and at the time I was at his house he was absent on duty. The inspecting officer and his aid-de-camp were expected at Penny Cross the night I arrived there, but they did not come.

I took my leave of Mrs. McLean and family, with grateful thanks for her hospitality, and proceeded on my way to Mr. Campbell's. The morning was not clear, though it was fair when I set off; but I had not gone above two miles before it began to rain, and when I arrived at my friend's house, I had not a dry thread about me.

The road between Penny Cross and Busessain, near which is Mr. Campbell's habitation, exceeds, in point of danger for a horse, every track I had before entered. I am astonished how the inhabitants of that quarter escape breaking their bones and necks, in scrambling over that distance of nine or ten miles.

CHAPTER FOUR

I-Ona signifies the Island of Waves: I-Columbkill, the Island of Saint Columba's Church, burying place, or cell: for kill signifies all three. I is Gaelic for island, and by way of pre-eminence, I-Ona in the west is commonly called simply I.

On the 10th of August a strong party of us set out for I-Ona, consisting of Mr. Campbell, his two sons, Mr. Gillis, three females, and our attendants.

From Bunessain to the point of Ross by land, may be eight miles of country, (road there is none,) similar to that between Penny Cross and Bunessain, but more island. At about a mile before we arrived at the Sound of I, we came upon a black dreary desolate moor, on which is an excessively pretty fresh-water lake, nearly surrounded by rocks covered with alpine wood, chiefly birch. In the lake are many rocky islands. Those islands, and all the rocks around the lake were, when I passed that way, completely covered with sea-gulls, which by their noise and fluttering caused a very extraordinary effect. It was like a general motion of all the component parts of the lake, and a confusion of sound not to be described.

From the fresh-water lake to the sea is about a mile of the most dreary black moor I ever went over; so that I began to be very much tired of my ride; when, without suspecting it, I found myself within two hundred yards of the Sound of I. The coup-d'oeil of I-Columbkill, and the extraordinary rocky shore of Ross, to which I was approaching, astonished me beyond measure. I did not expect to see any thing from Ross but merely the outline of I-Ona, because I had conceived the Sound between Mull and I-Ona was far broader than it is, therefore when suddenly my eyes, from a black moor, were fixed upon a view so wild, and yet so sublime, I sat for a few moments on my horse, like a statue, dumb with amazement; occasioned by the huge fantastical rocks of fine red granite, similar to the Egyptian, standing and lying in every imaginable form, all along the Mull shore for miles; and on the other side of a narrow sound, ruins of grandeur, that made the mind revert to ages past, and reflect how frail and uncertain is human greatness.

A boat had been ordered to meet us at the point of Ross, opposite the harbour, near the town in I-Ona. The day, from a very doubtful morning, became as fine as possible, and quite calm; we therefore embarked with pleasure, leaving our horses to get what food they could amongst the granite masses, until our return. We crossed the Sound to procure an addition of two rowers, that we might go by sea to Port-a-churaich, so called because Saint Columba first landed on I-Ona, in his wicker boat, at that small bay on the south side of the island. It is at least six miles to walk from the town to Port-a-churaich, and back again, which in the heat of the day would have been very fatiguing; I was therefore much pleased with the plan of going by sea. We rowed as near the shore of I-Columbkill as possible, and a bold shore of rocks it is, particularly near the marble quarry, where vast cliffs of marble rise in irregular masses from the sea to a great height.

The young men of our party, and three of the boatmen, ran up and down the broken points and sides of these tremendous cliffs like goats; it was quite terrifying to look at them.

They reached the marble quarry, and returned to the boat laden with marble of three kinds; pure white, white veined with bright light green, and a light gray or rather dove colour. The quarry was worked only for a short time; why it was discontinued I cannot say.

When we came near the southern point of I-Ona the rocks became wonderfully bold and sublime; innumerable rocky islands too are scattered near to Port-a-churaich, which, with huge cave-like, hollows in the broken masses around the bay, render the scene at that point very grand indeed.

Port-a-churaich, Like Fingal's cave in Staffa, is open to the south-west, and receives the violent blasts from America, so that in a storm blowing from that quarter, the billows rise mountains high on the west and south sides of I-Ona, and rush into the small bay of Port-a-churaich, I was told, with a noise like thunder. We entered it peaceably, and landed on the sloping pebbly beach, and there I picked up gray pebbles, beautifully marked; fine lapis nephriticus; jaspers, green mixed with red; serpentine stone, gray and other porphyries; pure white marble, and many other rare stones, of which I do not know the names, all rounded and in some degree polished. I also found one small amethyst, but not a clear one. I have many of the lapis nephriticus of a beautiful green, quite transparent, and very rare; these also are from Port-a-churaich, and I believe they are no where to be found except I-Ona.

From Port-a-churaich we rowed back to the town, for we had not time to go round the island; and landed at the bay where the corpses of kings and heroes "of other days" were received in I-Ona for interment. Their bodies were taken from the vessels conveying them, and placed on land at the head of the bay, from which they were carried in great funeral pomp over a broad causeway, leading from the bay to the cathedral, nearly a quarter of a mile. There are parts of the causeway remaining, but most of it has been taken up by the poor people, in order to build their huts with the stones. One would imagine it were as much labour to destroy the causeway as to procure the stone from the rocks, the chief commodity of I-Ona; but the stones forming the causeway were already broken, and on the spot; these were, I imagine, to indolent folks, sufficient reasons for the destruction of the causeway.

The huts forming the town in I-Ona, (and there are no other habitations on the island,) are scattered amongst the ruins; chiefly around the nunnery, and along the causeway; but as far as I can recollect, there are no huts within the ancient pale of the monastery and church premises, which were pretty extensive, running on every side, except the one adjoining the town, to the sea.

If a judgment may be formed from the remains of the cathedral, I-Ona was once a great seminary of ecclesiastical learning. The ruins of this famous island, and their dimensions, have been described and made public by far abler pens than mine, I shall therefore confine my account chiefly to local circumstances, and observations beneath the classical pens of my predecessors, in the mixed, uncertain, oral, legendary, history of I-Ona.

Some of my readers may not have read its history, written by Dr. Johnson and others, I will therefore give as laconic an account of what is current in that country, as I possibly can, which I collected upon the spot.

In former times, I cannot say when, Saint Columba with his

friend Oran, accompanied by as many followers as their wicker bark could contain, landed from Ireland at Port-a-churaich.

Tradition says that Saint Columba's boat was formed of bended oziers, covered with hides; and the length of it, as marked on the beach at Port-a-churaich, was forty-six feet.

It is related, the motive of Saint Columba, and his friend and followers, for leaving Ireland, was either disgust at something in their own country, or zeal for the propagation of the catholic faith. I will suppose the latter, as it is the most charitable, and redounds most to the honour of the saint.

Reformers in all ages, and upon all occasions, have experienced more or less persecution; therefore Saint Columba would expect his share of difficulty and danger, in the wild region to which he had voluntarily transported himself, out of zeal for the salvation of souls. He therefore, like a wise man, deep in forecast, pitched upon the wildest and most inaccessible spot of the wild region to which he had bent his course. Had he any ideas similar to those I imagine him to have had, he could not have chosen a situation more applicable to his purpose than I-Ona, for the seat of his future ecclesiastical sovereignty; for such it afterwards became, when kings, chieftains, and heroes, implicitly obeyed him, and humbly kissed his rod, if ever he deigned to use it.

It is reported, and written too, that the holy Saint had an aversion to women; I will endeavour to clear his reputation on that subject, and vindicate the honour of the female sex by a query. If the females had been all banished from I-Ona, why did Saint Columba erect a beautiful edifice, called the nunnery? of which there remains sufficient to prove, that it was a fine piece of architecture, although built, probably, in the latter part of the sixth century. Besides, if in process of time, a great town arose at the very gates of the monastery, how could that town be peopled without women?

The island which has been called the Nuns Island, to which the females were said to be confined, through dislike of the Saint to the sex, is, in the Gaelic language expressed the Island of Women; not on account of their having been banished thither for life, but only for a while, during the time the foreign colony of holy men were erecting the buildings, lest their charms and allurements should, by rendering the men less industrious, impede the great work. I am sure if the Island of Women in those ages past was, as it is now, I lament the horrible state the poor females must have been in, during their abode upon it, for at present it is only a rugged huge mass of red granite, without any appearance of soil; at least that came within my sight as I rowed close to it, through the narrow sound between it and Mull. I was told that from the Island of Women came all the stone with which the buildings on I-Ona were constructed.

There are near the cathedral, (and one in the middle of the

street or causeway,) several large hewn pieces of granite standing in the form of crosses; one in particular, called Saint John's cross, is more perfect than any of the rest, and the carving on it, I was told, is very fine, but I did not examine it, or if I had, I might not have understood it.

At the reformation, when the ecclesiastical inhabitants, both male and female, were persecuted, and obliged to fly from I-Ona, it is said, above five hundred crosses, similar to Saint John's, were found upon the island.

In the days of Saint Columba, as well as in more modern times, monks loved good eating, if their fish-ponds and other marks of luxury may be allowed signs of their nice sense of palate. From the monastery to what is now a marsh, is a tolerably perfect broad causeway, which in prosperous times led to a lake, probably made by art for the preserving and easily taking fish at pleasure.

The causeway from the monastery to the lake, was also formed around it, and finely shaded by plantations, (of which not a bush remains,) so that the holy men might indulge themselves with a beautiful shady walk, contemplating the delicious meal the pond would afford them.

I was told the first edifice raised, or at least attempted to be raised on I-Ona, was Saint Oran's chapel, but finished it could not be, for when it came to a certain height, what was built in the day was tumbled down in the night. An oracle was consulted, and by the voice of Saint Columba it declared, that no building would ever be completely reared, until a human being were interred alive. Saint Oran's zeal led him to offer himself the victim, and, in appearance, he was under ground for three days. Saint Columba, at the end of that period, was desirous of seeing the state in which his friend Oran remained, and to gratify his curiosity had the sod which had been laid over his grave removed, when behold Oran arose, and began to preach to the astonished spectators.

He informed them that in the grave his eyes had been opened in a wonderful manner, and that he was compelled by an invisible power to declare to them, that every tittle that had been promulgated by Saint Columba and himself, of a future state, and hell and heaven, was false. Saint Columba cried out in a loud voice, "cover him, cover him with dust, for the devil has taken possession of him!" He was covered, and then in reality buried alive; thus the oracle was satisfied; Saint Oran's chapel was completed, and the cathedral, nunnery, and town in due time also, rose in grandeur.

It is a great pity that both the cathedral and the nunnery are going fast to decay. Part of the ground around the cathedral, when I was at I-Ona, was planted with potatoes and other vegetables; the rest of it was over-run with the most luxuriant weeds and wild plants, I ever beheld.

CHAPTER FIVE

Although the town in I-Ona appears an insignificant irregular cluster of huts, thatched with turf or heath; it contained, at the last enumeration of its inhabitants, two or three years since, four hundred souls. As for their morals, such has been their general good behaviour, that none have suffered capital punishment in the memory of any person living, or even imprisonment for inferior crimes, except one man in the year 1793.

I-Ona to its proprietor, the Duke of Argyle, is worth about one hundred and forty pounds a year; consisting of two equal farms, and these are subdivided into about thirty farms.

The extent of the island may be about five English miles long by three broad. It is very rocky, particularly on the west side of it, although in many parts there is fine grazing land. The soil of it is very productive of barley, oats, and potatoes; the profit arising from the latter is often sufficient to pay the whole rent of a farm.

Cattle are fed on I-Columbkill, but sheep are forbidden by the proprietor, on account of the smallness of the island. A very few sheep are, however, reared on I-Ona; but it is in secret.

There are no trees on the island, nor fuel of any sort. At the proper season the inhabitants cross over to Ross, where they find plenty of peat mosses. From these mosses, or black bogs, they cut, dry, and pile vast quantities of peat, and let them remain in stacks upon the mosses until completely fit for use; they then set all their boats and hands to work to convey their yearly store of fuel across the Sound to their houses.

The inhabitants of I-Ona, as well as those of Ross, are healthy, but subject at one season of the year to putrid fevers brought from the low countries, (around Edinburgh and Glasgow,) where numbers from the Highlands go every year, at the time of harvest. In the low countries the harvest is over before that in the Highlands begins, which enables the Highland men and women to profit by two harvests. A traveller in June will continually meet groups of Highlanders trudging south; the women with cloth cloaks on, bare feet and legs, their petticoats pinned up, their sickle on their arm, and a snow white mob cap on their heads, without any hat; thus they march on, for perhaps, a hundred miles to the earliest harvest districts, and work their way back to the north and west by degrees, as the climate retards the ripening season, and arrive at their homes in good time for gathering in their own crops.

The parish of Ross is famous for longevity. In 1800 there were three brothers and a sister, of the name of McGilvra, whose ages together made near four hundred years. In the same year a man of above a hundred years old came from I-Ona for me to

Iona - this famous island.

see him; and when he had crossed the Sound, he was stout enough to walk from the shore to where I was in Mull, a distance of at least eight miles. I gave him half a guinea; a coin he never had in his possession before. He felt it, his eye-sight being dim, and took it for a sixpence; nevertheless he was thankful, but not so much so as was expected. The lady of the house explained to him in Gaelic, that the piece he held in his hand was gold, and worth ten shillings and sixpence. His joy was then beyond description, and he poured forth more Gaelic blessings upon me than I can repeat. Were I superstitious, I should fancy the old man's prayers, in my behalf, were efficacious, for luck like mine in those quarters was never, I believe, equalled.

After visiting the ruins of the cathedral and the nunnery, and surveying the ancient tombs of great men long forgotten, our party reached the inn, not equal to a hotel, but by no means in so despicable a state as when Dr. Garnet and Mr. Watts were in danger of being suffocated with laughter, excited by the crowing of a young cock, perched over their heads. Since that time the public room in the inn at I-Ona has acquired a new ceiling, which now excludes the rain, which when they were there, (they said,) rendered the floor of it liquid mire. In my time the room was dry, and as clean as I expected to find it, in such a secluded situation; there were two beds in it, which I did not examine, having no intention of passing a night at I-Ona, but I was told they could accommodate travellers with sheets, which puts me in mind of a boast, made by a worthy minister of an extensive parish in Perthshire. "I can now, (said he,) go through the whole of my parish, and be certain of finding a feather-bed and sheets to sleep in, and a tea breakfast in the morning." It is owing to the more frequent use of linen, (I have been told,) that the itch is much decreased in Scotland. I saw but very few afflicted (or, as they call it, smitten) with it, in all my travels through the Highlands; and although I was three weeks at one time, and fourteen days another, in the habit of taking meals at the same table with persons diseased with the itch, I was not smitten, for which I was most heartily thankful, when it came to my knowledge what a risk I had run.

The good woman at the inn at I-Ona, when we returned from our long and fatiguing peregrination, furnished us with a meal of fine fish and excellent potatoes; hunger added the best of sauce.

When our dinner was concluded, the young ladies of our party and I went down to the bay; while we were seated on the rocks impending over the bay, numbers of women and children came after us, and by degrees some of the old ones crept from one piece of rock to another, until they were close to us. The men and boys kept a respectful distance, not that they had less curiosity, but were more bashful than the women. The manners of the females appeared to me to be innocent, simple, and crouching, like spaniel dogs approaching their masters. If fear had not deterred them, I verily believe the poor things would have gladly fondled us. Very seldom indeed are their eyes accustomed to look upon strangers of either sex, and a few shillings distributed amongst them afforded a transient joy not easily described.

The habiliments of the commonalty, both men and women, in most parts of the Highlands, are chiefly made of a thin coarse woollen cloth which they fabricate, and dye of indigo colour blue.

The form of the womens' dress is generally a petticoat, and a sort of bed-gown of that cloth, and a white mob cap, or an handkerchief wrapped closely round their heads and under their chins. The men wear waistcoats and trousers of the same sort of cloth, and beaver hats.

The manners and dress of the modern females of higher ranks in the Highlands, are precisely the same as those of ladies in other parts of Scotland and England.

In undress, the gentlemen most commonly wear short coats, like shooting jackets, made of tartan, (the stuff in England called plaid,) instead of a broad cloth coat, and sometimes trousers of tartan; otherwise their dress is the same as in England.

The true Highland dress with the belted plaid, is now seldom worn; and even the kilt is discarded, except by sporting gentlemen, and farmers, who find it convenient for walking in all places and weathers. The Scotch bonnet too, I am sorry to say, is seldom worn; and I fear within a few years the Highland dress and language too, will be wholly laid aside.

No man will be seen in Scotland without shoes and hose of some sort, although very many women of the lower class go without.

Boys and girls, children of chieftains and lairds, may be seen in the Highlands running about without shoes or stockings, but it is in early youth, and it makes them hardy.

It was soon time to return to Mull and we gladly quitted our new made friends of I-Ona, and set out in our boat. We put some of the lads on shore in Mull to seek and ride our horses to Bunessain, because we determined to return thither by sea, and a fine voyage we had, although a long one; for it was half after ten o'clock at night before we reached the head of Loch Laich.

Between the Sound of I and Loch Laich we enjoyed a solemn pleasing scene, which a clear sky and a bright moon-shine afforded, of the region through which we were gliding in the tranquillity of the night, and saw now a rock, and now an island, grow gradually conspicuous and gradually obscure.

After we landed at Bunessain we had a mile to go before we reached Mr. Campbell's house; I chose to walk it, others rode.

One of the young ladies who was of our party to I-Ona, is an amiable daughter of the worthy minister of whom Dr. Johnson speaks so highly, but by mistake he calls him, in his Journey to the Western Islands, McLean, whereas the then minister of Ross was McLeod; his house was situated by the sea side; that of the present minister is on the bank of a fresh-water lake, about one mile inland.

Part Five

CHAPTER ONE

I believe no one has written any very particular account of the island of Mull. Dr. Johnson in his Journey to the Western Islands of Scotland says, "the isle of Mull is perhaps in extent the third of the Hebrides. It is not broken by waters, nor shot into promontories, but is a solid and compact mass of breadth nearly equal to its length. Of the dimensions of the larger islands there is no knowledge approaching to exactness. I am willing to estimate it as containing about three hundred square miles."

Dr. Johnson crossed Mull from Tobermoire to Lagan Ulva, and again from Bunessain by the head of Loch Buy to Loch Spelibh, but being much out of humour with the country, "for, (as he said,) road there was none," he made no observations.

I having travelled more through the interior of Mull than most other strangers, am able to form some judgment of its geography.

I was told that Mull is about forty English miles square. It is very broken by waters, and has many promontories, particularly Ross, which literally signifies in the Gaelic language promontory, or point of land, as does also the name of every place ending in inish, of which there are many.

Mull is so broken by waters, that it forms three peninsulas. The head of Loch-na-keall so nearly reaches the Sound of Mull, that the tarbart or isthmus between these two seas is scarcely four miles broad, and which serves as the boundary between the north peninsula and the middle one.

Loch Buy joins within one mile a large fresh-water lake, and the fresh-water lake meets within half a mile Loch Spelibh, running into the sea between the mainland and the western isles; these diminutive isthmuses and lakes form the boundary between the middle and the south peninsula, which is the smallest.

Each peninsula is also more or less broken by waters. To the north-west, in the parish of Killninien, there is a salt-water lake running a considerable way inland. Loch Scridain, also a fine salt-water lake abounding with herrings, runs from west to east for 12 miles. Also Loch Laich, and several lesser salt-water lakes. Besides there are a great many fresh-water lakes in the interior of the island.

Mull is very mountainous, and affords fine pasture for cattle and sheep; these and kelp, as I imagine, are the chief exports of that island. Of the particulars of its produce and population, I am an inadequate judge; besides, these topics are foreign to my plan, and beyond the scope of my talents.

The little anecdotes of manners, superstition, and opinions of the lower class of people, that I collected during my pleasant sojournment in Mull, and which I have here and there interspersed in this guide, will I hope give some idea, although an imperfect one, of the local customs of the inhabitants.

In former times a chieftain kept his family about him, and thought nothing of riches beyond his paternal inheritance. Hunting, shooting, and fishing, were the sole employments of the greater portion, and higher class of men; others cultivated land just sufficient to produce a crop of oats and barley, for the consumption of the clan of which they made a part. Every other pursuit was foreign to a Highlander's mind, as beneath the attention of a gentleman, for such they esteemed themselves, being related to, and bearing the name of their chief. They had no luxuries, consequently few wants. They had no ambition, therefore made no efforts to aggrandize their situation, or even meliorate, by industry, their hereditary possessions. But since the year 1745 a great change has taken place in the Highlands, for now every gentleman makes the most of his land by industrious cultivation, and cattle and sheep are reared for exportation, for which very considerable returns are made. He sends abroad his sons (and most of the chiefs, lairds, and taxmen, have tribes of fine children) to our fleets and armies. Many of these brave men are lost, but some return with spoils from the east and west; but alas! with them they have imported luxuries, and wants unknown to their forefathers, which have caused the downfall of some ancient clans, and many respectable families.

In other days, there was no example of Highland property being alienated, otherwise than by forfeiture or violence, because he who was born poor had no means of becoming rich, and if none were able to buy estates, he that was born to land, could not annihilate his family by selling it; but since money has been brought amongst the Highlanders, they have found, like others, the art of spending more than they received, and to pay their debts many estates which had descended lineally from generation to generation, are now yearly brought to the hammer.

I suppose the generality of the inhabitants of Mull, must be either very healthy or individually skilful in medicinal science, I say individually, because there is not a professional medical man in the island; a strong proof he cannot there gain a maintenance. It sometimes came across my mind, when scrambling in the terrible tracks of Mull, what shall I do if I fall and break a bone?

In days of yore every chieftain had his bard and sceanach-aidh, (historian.) The works of the bards have been orally preserved from one generation to another; but what became of the historical page from the pens of the sceanachaidhs, I know not.

Ossian was the Homer of the western mainland Highlands and Hebrides. He too, like the sage Greek, has had imitators. I was told by one well versed in Ossian's style, that the genuine poetry of that bard may be discovered from its imitation introduced in the west by subsequent poets, by their frequent use of magical machinery; whereas Ossian never called to his assistance any of the supernatural powers.

Many believe that such a poet as Ossian never existed. It may, or may not be so. I saw in one of the islands a gentleman of great veracity, who assured me that in his youth he had heard an old person in the island of Lismore repeat the history of the "sons of Usnoth chief of streamy Etha." It is a tale of woe sweetly sung in the poem of Dur-thula, published as Ossian's by Mr. Macpherson. My friend heard it repeated before Mr. Macpherson's publication of Ossian's poems saw light. I myself met with many old people in the isles, who, I was told, could neither write, read, nor had ever heard of Mr. Macpherson, yet could repeat and sing fragments of the identical poems published as Ossian's by the English translator, who certainly deserves credit for his production; but from all I could learn from Gaelic scholars in the Hebrides, it falls very short of the original poetry, which must be the case with all translations from one language to another.

One day whilst at my friend Mr. Campbell's I expected to be present at a wedding; a message having been received that a couple were in their way from Kilfinechen, to be joined together in the bonds of holy matrimony at the minister's house, but they reached not thus far; having met a missionary minister at the head of Loch Scridain, they beseeched him to save them a long walk by tying them together on the spot, (the bank of the lake,) which he did, and thus arose my disappointment.

The marriage ceremony of the commonalty in the west Highlands, is very laconic, consisting of joining of hands, and a short exhortation from the minister for their future behaviour.

Their feasts at weddings in Mull, where there are means, are not dispatched so quickly, for they give breakfast, dinner, and supper. The guests invited are sometimes so numerous, that no less than six sheep are slaughtered for one entertainment. A very long table is placed in a barn, or out-house, on which is set meat at different distances; with potatoes, eggs, and oat bread in abundance; also near the seat of every third person a whole cheese, and a lump of butter. The liquor, whiskey or rum, is provided by the bridegroom. The rest of the entertainment is furnished by the parents of the bride.

The poorest people will always have a feast at Christmas, and kill a sheep. Their usual food is potatoes, fish, milk, eggs, and oat bread, and drink from the clear stream.

In times past too, in the Highlands, parade and feasting were carried to great lengths at burials; and what was still worse, the nearest a-kin were obliged, by the etiquette of the times, to preside at the ceremonial. The finer feelings of humanity on such occasions were laid aside, for even if a lady had the misfortune to lose the best and most affectionate of husbands, custom obliged her to lead down the first dance, let her sorrow be ever so acute.

Not a great number of years past, a respectable person of rank died; a numerous company of relations and friends were invited to the funeral, and as means were not wanting, they regaled themselves plentifully, even to excess. At length, the procession began, and arrived at the burying-place with tolerable order and decorum, but behold, the corpse was forgotten, and they were obliged to return for it.

This is a fact known to some now living.

Much kelp is manufactured in the islands, and on the west coast of Scotland; it is an alkaline vegetable salt, produced from calcined sea weed called ware. It is sent to Liverpool, Bristol, and Greenoch, and is an ingredient in making soap and glass; chiefly the former; the price varies, but it has been sold for ten pounds a ton. Men and women, at low water, walk into the sea, and cut this weed from the rocks. The weed when dried is burnt in stone troughts, like large coffins.

The chief exports of the Isles and the western parts of Scotland, are kelp, sheep, wool, cattle, and slate.

I have already lamented the want of inns in Mull; I will now notice the sad deficiency of religious buildings for public worship.

I saw one kirk on the banks of the Sound of Mull, in the parish of Torosay, and I believe there is one in Killninian; but not one covered appropriate place is there in the extensive parish of Ross, for the minister of Christ's gospel to preach in; even I-Ona does not afford a better shelter than a barn, for the performance of divine service. It would be an act of piety, and great humanity too, if his Grace the Duke of Argyle would set an example to proprietors throughout the western Highlands, by building kirks on his extensive property in that quarter. Barns, tents, and fields, are improper places in which to preach the Christian faith; and in winter, by this neglect, inhumanity to man is added to impiety towards the Deity.

As I have taken the liberty of giving a few hints concerning churches, and inns to the proprietors of land in the Hebrides, I cannot, and ought not, to withhold my admiration of the noble proprietor of I-Ona, Ross in Mull, &c. for his goodness to his dependant people there, and elsewhere, who look upon him as a benign father rather than master; and well may they do so, for there cannot be a better landlord in every respect. He never removes a tenant but for flagrant bad behaviour, and his farms pass from father to son without raising their rents; allowing besides many indulgencies which other proprietors, not having the disposition, or means, do not, or cannot afford to do, particularly in the article of Kelp. The Duke of Argyle, (I have been assured,) suffers his tenants to burn, if they please, all the kelp on their farms for their own emolument.

CHAPTER TWO

I waited at my friend, Mr. Campbell's, for a calm fine day, that I might see the grand rocks at Inimore; and such a day was the 12th of August. I entered a boat, with two oars, at Sherba, accompanied by Mr. Gillis, and Mr. McLeod, brother to the lady who went with us to I-Ona.

Inimore is little known, consequently has never been seen or noticed by travellers, although nearly equal in stupendous grandeur to Staffa, but in a very different style. There are columns in abundance on the face of Inimore, though I did not perceive any of them to be prismatic. We put off from Sherba with only two boatmen, who proposed taking up another rower at some little distance, that they might in turns relieve each other, We kept close to the shore in a bay, half encircled by almost perpendicular cliffs, rising to a wonderful height, having cascades, (some of them enormously high and full, although a dry day,) dashing and rattling down their lofty sides.

In storms of rain and wind, what a glorious sight must Inimore exhibit! but few see it in that state from the sea; or if they do, their own extreme danger renders that scene a matter of terror rather than admiration, because if any vessel be unfortunate enough by stress of weather to be driven to Inimore, it is a thousand to one it escapes a wreck. A shelf of rocks was pointed out to me, on which a large ship was unhappily lost in the spring previous to my passing that shore.

About half-way in the curve of cliffs, round the bay, one of our seamen exclaimed, "Here he comes:" I raised my eyes, and saw a man diminished by distance to the size of a child, stepping and slipping down the cliffs. I every instant expected he would come rolling like a bottle, and be dashed to pieces like glass, upon the huge stones on the beach. The boatmen smiled at my fears, and their comrade sure enough, slipped down the lowest crumbling hollows with perfect safety, as if he had been sitting upon a sledge, and then waded to the boat with the utmost composure.

Every length of the boat brought us something new to admire; but when I came to the point called Bein-an-Gore, (peak of Godfrey,) I was lost in admiration. The height of the peak, and the formation of the rocks, from the top to the bottom, many of them columnar, amazed and delighted me. The seamen lay on their oars while I gazed; and they were almost as much astonished at my raptures, as I was at the wonderful appearance of Bein-an-Gore. What a leap, thought I, was that of Godfrey!

In ages past, the McLeans of Loch Buy were absolute monarchs of the south side of Mull, and in those days hunting deer was their amusement and support.

Loch Buy commanded a great chase, and gave strict charge to an attendant named Gore, (Godfrey,) not to suffer a stag to escape through a certain pass, and at the same time declared, if such a thing did happen, Gore should forfeit his life.

Gore took his station, but notwithstanding all his caution, some deer forced the pass, and made their escape.

Gore did not lose his life, but he was ignominiously chastised in the presence of the chieftain, and his assembled clan, on the summit of the peak.

The proud Highland blood of Gore boiled at the indignity he had sustained in the face of his chief and clan. Death, in his opinion, would have been honourable, but the sting of disgrace was more than he could bear.

Young and old were assembled to see the chase, and poor Gore's shameful chastisement. Amongst the rest was a nurse, with the infant son of the chief in her arms. Gore watched his opportunity, snatched Loch Buy's child from the arms of his nurse, and with him in his hand leaped amongst the rocks of the peak to a shelf far below the astonished spectators. Gore came safely upon his feet, with the babe in his hand, and there held his victim in triumph. Rewards and honours were offered; tears and entreaties were poured forth by the distracted parents to Gore, to save and restore their only son. At length he seemed to relent, and declared if Loch Buy was brought within his sight, and chastised in the same ignominious manner he had been, he should be satisfied.

The parent, for the sake of his child, readily submitted to be treated precisely as Gore had been, and then required the restoration of his son; Gore, with a smile of triumphant contempt, raised the child in his hand at arms length in the air, and with a shout threw himself over the peak. Both Gore and the child were dashed in pieces long before they reached the sea.

Such deeds wear the resemblance of fable; but those who are well acquainted with the life and manners of remote High-landers before the year 1745, will not think them wholly incredible.

Somewhat to the east of Bein-an-Gore we came to irregular huge rocks, with cliffs rising to the clouds, at about twenty or thirty feet behind them; the intermediate space is strewed with huge stones, amongst which stand stupendous and beautiful arches, and through them from the boat, the cliffs behind form a most picturesque appearance. These arches seem as though formed by the nicest chisel and in perfect symmetry, but far too sublime for human art to reach.

Off the shore, at a small distance from these arches, a huge rock lifts its head above the sea, by which it is surrounded. One end of it faces the south-west, and is open like Fingal's cave in Staffa, and Port-a-churaich in I-Ona, to receive the full force of the American blasts. This rock has been probably perforated by waves strongly beating against it, by which means two arches are formed, one at the south-west and the other at north-east. The sea flows in at the south-west arch, and passes out through the north-east one; and vice versa at ebb tide. The facades of these arches are amazingly beautiful, grand, and curiously (as it were) chiselled. The sea rolls with considerable noise through this rock, even in calm weather. Near this sublime, grand, terrific scenery, (for such it must be in a storm, though beautiful in a calm,) is situated a shepherd's hut, the only human habitation on the shore, between Sherba and Carsaig Bay. Indeed I believe it is the only spot on which a hut can be placed. It looks like a brown dot in the midst of scattered huge stones, fallen from the stupendous cliffs behind it, having a rough rocky shore to the sea, at about twelve yards before it. A family however lives in this secluded tremendous place, all the year, and it is amazing how such a situation can be borne by human beings, for so rugged is the shore of Inimore for several miles, that one would think not even sheep could find food, or safe ground whereon to place their feet.

At a mile or two after we quitted the wonderful arches, and the shepherd's hut, we came to the nun's cave, now a fine shelter for cattle from heat and snow. When I entered it, it contained, as I guessed, (for I did not count them,) near a hundred head of cattle, there screening themselves from the scorching rays of the sun. The filth they made in the cave deterred me from going to the end of it, where I was told I might see carving on the rocks, executed by the persecuted nuns, who, it is said, took shelter in this cave, when they were driven from I-Ona at the reformation.

This cave is neither pleasant nor terrific, nor is it a place of great concealment. As nearly as my eye could judge, the width of the mouth of it must be about forty feet. The arch of it is higher at the entrance than in the interior parts of it, which renders it light to the end. I had a terrible scramble over slippery rocks to land, in order to enter it, and after all I was much disgusted with it.

I suppose the fame of this cave arises from its size. I was told, (although I do not credit it,) that three hundred armed men at a time had been known to conceal themselves there. In rude times, perhaps, this cave might have been a den for pirates and purloiners of cattle. It is now used much more innocently as a shelter for them.

The next place we came to, worth notice, was the bay and vale of Carsaig. The bay is a safe anchorage for vessels. The glen is productive and beautifully pastoral, and there is a track through it to Penny Cross, not above six miles from it.

When I came within sight of the southern point, at the mouth of Loch Buy, the rocks appeared to me similar to those of Inimore, but I was not near them, keeping as close to the north shore as possible, until we entered Loch Buy, the mouth of which is of considerable breadth.

I had not been informed a tittle of what I should meet with at Moy, the residence of Mr. McLean, chief of the Loch Buy family; judge then of my surprise and pleasure when my eyes first caught the lovely scene at, and at the head of Loch Buy. It is a vista of grand mountains on each side the lake leading to the head of it, where stands on the margin of the sea, the ancient and picturesque castle of Moy, near which is an excellent modern house surrounded by trees, and backed by the stupendous mountains of Ben Buy, and others rising around the head of the lake, some with craggy, towering tops, others with verdure and heath, claiming an equal height with Ben Buy.

I also had good reason to be pleased and thankful too, for the hospitality shewn me (although a perfect stranger with an introductory letter) by Mr. and Mrs. McLean Loch Buy, and their numerous family of amiable children.

Mrs. McLean told me that to her knowledge the scenery at the head of Loch Buy, had never been delineated by any one, but a carpenter, while the new house was building. She shewed me the carpenter's sketch, and it is such an one as might be expected from the pencil of an ingenious workman.

The idea that the beauties of Moy had never been delineated, but by a carpenter, sharpened my pencil's pretty talent. I also thought it a pity that such scenery should exist, and remain unnoticed and unknown; I therefore on the spot took up my pencil, as I now do my pen, to bring those beauties to light, that is as far as my feeble efforts extend; but alas! they are inadequate to the subject.

I drew five different views of the head of Loch Buy, and in all of them I have inserted the old castle; for in every direction it forms a picturesque object.

One day when I returned from a station where I had been sketching for an hour or two, I asked one of my young friends, if there were many serpants at Moy. "Aye," (she archly replied,) "the rock on which you have been sitting is a nest for them."

Fortunately these venemous adders, (for such I believe is the reptile the people in Mull call serpants,) did not creep out of their nest to molest me. I cannot say I was without fear of them when I placed myself for drawing; but I took the precaution of beating the heath with my stick, all around the piece of rock on which I perched myself.

The castle of Moy, in days of yore, was the habitation of the chieftain of Loch Buy, but now it is the storehouse of the family, and a very nice one it makes. It is a high square tower, and only one door to it. The windows are very small, and most of them like slits in the wall at irregular heights and distances. There are short round towers on the angles of the castle at the uppermost floor of it, and battlements at the top of the square fabric, having small high chimneys and ridges of roofs within the square, rising somewhat above the battlements.

When the door of the castle was opened, I entered a small vestibule surrounded by exceedingly thick walls, in one of which is a space which formerly contained the bed of the porter, his bedstead a huge stone. I then entered by a strong portal a room nearly the size of the whole building, in one corner of which Loch Buy led me to the hole over the dungeon. It made my blood run cold to look at it. The depth of it I did not attend to, but probably it is to the level of the sea, which washes the base of the castle on the side where the dungeon lies. No steps ever led to the bottom of it. Culprits were let down by ropes, and over the aperture a huge flat stone was laid, which no single human strength could move. I went to the upper rooms by close, dark, and narrow stone stairs. I found the kitchen, which was also the common eating room, very spacious, but the bed rooms in the stories above it so small, that I cannot conceive how even one person could sleep in the beds the rooms could contain.

Not far from Moy, on the west side, lies a beautiful small glen, having the most sequestered pastoral appearance imaginable, particularly when viewed from the track, as it winds over the hill, at the head of the glen, from Penny Cross to Moy. To travellers in that road, the glen and its inhabitants far beneath them, appear like a lovely soft landscape, painted finely in miniature; so much does the great distance down the precipice lessen the size of the glen and every object in it.

On the summit of the hills hanging over the eastern side of this glen, when travellers come within sight of Moy, they will gain one of the finest bird's eye views that the imagination or reality can furnish. I will endeavour to describe it, but the landscape is so fine and so extensive, I can give but a very faint idea of it. It includes Mr. McLean's house, plantations, and castle, at the head of Loch Buy, with stupendous mountains of every shape and description encircling them and the lake, except at its mouth, which is open to the ocean on the south. To the east, immediately behind the buildings, the eye perceives, over a comparative low range of hills, a spacious hollow surrounded by mountains, some craggy, others smooth, to a vast height, equally having wood at their bases, and growing up their sides to the summits. In this space is a large fresh-water lake, and its banks beautifully broken on each side by numerous promontories, and windings. Here gentle slopes rise up the sides of the mountains covered with wood; there bold perpendicular cliffs with jagged tops, seem to touch the clouds, with trees and shrubs growing out of every chink from the summits down to the edge of the lake; beyond which, at the distance of three quarters of a mile, is an arm of the sea, bounded by mountains, till the view is closed by the peaks of Cruchan, on the main land of Lorn, just discernible in the clouds of the distant horizon.

The day I proposed to leave Moy, proved a very rainy one, which obliged me to defer my ride to Ach-na-craig till the next morning. This was much against the inclination of my man Dugall, who wished to be at home, thinking Ach-na-craig a scene of gaiety, in comparison with the secluded, out of the world regions of Ross and Moy. He expostulated with Loch Buy, when he told him the day was too bad for me to travel. "In troth, sir, it can't hurt her, for the rain will only drive on her back." My idea of the rain on my back, did not coincide with Dugall's, so I remained comfortably at Moy for another night. The day following proved as fine as I could wish it to be, and I had a most delightful ride to Ach-na-craig, by the above described fresh-water lake, and the two heads of Loch Spelibh, riding almost all the way through groves of birch, young oak, alder, mountain ash trees, and a great variety of brushwood.

I arrived at Ach-na-craig to dinner, and my kind friends there treated me with a brace of the finest moor fowl, or grouse, I ever tasted.

After dinner I walked to the bay, south of Ach-na-craig, where the cattle bred in Mull are embarked for sale in the south. I returned by the base of the cliffs hanging over the sea, which are very fine; but I have reason to remember my visit to them, with regret, as amongst them I dropped out of my portfolio, a cargo of dried wild flowers, and leaves, collected in Mull, I-Ona, and Staffa.

CHAPTER THREE

The following morning I took leave of my good friends at Ach-na-craig, and went down to the bay of embarkation, a walk of more than half a mile, where I entered the ferry boat, which contained only two seamen who spoke very little English. As soon as we got out of the shelter of the bay, the sea was rough, and the wind rather high and unfavourable, which put the two seamen in a bustle with the sails. At that time I was not so conversant with nautical business as I have since been; so that the seamen's bustle with the ropes and sails threw me also into a fuss, and I questioned my companions first one, and then the other, with earnestness, if we were in danger of going to the bottom; "Oh! yes", was the answer repeatedly given by both the men; but as I perceived their countenances did not accord with the signification of their words, I was not much frightened, and concluded they did not understand what I asked them; I therefore by signs and a change of words, made them comprehend my meaning, and they both smiling exclaimed, "Oh! oh! no fear, no fear."

As soon as the sails were hoisted and in order, and the boat set in her proper trim, the boatmen took their stations one on each side of me, and began to examine the parcels I seemed to take the most care of. A bag containing stones lay at my feet, which, without ceremony, one of the sailors placed upon his knee, untied it, and took out of it a stone, which he looked at, and laughed. I told him it came from Staffa. His laughter increased; and he made me understand I had been at very useless trouble in conveying stones from such a distance, when I might have gotten plenty of the like in his island of Mull. My left hand companion perceiving my little mahogany box, and perhaps never having before seen so neat a piece of workmanship, took a fancy to take it in his hand, and viewed it with admiration. Besides its usual contents, it included some precious nephritic stones, which added to its common weight, and gave rise to an idea in the sailor's mind that nothing but gold could make it so heavy. After balancing my box for some seconds in his hand, he said, "is monies?" I laughed in my turn, and took out of my pocket the key of the box, and presented each of them with a small tumbler of wine out of it. Their surprise was extreme; the construction of the box, the bottles, the knife and fork, spoons, and other nick-knacks it contained, seemed matters of as much curiosity and astonishment to them, as Staffa and its prisms had been to me.

Some of my English friends have commended my presence of mind, (as they call it,) on this occasion; for, say they, had you not opened your box, and shewn its contents, the sailors might have given you a watery grave, in order to secure to themselves the imaginary treasures in it.

By the Lowlanders of Scotland the Highlanders are accused of a strong inclination to take what they have no right to; but such opinions are very erroneous and unjust. Previous to the Union and the year 1745, they might perhaps have sometimes deviated from the rule of right with respect to cattle; but in these days, they may be trusted as far as fallible beings ought to be. No greater proof of their fidelity, and my confidence in it, can I adduce, than that on all occasions I have entrusted myself to their sole care without having had the least cause of fear for my own safety, or a doubt arising of their integrity, even amongst the lowest class of Highlanders. I considered myself in the hands of men whose fathers had honour and honest sufficient to guard them against perfidy, when the temptation of thirty-thousand pounds for the head of an unfortunate wanderer was in vain held out as a reward for his discovery.

The time requisite for me to write from Oban to Perth, and for the chaise from thence to come for me, was ten days; which time I employed in going south of Oban.

The 23rd of August, 1800, I hired a small cart to carry me to Esdale, having a scheme in my mind few would venture to execute, namely, the going into the Gulf of Coire Vreaikain. This Coire is a whirlpool somewhat similar, I am told, to Maelstrom, off the coast of Norway.

The driver and owner of the cart was an honest Chelsea out pensioner, commonly called Gibraltar, owing to his having been wounded and mangled at the siege of that place in 1779 by the Spanish floating batteries. He highly entertained me by a very particular account of that notable day, and related very pathetically many instances of the extreme humanity, generosity, and daring perseverance of the Britons, from the highest to the lowest rank, in risking their own lives to save those of their enemies, who were in danger from both the elements of fire and water.

Mr. Campbell, of Esdale, had the goodness to entertain me at his romantically situated house, under the shelter of the high towering crags at the south side of the island of Seil, and he also hired a boat with four oars, for my voyage to Coire Vreaikain. His own business on the mainland the day I set off prevented his going with me, he therefore engaged Mr. — to accompany me, that I might not be left at the mercy of the four sailors and the rapacious Coire.

Mr. — attended me in the quality of a friend; therefore I could not object to his appearance, which denoted rather a weakly frame, although his face was ruby colour.

Very fortunately for me Mr. Campbell had the goodness to endeavour to secure me also the company of Mr. McDugall of Loing, an island not far from Esdale; he therefore wrote a letter to that gentleman, requesting him if he possibly could, to go with me himself, into the gulf.

The 25th of August being a very fine morning, and promising a continuance of fair weather, I and Mr. — entered the boat, having previously insisted on the sail being left on shore, being sensible if it remained in the boat it would be hoisted whether I chose it or no, or it should suit the sailors to do so, when we were at sea. The tide and wind were for us, and we went rapidly on through the Sound between Scarba and Loing, not however without a continued lamentation for the want of the sail, which, said the men, as the wind was brisk in our favour, would carry us along like lightning. I silently listened to their jargon, and inwardly rejoiced at my precaution in having had the sail left on shore.

When we came to the landing place in Loing, near Mr.

McDugall's house, I went on shore, and presented Mr. Campbell's letter to that gentleman, whom I found in a field in the midst of his hay-makers.

At the hay harvest, in the uncertain climate of the west of Scotland, time is of great importance; so is the close attention of superiors to the keeping their people hard at work, whilst they are making their hay; notwithstanding Mr. McDugall most friendlily said he would with pleasure attend me; and I have the greater satisfaction in having it in my power to acknowledge my gratitude to him, for his goodness and service to me on that occasion; as, had he not done so, I verily believe I should have found a grave in Vreaikain's Coire. Coire in the Gaelic language signifies a hollow, and Vreaikain a person's name; but I could not learn who Vreaikain might have been, nor why the Coire in the Gulf between Scarba and Jura is called by his name.

Mrs. McDugall had the goodness to order a basket of provision for our dinner, and I re-entered the boat, adding to our party Mr. McDugall, and a young gentleman who was on a visit at Loing.

No boat or vessel of any size whatever, can with entire safety enter the gulf of Coire Vreaikain, either from the east or west (the gulf runs nearly in that direction,) at flood tide. At ebb tide all boats and vessels may row or sail through it, and there find the sea as smooth as elsewhere.

The cause of this whirlpool is unknown; some suppose it is occasioned by a vast hollow at the bottom of the sea with its concave side to the east, and therefore at flood tide, the water being retarded or interupted by the concavity, the swells commence at some distance from the hollow, and gradually rise in billows, which successively break over the highest part of the cavity. It is imagined also, that on the west side the hollow is convex, and therefore at ebb tide it passes over the obstruction in the same manner as it does over other rocks without agitation, except in a very high east wind.

This gulf lies between the south-west side of the island of Scarba and the island of Jura. The coast of Scarba from the south-east point to the north-east point of it, is a continued range of the roughest perpendicular, jagged, bare cliffs I ever saw, rendering it impossible for many miles, in that quarter, to gain land from the sea, or the summit of the island.

The mountains of Jura, on the opposite side of the gulf of Scarba, rise very high and abruptly from the sea, and are of course verdure, such as afford, amongst innumerable springs, heath, and fern, very fine pasture for cattle and sheep. The five huge conical hills, called the Paps of Jura, lie so much to the west side of the island that they are not seen from any part of the gulf of Coire Vreaikain.

As soon as we were all seated, the boat put off from Loing, and we crossed the Sound to gain the shelter of the Scarba shore, and doubled the south-east point of that island. We there entered the gulf, and proceeded as close as possible to the rocks on Scarba, keeping out of the current of the tide, which was still ebbing. We proposed rowing to some very high pointed rocks, but rising less abruptly than the rest of the range, or rather broken in ridges one above another, nearly opposite to the Coire. When we had reached about half way to this station we had a chase of a brace of otters, whose skin, the sailors said, would sell from twenty to twenty-five shillings each. The gun was fired, but nothing was done, except frightening one of the otters from his half made meal, on a very large lobster, the mangled remains of which he dropt on a rock as he fled from his enemies. When the chase was given over as fruitless, we landed on rocks at some distance from those we meant to occupy, opposite the Coire; the boat was ordered to carry the provisions to the base of those rocks, and we began our laborious rough march, and arrived safe at the destined station. My guardian, Mr. — , instead of assisting me, had the utmost difficulty to poise himself on the edges and points of rocks, over which we were scrambling. All difficulties were at length removed, and high above the sea we perched ourselves.

The sailors brought up our provision basket, &c. and as we were determined to gain as complete a view of the frolics of the Coire, as the tide and wind would give us, we decided to remain on the rocks till after the mid flood tide. The wind blew from the northward; it should have been west, and strong, to afford us a complete specimen of the whirlpool's fury, but we could not command the wind.

As we were preparing to regale ourselves with what our basket contained, the boatmen observed a large vessel entering the gulf at the west end of it. Like goats the sailors bounded from rock to rock until they reached the boat, and then rowed under the shelter of the shore as hard as they were able, until they came alongside the vessel. They hailed her, but her crew were sullen, and no answer did they obtain to their friendly advice and caution, except, "We well know where we are, and what we are about."

It was plain to our boatmen that the vessel was from Dantzic, and heavily laden. On she sailed in spite of the then commenced flood tide, and beginning of agitation at the Coire. The wind fortunately remained favourable till she was fairly out of the gulf; my heart beat violently from the time I perceived her enter the gulf, till I saw her struggle out of it, for I every instant expected to see her drawn within the suction and sunk in the vortex of the Coire. Had the wind slackened I should have been an eye witness of such a shocking catastrophe.

A gentleman, I was told, having a wish to see in what manner a boat would be destroyed by Vreaikain's Coire, purchased a condemned vessel, and towed her to the mouth of the gulf at flood tide, and then set her adrift. He and his party were on Scarba, and saw the vessel carried by the current with encreasing velocity till it came within the suction of the Coire, and then it was whirled like a totum in the vortex and sunk; not a trace of its wreck was ever found.

The gulf is not broad, and the tide rushes in with great force, so that it is with infinite difficulty any kind of vessel can stem it, even with the wind in their favour. We to our cost found it, in our small boat, a tremendous struggle to master the tide sufficiently to escape the suction of the whirlpool's whisking, for a considerable distance around the Coire.

When the boatmen quitted the Dantzic vessel, they anchored our boat in the creek where they set us on shore, and joined us to share our dinner.

The object for which I was likely to forfeit my life is grand, and, perhaps, unique; and what is not ungrateful to a feminine mind; I do not think one woman, except myself, has ever seen the Coire of Vreaikain raging; many have heard its roaring at Craignish castle, at the distance of twenty miles, but I was at the scene of action.

I can but ill describe its appearance; its effect is beyond description. When the tide had been flowing about two hours, small billows rose and burst over the Coire; but at mid tide I saw, particularly if any wind met the tide, the sea begin to rise a great way below the Coire, and then gradually swell to vast billows rolling on, some white and foaming, others glassy and smooth, still getting higher and higher, till they came to the grand whirlpool, where they burst with an amazing noise, forming hundreds of small whirls in the surf around, and for a quarter of a mile in a direct line, in the current of the tide. Thus I beheld, for an hour, a succession of rising and breaking of billows, some low, others, if a gust of wind met the coming wave, to a vast height; and the noise in breaking was proportionably tremendous and loud.

The best station to witness and view the rage of Cloire Vreaikain, is on the summit of Scarba, immediately above the cliffs, on the lower points of which we perched ourselves; but to gain that eminence is impracticable for any but shepherds and young Highlanders, who are able to encounter a walk of perhaps more than twenty miles there and back again, amongst rocks, over hills, and through extensive bogs, and heath, up to their chins; for such I was told is the ground on Scarba, from the house on the east side of the island, quite across it to the point above Coire Vreaikain. What adds to the difficulty of a journey through Scarba is the labour of carrying a day's provision; a necessary not to be without. It is a pity they cannot tame goats sufficiently to carry small panniers on their backs for such scrambling expeditions, where a man has enough to do to surmount the impediments in his laborious fatiguing walk, without the incumbrance of a satchel.

After we had sat between three and four hours admiring the grand scene beneath us, we retraced our steps from one ledge of rock to another, till we gained the creek in which our boat was moored. Our wisdom failed us, when our impatience led us to quit our solid firm seat before the tide slackened; had we waited on the rocks for that event, we should have got out of the gulf with ease and smooth water; whereas the contrary happened, for in a very short time the seamen had no use of their oars, and we began to go backwards instead of forwards. It was absolutely necessary, in order to keep out of the strong current, that we should row as close to the cliffs as possible; the men strained every nerve to get the boat round the projecting points of rocks, till they were nearly exhausted. The confusion was not little, and all tongues, but mine, were clattering pellmell in the Gaelic language, with which I was unacquainted, consequently it was to me like the confusion at the Tower of Babel

When nothing could be done with the oars, the sailors fastened one rope to the head, and another to the stern of the boat, and leaping on the jagged rocks, began to tow it. Sometimes they were able to be alongside of us for a few moments, then forced (by pointed or perpendicular rocks,) to lengthen the rope, and skip over chasms, and from point to point of rocks, to get to eminences at a great height above us. Then smack went the head of the boat (driven by the sea), against the rocks, which obliged the seamen to leap to the rope at the stern to pull her off; and then scramble back again to their towering stations. Thus we slowly advanced, alternately dashing against rocks, and being pulled from them, till we doubled five or six points, and got out of the influence of the tide.

Nothing could equal the dexterity, the perseverance, and activity of the four seamen; the danger, sometimes, was very great, both to themselves, and to those in the boat, because had they slipped, or made a false step, when leaping the chasms, and from one point of rock to another, they must have been drowned, or have broken their bones. Their assistance to us would thereby have been lost, and the boat carried by the tide to the vortex of the Coire; the like catastrophe must have happened had the rope by which the boat was towed, either given way or broke.

I know not why, but I certainly was not frightened; no dount I did not see the extent of our danger. I knew Mr. McDugall had been to the East or West Indies, and I therefore concluded he was somewhat versed in nautical business. I observed he gave orders, though I did not understand them, with composure; and his countenance, I thought, indicated no signs of danger, so I sat quietly watching the issue of the struggle, not without now and then looking back to admire the grand breakers at the still raging Coire.

One person in the boat shewed far greater signs of fear than I did; for poor Mr. — , wrapped in his tartan cloke, as soon as the confusion began, slipped off his seat to the bottom of the boat, and silently watched for the moment that (as he probably imagined,) was to whirl him to a better world; and so great was his internal agitation, that his face was the colour of crimson, with drops of perspiration as big as peas, running down it.

My protector, and now my friend, Mr. McDugall, would not suffer me to return immediately to Esdale, but insisted on my passing a night under his hospitable roof; luckily for me I did so, for the boat could not reach Esdale till two o'clock the following morning. I desired the boatmen at their return to get a bottle of whisky to drink, and be thankful for my escape. My heart first glowed with gratitude to the source of my preservation, and then descended to the second causes of my safety, the exertions of the seamen to whom I was so much obliged.

After the fatigues of the day, I was solaced by the kind and most friendly attentions of Mr. and Mrs. McDugall, and we greatly amused that lady with our adventures, not forgetting Mr. — , and his terrors.

The next day Mr. McDugall asked me if I would return to Esdale by land or sea: I had recently gotten such a surfeit of salt water, that I immediately embraced the offer of his cart, in preference to his boat. One of Mr. McDugall's daughters asked permission to accompany me to the narrow ferry between Loing and Seil. On taking leave of my little companion, who could not be more than nine or ten years old, she very civilly addressed me, "Madam, I am very sorry I cannot cross the ferry, and see you safe to the minister's, but my father and mother desired me not to detain the car." As a proof of her useful knowledge, she surprised me during the course of our drive through the island, by her clear and pertinent account, considering her age, of the produce and profit of the land belonging to her father.

Very near the ferry from Loing, on the Seil side, is the minister's house, to whom Mr. McDugall had given me a letter, which requested him to forward me in his cart to Mr. Campbell's of Esdale, which request he kindly and cheerfully complied with, although it must have been inconvenient to him, he being also in the midst of his hay harvest.

When I was thus consigned from one gentleman to another, I sometimes amused myself with comparisons, and the different situations in which I so frequently found myself. Sometimes in palaces, surrounded with delicacies, luxuries, and refinements; then in humbler walks, with somewhat humbler fare, I enjoyed equally good society, gained useful information, and had the fascinating charm of simplicity in manners, and plain rational conversation, which led my mind to investigate happiness beyond the passing hour. Then again in a hut, or mounted in a cart, which last situation brought to my recollection, that I then

173

somewhat resembled paupers in England, passed from one parish to another till arrived at their own, but experiencing a difference in treatment; for I, although franked from one place to another in a cart, or other convenience, never failed to meet at every stage with friendship and hospitality. Whilst the distressed paupers at their different stages are frequently ill accommodated, and treated with cold neglect.

The Perth chaise came for me to Esdale, and conveyed me to Oban but before I take leave of that town, I must carry you to Dunolly castle, a very pleasant walk of about a mile, and describe some other places. The first time I had the pleasure of taking that walk, I was accompanied by one of the Mr. Stevensons, who, in order to surprise me, did not mention what sort of scenery I should find at Dunolly. We walked through a beautiful field, bounded on one hand by a craggy hill covered with wood, on the other by the sea and a rocky beach. As I advanced and turned round a projecting rock, I was suddenly and highly gratified by a view of the picturesque ruin of the old castle on a high crag hanging over the sea, whose rough sides were covered with wood, and its base washed by white waves.

Dunolly house was hid from my view by fine trees, others, also partially concealed, not only the rocks on which the ruins stand, but also covered the rough sides of a craggy mountain rising high on the east side of the little hollow in which the present habitation is built. The sun shone finely, not only on the near scene, but also illuminated the distant tops of the Morven mountains, and the numerous little islands lying between them and Dunolly.

In the foreground of this enchanting landscape, a single rock, rising high above its neighbours, of an uncommon shape, makes it appearance, covered with brush wood and fern. It had a fine tree upon its summit; but unfortunately a lady of other days, of the house of McDugall, dreamed that on the summit of this rock, and under the fine tree growing there, a treasure was concealed. Men with mattocks and spades were set to work to discover the gold, but alas! they destroyed the tree, and found no treasure.

I was told that the laird of McDugal has in his possession at Dunolly the mantle and broach of king Robert Bruce, taken from his person when he fled from the field of battle in Strath Fillan near to Tyndrum, but I could not procure a sight of those relics.

Amongst the lower class of people there still exists many superstitious ceremonies, particularly in child birth, two of which I recollect. When a woman is near her time, in order to procure a safe and easy delivery, she causes to be laid under her bedstead a large knife and a spade, and under his pillow the bible. Salt is strewed about the windows and doors to prevent evil disposed fairies from entering where the new-born babe is.

Every old castle has its household brunies, and green maids.

Brunies are invisible spirits, guarding and protecting the families, dependants, and possessions of the lairds. These brunies are said to be every where, but never seen.

The green maids are kind fairies, who during the night enter the castles, and clean and set every thing to rights whilst the families sleep. These are most convenient little beings. I wish they would extend their good offices to England.

CHAPTER FOUR

Since the publication of my Tour taken in 1796, I have in four subsequent journies added to my stock of information, concerning Scotland, and I shall here give a short account of my visit in 1802 to the islands of Coll, Tirii, Eigg, Rum, and Skye, together with a description of St. Kilda, before rejoining my road to Inveraray.

To take a slight view of the island of Coll you would imagine it a bed of low rocks, for the length of twenty miles, with now and then a small patch of verdure between them, without cultivation; but notwithstanding appearances, at first sight, it is tolerably productive. I saw in the island of Coll the Egyptian desert in miniature, when I past over a small plain of fine white sand. It was in its gayest dress, being in July, thickly covered with a wild geranium of the finest purple colour I ever saw. Around this enamelled plain a great number of sand hills were scattered, which change their situation at the pleasure of the wind. This plain and these hills are very near the west shore, where the south-east wind has vast power. The foundation of the sandy plain is tolerably firm, but the tracks between the sand hills are very soft, so that in passing them man and beast sink to a great depth, which makes it very fatiguing to walk or ride through them. If there be the least wind blowing, the sand is very troublesome, and the sun shining on it, is extremely hurtful to the eyes; so that I can now very satisfactorily to my own mind, account for the loss of sight to many individuals of our brave army in Egypt.

Tirii belongs to the Duke of Argyle, and is about 16 English miles long, and in some places about eight miles broad; in one part perhaps, not more than half a mile broad. It contains about 3000 inhabitants. Its soil, like that of I-Ona, is a light sand, and the crops are seldom longer on the ground than six weeks. The seed time is June.

Potatoes too in Tirii vegetate quickly, and are very fine.

Tirii affords a scanty portion of fuel for the number of its inhabitants, which sometimes puts them to very great inconvenience. Their peat mosses are nearly, if not quite exhausted, which has obliged them to go to Mull for peat, where they cut and dry it, and then with great risk and loss of time convey it to

Tirii, a voyage of 11 or 12 leagues. The formation of their houses may preclude them from burning coals; for without chimnies to carry off the sulphureous smoke of coal fires, I should suppose it would be dangerous to their lives and health.

The walls of the huts in Tirii are double, and the space between them is (like the great Chinese wall,) filled with earth and sand to make them the stronger, to bear the western blast, which sometimes makes dreadful havoc. Most commonly every hut has two doors, that when the wind blows hard, the one to windward may be shut, and that to leeward opened. It is not always these poor folk have wooden doors, they then stop the gaps in their huts with thick bundles of heath or straw, tightly tied together.

There is on Tirii a beautiful plain of twelve hundred Scotch acres of grazing land; it is, I was informed, a perfect level, without a rising spot or a shrub upon it; and at one season of the year, when the white clover and daisies on it are in bloom, it looks like an enormous bleaching field covered with linen. I should prefer it when it is decked with green. This plain is a common, for the benefit of the inhabitants, whereon to feed their cattle.

The manners of the people of Tirii, I have been told, are less degenerated from the manners of the aborigines of the Highlands, than any of those of the other islands. They are great composers of songs, both of tunes and words, and are noted for gaiety, and an excessive fondness for singing and dancing. They work hard (being very industrious) all day, and dance the chief part of the night, as the best receipt for taking off fatigue. If hearsay may be credited, they verify the golden age, and must be the happiest people existing. They have dancing assemblies once a week, which are held in a barn. There is one of these assembly rooms at each end of the island, where the young and the gay part of the inhabitants meet alternately.

They have numerous fiddlers and pipers on the island, so that they are never at a loss for music. They have much health and little money amongst them, consequently ever gay and lively; for as Patie says in the Gentle Shepherd,

"He that has just enough can soundly sleep;
The o'ercome only fashes fowk to keep."

The scarcity of money however, carries the lassies over sea to the low country to the harvest, not for the pleasure of being richer than their neighbours, for they never import silver or gold, but dispose of their cash, arising from their labour, at Glasgow or any other great town, in personal habiliments; and she who can purchase a white muslin gown and petticoat, is the happiest of beings.

I was also informed, that as soon as a stranger was announced to be arrived on a visit to any family living on the island of Tirii, the joyous news quickly reached all quarters, and every one was in haste to join and welcome the newly arrived guest. The fiddles and pipes were put in tune, ponies were collected, the turf cutters were taken in hand, and off went the green sod to serve for saddles, which were placed upon the backs of the ponies, on which, men, women, and children mounted, and without either bridle or stirrup, scampered away to the scene of action. Thus the feast and dance went round from one house to another, till the stranger quitted the island.

I was assured for a fact, by several persons of veracity, that in Tirii, not more than eight or nine years since, was found buried very deep in a sand bank the skeleton of a horse, and a warrior in complete armour; both horse and man when discovered were

in a lying posture, but their skeletons were not separated from each other. The blade of the warrior's sword was somewhat rusted, but the hilt of it, which was silver, was not in the least injured; the bit of the bridle also being of the same metal, was in equal preservation, and the stirrups the same; but what was still more surprising. the skeleton of a woman was found by that of the man, and appeared as if at the time of their sinking into the sand, she had been riding behind him. The oldest person living in Tirii, has neither by writing, nor oral tradition, ever heard of the disappearance of any such warrior or lady. Query then, who could they have been? and for how many ages had their remains been concealed, and preserved in the sand? or whether the warrior was the lady's protector, or another Paris from Lochlin, (Denmark,) in the act of conveying a fair Fingalian Helen to a vessel, in order to transport her to his native land? Their flight was probably in obscurity, which prevented their seeing their danger from the sand mounds in their way, which on Tirii, like those in the deserts of Arabia and Egypt, move their stations at the pleasure of Aeolus.

Tirii produces a race of ponies which are very pretty, and although not much larger than Newfoundland dogs, are extremely strong. Several sets of them have been sent to England for light open carriages. There was one Tirii pony at Penny Cross when I was there, on which Mr. McLean's children rode, which was so docile, that it walked up and down stairs (I was told) like a domestic animal.

Eigg signifies in the Gaelic language a gap or notch. At a distance in some directions, the island of that name looks like a notch in a huge mountain, and that appearance is occasioned by the flattest land lying between the towering Scur, and the north west cliffs of the island. Eigg belongs to Clanranald, and is about 10 miles long, and from five to eight broad. It is let in small farms producing good cattle, but except the land within the crescent of columnar rocks to the west, I believe Eigg cannot boast of a very rich soil. The greatest part of the inhabitants are of the Roman Catholic religion, having a priest living amongst them. The worthy Protestant minister's flock in Eigg is but small, but his duty, upon the whole, is exceedingly hard. He is the minister of the small isles, namely Eigg, (where he resides,) Mucdh, Rum, and Canna. He attends these isles alternately, at the risk of his life almost every time he visits the two last named. Fortunately for him he is fond of the sea, and is reckoned the most skilful mariner in the Hebrides.

Almost every minister in the Highlands has a farm, besides his glebe land, otherwise he could not maintain his family, particularly in the islands, for as there are no markets, a farm is absolutely necessary to produce cattle, sheep, and grain, suffic-

The poor people are servants to the Laird.

ient for the consumption of every family.

There are three ranks of people in the islands, the lairds, taxmen or gentlemen farmers, and the very poor. There being no towns, or manufactures carried on, there are no tradesmen or artificers by profession.

The poor people living on each farm are servants to the laird, or taxman, who pays them a small portion of wages, and allows them oatmeal sufficient for the consumption of themselves and families. Around their huts they have each a patch of ground in which they carefully cultivate potatoes and cale. Household servants in the islands have but two meals a day; on the mainland they have three. An island lady married a gentleman on the mainland not a league from the isles, and she began to regulate his family as was that of her father, by introducing two meals a day; but her husband was soon obliged to request that the customs of his household might remain as she found them, or his servants would rebel and leave him.

Oat meal porridge, (a thick hasty pudding,) eaten with milk, is generally the Highland breakfast for children and the lower classes of people, but when meal runs scarce, the servants and the poor feed on herrings and potatoes, and they sometimes can afford to join their pence to buy a sheep or a lamb. The drink of the lower order of Highlanders is generally water, of which they take copiously throughout the day, and whether they are hot or cold, when travelling, their mouths are regularly applied to every stream in their way. A glass of good whisky however, is to them a superlative treat. They cultivate flax and hemp sufficient for their own use, and sometimes sell yarn to purchase luxuries, such as shoes, tea, and sugar, or wool, which they fabricate into blankets, and dye and weave for their outward garments.

Glasgow, Greenoch, and Inverness markets, supply the laird's and taxmen's families with tea, sugar, grocery, biscuits, and all wearing apparel, except what is spun or knit by their children and servants.

Every laird, and every considerable taxman, is a patriarch in his small or extensive territory; and if he be a good man and kind to his people, they look upon him as a father, master, and friend, and would go through fire and water to serve him and his relatives.

What a grievous reflection it is, that such faithful dependants, who from generation to generation have imbibed from father to son the strongest attachment to the proprietor of the land on which they were born, and probably whose name they bear, should from oppression be obliged to banish themselves and families, and also thereby deprive their king and country of their assistance when they stand most in need of brave soldiers!

It is not new roads, nor agricultural improvements, nor yet the interference of Government that will keep Highlanders from emigrating. They are idolaters of their native soil and hills, and nothing but dire necessity could force them from their country.

What is the cause of that dire necessity? The first cause is luxury; the second, oppression. The remedy, I am afraid, is scarcely now practicable; because, when proprietors of land have learned how to spend on luxury, more than their property can fairly and justly produce; and they have screwed up their poor tenants to a far higher pitch than they can possibly bear, is it likely that they will relax in their oppression, or retrench in their luxurious mode of living? The poor Highlander's alternative therefore is, either to starve in, or fly from, his native land.

When proprietors lived on their property like patriarchs of old, spending their incomes amongst their tenants, connections, and dependants, they were rich in love and money; but now, almost every laird with his family must in winter reside in London or Edinburgh, where he spends more than he can afford, and gets deeply into debt. This is the cause of the alienation of estates as well as the oppression on poor tenants, and the source of emigration.

The landlord may not at present be hurt in pecuniary matters by the great emigration from the Highlands of Scotland, but he and the country at large will ultimately feel its bad effects, unless a desert could be as profitable as an inhabited country.

If land holders in the Hebrides and on the main land near those islands, do not alter their present plan of letting their property in that part of the kingdom, in a very few years it will be deserted, and the honest and brave race of Western Highlanders be totally extinct, as well as their language. It is the practice of almost all proprietors, whenever leases expire, to let their property in very extensive sheep farms to rich Lowlanders; and in order to make room for one overgrown shepherd, with three or four herdsmen in his train, three or four hundred poor people are dislodged from farms which they had enjoyed from father to son for centuries. This is one of the millions of mischievous works performed by luxury.

Emigration from the Highlands is not the work of a day, it has been progressively coming on, and the proprietors of land have actually put into the hands of their people the means of transporting themselves to America; for the greedy desire they have had for some years past of increasing their income has induced lairds to turn most of their land into sheep farms; and rich Lowlanders having offered a hundred or two pounds a year more than the Highlanders were able to do, the Lowlanders have had the preference. The great and rich farmer can always reserve his commodity until the market comes up to his price; whereas, the little farmer is obliged to dispose of his produce in order to pay his rent, let the market be low or high. Drovers, at stated times, go to the Highlands of Scotland, purchasing cattle and sheep for the English market; and for a few years past, have been obliged to comply with whatever demands the great and rich farmers have thought proper to ask, because they could afford to keep their stock in hand if the drovers would not purchase at their price. The still remaining petty farmers have certainly shared the advantage of the high price of cattle within the last three or four years, and have been enabled, by the sale of their stocks, to raise a sum of money sufficient to pay their expences to America. Thus from the luxury and increased expenditure of the proprietors of land, may be traced not only the cause of emigration and the means of accomplishing it, but in some measure also of the present high price of butcher's meat all over the kingdom.

It has been said, Government should interfere in order to prevent the Highland emigration. In this free country can Government interfere? Can it dictate to a proprietor of land to dispose of his property in any given mode? Or can it say to a free born people, you shall not leave the Highlands?

When I was in the Hebrides in 1802, I was an eye witness of the melancholy departure of many of the Highland emigrants; and I am informed, a greater number are gone this year, 1803.

The only way to prevent emigration seems to be, to persuade proprietors of Highland lands to let their properties as formerly, upon fair and reasonable terms, in small farms, on which numbers of families may exist.

Let the dreadful consequences of non-compliance be sounded in their ears, as was the echo at Dunstaffnage Chapel in the ears of the Argyleshire farmer; and that an equally good effect may be produced on their minds as was on his, I most sincerely wish.

Our first excursion on Eigg was to the caves on the south side of the island, which are very fine, so is the whole shore, but I had no temptation to enter the bone cave, although I passed close to its mouth. It is called the bone cave, because in it there are heaps of human bones, which I had no inclination to see.

In barbarous ages past, a party of McLeods from Skye landed on Eilan-a-hasel, on which at that time some of the Eigg women were at work. The McLeods behaved very ill to these females, notice of which was soon conveyed to their male relatives in Eigg, who came instantly across the small sound, seized the offenders, chastised them, and bound them so strongly in their boat, that it was impossible for them to extricate themselves from their bands, and then set the boat adrift. The men were not all destroyed; the few that survived were driven to some shore where they were unbound, and in time returned to their own clan.

The McLeods were exasperated at the treatment of their name-sakes, whose punishment they thought had been too severe for the crime they had committed; they therefore sent a deputation to the Macdonalds of Eigg, to require they would deliver up as many of the men who had bound the McLeods, as were lost of that clan in the boat which the Macdonalds had set adrift, threatening, in case of non-compliance, that they would come in a body and destroy all the inhabitants of Eigg.

The Macdonalds refused to comply with the demands of the McLeods, and accordingly a party of them set out to execute their threats. The Macdonalds perceiving the Skye boats advancing towards their island retired, men, women, and children, to a vast cave on the south side of the island, into which they had previously conveyed provisions. The McLeods landed, but finding Eigg deserted, concluded the inhabitants, being sensible they could not cope with them, had retired to the main land belonging to Clanranald; they therefore re-imbarked and were on the point of setting sail, when they espied a man on the summit of a high cliff; they re-landed, and expeditiously climbed to the eminence whereon they had seen a Macdonald. Unfortunately some snow was lying on the ground, by which they traced the Eigg man to the cave, the mouth of which being extremely small, might be easily defended. The McLeods did not attempt to enter it, but procured heath, and other fuel with which they completely stopped up the mouth of the cave, and then set fire to it, which suffocated the poor wretches within, to the number of about three hundred.

The vast veins of pitch stone was our next scramble; the rocks down which these veins descend, are very stupendous, forming a most sublime scene all round. I visited these rocks several times during my stay in Eigg, and once after having handled the pitch stone, I perceived marks and smell of pitch on the finger of my glove.

The first clear morning after my arrival in Eigg, I mounted a pony and began my journey to the Scur, (a hill so called, composed of prismatic pillars,) accompanied by my friends on foot, one of whom was a gentleman of eighty years old. He walked early from his farm on the other side of the island to pay his compliments to me, and then set off with us to mount the summit of the Scur.

I had heard that the Scur in Eigg was superior to Staffa, I was therefore very eager to ascertain the truth of that assertion, and can with certainty bear witness it is no such thing; in beauty, no comparison can be formed of any prismatic pillars in the Hebrides with those at Staffa.

When we reached the base of the Scur at the south side of it, I quitted the horse and began to scramble amongst fragments of pillars, till I got to the pillars themselves, rising sublimely to a vast height, and running in a range from east to west. The base of the Scur is about a mile from the sea shore, having a small farm lying between it and the sea. The summit of it is oblong, of no great extent, which is not like that of Staffa, covered with pasture, with some stones. It is a bunch of prisms, not of basaltes, but a kind of porphyry. The perpendicular pillars are

higher and have fewer joints in them than those at Staffa, but they are in a more crumbling state, probably for want of the sea preservative, which Staffa has, and therefore more exposed to decomposition. It is not more than eight or ten years since the prismatic pillars of the Scur were noticed. The Rev. Donald McLean was the first person on that island who had taste sufficient to discover nature's sublime works; the Scur is therefore solely indebted to him for bringing its information to light.

After we had refreshed ourselves on the top of the Scur, we began to descend on the contrary side from that we had ascended, and after a walk of about two miles, we suddenly came upon the summit of the crescent of cliffs surrounding a fertile plain, open to the sound between Eigg and the island of Rum. In this picturesque crescent-like plain, lives on a farm called Laig, the old gentleman who had been at the trouble of walking 10 miles to accompany me to the Scur, and under his roof I had the pleasure of passing one night, and being pleasantly entertained with many anecdotes of the memorable year 1745.

Mr. McLean had the goodness to order his boat to carry me to Rum and Skye, and we set sail on one of the clearest days I ever was out in, which procured me the finest treat imaginable of mountain scenery, for nothing can surpass in picturesque form the hills of Culin, and of Strath in Skye, and those in Rum, and the Scur and cliffs in Eigg.

We arrived at the head of the harbour in Rum in the afternoon, and left it at six the next morning. That island is so excessively wild and rugged, I was unable to explore any part of it. It is at the head of this bay where Mr. McLean preaches in a barn to his Rum flock. This isle is larger than Eigg, but I imagine it is but thinly inhabited. It is let in six farms, at the rent of about £500 a year. Colonel McLean of Coll is the proprietor, who insisted that one of the farms should be stocked with sheep. The farmer with much reluctance complied with his landlord's injunction, but instead of stocking his farm fully, he only put one half of the number of sheep the farm would feed; notwithstanding, he sold the wool of the half stock of sheep the first year for £50 and the rent of the whole farm was only £60.

One of Coll's ancestors, many years since, when might instead of right prevailed, meeting Clanranald unexpectedly at sea, without ceremony took him prisoner and carried him to his castle in the island of Coll, and confined him till he gave a deed for his ransom, wherein he made over the island of Rum to Coll and his family for ever.

I was unable to reach the island of Canna; I was told, it is a very pretty island; I should have been pleased to have been an eye witness of the effect the hill in Canna has upon the compass.

Canna is a very pretty island.

I have a small piece of a trunk of a tree found a year or two since, incorporated in a solid huge pudding-stone rock in Canna; the stem when found was in diameter about nine or ten inches. The wood is not petrified, and has undergone no change, except as if it had been charred.

CHAPTER FIVE

In the Gaelic language the island of Skye is called Eilan-a-Schiathanach, (island of wings,) because being indented by extensive arms of the sea called Lochs, they form a number of promontories resembling wings. Although Skye is at least in extent 100 miles, there is not a town in the island. Formerly (I believe) there were but two proprietors of land in Skye, namely, McLeod of McLeod, and the chief of the McDonalds.

McLeod has alienated some of his property, which has introduced into Skye some new lairds, but still the possessions of his family and Lord McDonald's are very extensive, and are let in a multiplicity of farms. Every farm has a house upon it, for the taxman's family, and huts sufficient to contain the servants and dependants of the taxman, but not in number sufficient to be called a village, consequently, there are no shops in Skye, except one at Oransa; and perhaps a few useful articles may be purchased at Portree, where some new houses have lately been erected.

On a charming clear morning we left Rum for Skye, sailing in sight of the sovereign of hills called Culin, and the jagged top of Bla-Bhein, (pronounced Blaw vein,) with the rest of the Strath mountains, till we came under the gold cliffs near the mouth of Loch Einort, where Mr. McLean's maritime skill was somewhat put to the test, for we experienced several great squalls, which made me shrink from the blast from Culin's towering crags, and seat myself at the bottom of the boat to be out of the way of the gib sail. Angus Cameron exclaimed, "Oh madam, look at the great pillar!" Pillars had no share at that moment in my attention, but when the squall was past, I opened my eyes and beheld in Angus's pillar one of the most singular formed rocks I ever saw, standing singly in the sea at some distance from the shore. I had on my head at that time a very large beaver hat, such as were worn in the year 1778. I had kept it by way of curiosity, till I produced it for my seafaring campaign in 1802, to shade me from the sun beams, and keep off rain. This large hat was tied down with a ribbon on the outside, forming altogether an antique and droll appearance; and to my surprise, when I looked at the singular rock, I viewed the shape of my own head on the top of it. I had passed to the north of that rock when I first perceived it, and in that direction saw a huge mass, in form like a lady dressed in a monstrous sized hoop and petticoat, such as are worn at the court of St. James's having a very large hole quite through the middle of the hoop. I suppose it is a strayed sister of McLeods maidens (rocks standing at the mouth of Loch Bracadale). I was very sorry I did not attend to Angus's exclamation, when I might have had a nearer view of this curiously shaped rock.

We were a long time tacking and working the boat to its anchorage in Loch Einort, which is surrounded by a shoulder of Culin and other cliffs, and we found that spot as silent and forlorn as an uninhabited island. We landed, and were espied by one solitary man, who came down the mountain to ask if he could assist us. He was useful in aiding our people to carry my baggage to some huts at two miles distance. After taking a little refreshment and setting the boat in safety, we began our march, in number seven. When we got about half way we came to a river; it was too deep for me to wade, I was therefore conducted to where two rocks meet, within about two feet of each other, forming a deep chasm, through which the river was roaring with violence far below the top of the rocks. The Skye man who was our guide, told me I must give him my hand, and I skipped across the chasm, but I kept my eyes open.

As we advanced to the huts, the good folks inhabiting them came out to gaze at us, having taken us at a distance for a party of disbanded soldiers or sailors. It was a very fine day, and we found several very old men and women sitting upon stones and hillocs, near a rattling burn, with their grandchildren playing about them, and the mothers of the young ones sitting and knitting by the old ones, whom they had led out of the huts for the benefit of fresh air, watching and attending them with filial anxiety and affection. It was a pleasant sight. I entered one of the poorest of the huts, and there found a female, out of her place in society, for she was certainly born in a superior station to that in which I found her.

We were informed that from those huts it was no more than three miles to Talisker. Surely, I said, I can walk three miles. No, madam, said Mrs. McLean, (the name of the female in the hut,) you must not think of walking, our Skye miles are not like your English miles. I have two horses not far in the hill; I have sent a boy for them; one you may ride, and the other will carry your baggage.

The horses came, but as I knew my Eigg friend could not walk even three miles, I insisted upon his riding, which was soon settled, as the good woman assured us the tall horse would carry double; and for all this civility I could not prevail upon this Skye Mrs. McLean to accept of any recompence. She said she could not bear that a stranger who had honoured her country with a visit, should pay for any thing she had in her power to give. It is not often in the Hebrides that females ride double, but when they do so, it is on the bare rump of the horse; but as I was not accustomed to such a pillion, my journey from the hut near Loch Einort to Talisker, was laughable enough.

When I arrived at the house of Talisker, I fancied myself in Paradise; and when I became acquainted with those who resided in it, I was sensible they were deserving of, and fit for, such an abode.

The family of Talisker, when I visited it, consisted of — McLeod, Esq. his mother, and Mrs. McLeod, Dowager of Talisker, and a very amiable young lady, Miss McNeil. The Dowager is the relict of the colonel McLeod, who resided at Talisker when Doctor Johnson was in Skye, and of whom he speaks with great respect. Talisker is a picturesque place; it is a small plain, perfectly level, with fields of grass, grain and potatoes, and a large garden, at the east end of which is the house, surrounded and finely shaded by trees. The plain is encompassed by almost perpendicular mountains and cliffs, so that no way to get into, or out of it, is perceptible, except the opening to the west at the boisterous bay, where a charming view of south Uist is obtained at a great distance across the sea.

Down the cliffs at Talisker, in hard rains, cascades are dashing in every direction; and there I saw with delight the struggle between wind and water in the cascades tumbling down the high cliffs. It has the prettiest effect imaginable, and what no one can have a just idea of unless they have seen it. Sometimes the black rocks were foaming and white, then came a gust of wind and drove the water up again; the wind slackened, and the water again rushed down a step or two; then came a fresh blast and scattered it in smoke; in short, the wind and water are sometimes for hours thus tantalizing each other, the one struggling to fall, the other to prevent it.

The weather was very unfavourable to me throughout my journey, and particularly so the day I left Talisker. It was fair indeed when I set out, but soon came on a drizzling rain, which not only incommoded me in my ride, but destroyed my prospect of the country, which by intervals I perceived to be very sublime and beautiful; but what was more grievous, the mist totally covered the majestic tops of Culin, so that I did not see one point of it, although I rode quite across Skye, and very near its base for several miles. When I quitted the lovely plain of Talisker, I ascended the very steep path by which I had descended into it, and then rode three or four miles on the summit of a hill, where I gained a fine view of a branch of Loch Bracadale; I then descended a dreadfully steep boggy path to the level of that Loch, and crossed a river, and there joined the horse road from Sconcer to Dunvegan, which I found tolerably good to the head of Loch Sligachan, about four miles. I had some hopes of there gaining a boat, but they were all engaged in fishing, so that I was under the necessity of keeping on horseback, although it began to rain fast.

During the season for fishing herrings, it is a difficult thing to hire a boat in the Hebrides, because that fishing is of such infinite consequence to the lower class of Highlanders; herrings and potatoes, being their chief food both in winter and summer.

Talisker had the goodness to ride on with me till I could procure a boat, to carry me across to Raza. After we quitted the hut at Loch Sligachan, we rode along the shore for a mile or two, amongst huge slippery rocks, which a few hours before had been covered by the sea, and then ascended a shoulder of Glamig, in such a track, that I am astonished how the horses could scramble through it. On that eminence I obtained a view of Raza's house for the first time, and I was delighted with it. The sound between the island of Raza and Skye, is narrow, therefore Raza's house appeared from the shoulder of Glamig, at a very short distance from me. It is built on the declivity of a hill, at about a quarter of a mile from the landing place. It faces the south, and is sheltered on the north by a high hill, and a great many fine trees growing thickly around the house, forming a beautiful landscape from the point where I at first beheld it. Trees are great rarities in the islands, and except at Talisker, my eyes had been long unused to foliage; Raza's trees were therefore a charming treat to me.

At the mouth of Loch Sligachan I procured the small boat belonging to a large herring-fishing one at anchor in the Loch, and after engaging four oars, and the master of the inn at the head of Loch Sligachan to accompany me, I took leave of Talisker and launched. The wind was for us; but we had not rowed five minutes before it blew a hurricane, the rain descended in spouts, the sea was excessively rough with dreadful squalls, so that I was seriously apprehensive for our safety; the rowers were obliged to strain every nerve to stem the waves, which tossed our little bark up and down without mercy; I and Angus sat mute, revolving in our minds (at least I in mind) what effect our fate would have on our distant connections. I did not forget what a loss he would be to his wife and children, he being their sole support. We received no other harm however from our frightful voyage, but a complete wetting. Angus, when he brought my baggage into the room allotted me in Raza's house, "Oh! madam, I wish we were aince again on dry ground."

I was obliged to stay twelve days on the island of Raza, waiting for a fair day to convey me to the island of Scalpa, which made me very uneasy, as I soon discovered I was rather an unwelcome guest. At any rate, however, I am certainly obliged to Mr. McLeod for receiving me at all into his house, particularly as I could find no mode of making a return for his entertainment, which must have put him to some expence. I have to lament that the wet weather did not admit of my seeing Raza's beautiful possessions, beyond the limits of his house and garden, and I have also to lament that the urbanity and hospital-

ity of Dr. Johnson's Raza has not descended in full force to his son. His countrymen will not envy his being a solitary exception to the universal hospitality towards strangers, which prevails throughout North Britain. But before I quit this unpleasant subject, I am happy to do justice to the ladies of that family, who continued to treat me with the utmost kindness and civility, to the moment of my departure.

On the 29th of August I left the island of Raza, in a most dreadful day of rain and wind, much against my will, but necessity has no law. I was that day under the kind protection of two worthy gentlemen, — McDonald Esq. of Scalpa, and Lachlan McKinnon Esq. of Coire Chatachan, who kept up my spirits and dissipated my fears. Late in the evening we landed on Scalpa, within a hundred yards of Mr. McDonald's house, in which I was received by his amiable family with the utmost kindness, and cordiality. The island of Scalpa is not very extensive, and is rented of Lord McDonald by Mr. McDonald. The house on Scalpa, the only one I believe except huts on the island, was built by the present occupier. It is very pleasantly situated at the south end of the island. where a fine view of Bein-na-Cailich in Skye, across a very narrow sound, may be had. From the summit of Bein-na-Cailich, as well as from Glamig, at Sconcer, may be obtained extremely fine and extensive prospects.

On one of the highest points of Bein-na-Cailich is a heap of stones; it is the monument of a female Dane, who was nurse to a child of a Danish prince or general, while the Danes were in possession of that part of the Hebrides. She had followed her young charge to Skye, and there gained a promise from her lord, that if she died in a foreign land, she should be buried in such a situation as might admit of a breeze from Denmark to blow over her grave. She died; and as the summit of Bein-na-Cailich was the highest accessible point within reach, her body was carried to that eminence and there deposited, and on her grave they raised a vast cairn of stones, and called the mountain Bein-na-Cailich, the hill of the old woman.

My next voyage was from Scalpa to a new house, and a most comfortable one, built near Broadford, by Lachlan McKinnnon Esq. on Lord McDonald's property. Mr. McKinnon's father and family, when Dr Johnson was in Skye, lived at Coire Chatachan, at the base of Bein-na-Cailich. The present Coire Chatachan was born about two hours after Dr, Johnson entered his father's house; and I can bear witness the son has not degenerated from his father in the points of hospitality and attention to strangers. He is blessed with fine children, and an amiable and handsome wife.

Mr. McKinnon accommodated me with two horses to carry

The view from Bein-na-Cailich.

me and my baggage to Kylerai, at which in due time I arrived, not without having several times risked the breaking of my neck. At about three miles from Kylerai I came to a dreadful descent, down which a new road was partly made. I got off my horse and walked down the hill, but how the men got the horses over the channels, made by torrents, precipices, hollows, and rough ways, I cannot conceive. However they at last joined me on the pier, at the ferry, where were crossing a great number of sheep to the mainland.

There are two kyles, (in the Gaelic language spelt chul or ceiul, signifying narrow,) between Skye and the mainland of Scotland. The north one is the broadest, and is between a district called Loch Ailsh on the mainland, and Strath in Skye.

When I was in the neighbourhood of the kyles, I endeavoured to gain some information concerning the tides between them, but my enquiries met with little success; all I did learn was, that the sea flows through the south kyle to the north, and through the north kyle to the south, and meet in a basin between the two, where sometimes there is no visible motion of the tide; at others it flows and ebbs eight or ten times a day; in short, at and near the junction of the tides, in that quarter its course is quite irregular, and can never be depended upon.

I was cautioned not to attempt going against the tide at Kylerai, and was fortunate enough to arrive at the pier just as the tide began to flow; had I been half an hour later, I should have found the current rather too much for us to row to Eilan Riach, whither I was bound, thus terminating a most entertaining and adventurous expedition through the smaller islands of the Hebrides.

I cannot, however, conclude without relating of an incident concerning St. Kilda. It concerns the melancholy fate of the wife of an Erskine, a Lord of session, whose title was Lord Grange. It was suspected that the lady, by some means or other, had got at the knowledge of some state papers of consequence; and as poor women are set down, in the minds of all arbitrary men, to be incapable of keeping a secret, Erskine and his son were determined to secure the one contained in the papers in question, by putting it out of the lady's power to divulge any thing she knew of the matter. To accomplish their design, the husband and son privately conveyed her to the island of St. Kilda, there put her on shore, and left her to shift for herself; and sailed back again, without a living being having missed them, or suspected what they had executed; nor could the lady's place of concealment be discovered by her friends, although they made every effort in their power to find out whither she had been conveyed; consequently the unnatural husband and son could not be prosecuted for their crime. The island of St. Kilda afforded no implements for writing, and the lady's history would never have been known, had she not worked it on her muslin apron with her hair. Her family, by some means or other, after her death (which happened at St. Kilda, near thirty years after her banishment) got possession of this curious piece of work, and preserved it with great care, as a memorial to her sufferings, and of the tyranny of the times in which she lived.

The inhabitants of the island of St. Kilda, to this day, are no better than savages; they are few in number, and live upon stinking fish, and rotten eggs, laid by birds in the hollows of the rocks. They will touch neither eggs nor fish until they are in a state of putrefaction. They are little known to the rest of the world, and very seldom visited; and lucky for them that this is the case, ot the race of Kildaites would soon be extinct by frequent hemorrhages; for it is confidently affirmed that the instant a stranger touches the shore, the noses of all the natives begin to bleed throughout the island.

The isle of St. Kilda lies about fifteen miles west from the northern point of North Uist, the most westerly of the Western Islands. If St. Kilda be such at present, as it is described to be, what must it have been when poor Lady Grange was turned adrift upon it? Her husband probably carried her to the last rock that could be found to the west; and concluding that this rock was desolate, put her thereon, that she might perish for want of food.

CHAPTER SIX

I now return to my route towards Inveraray from Dalmally; and as I left the view of Loch Awe, and proceeded on my journey, I drove through a woody district; the road, from the hard rain, was continually crossed by roaring torrents, and burns swelled to rapid rivers. When I came to the bridge of Cladich, the stream there was so tremendous, that I was apprehensive it would wash away every thing before it. From that bridge the road takes a short turn towards the east, and immediately winds up, amongst mountains, to a very wild and dreary alpine country. The stream by the road side, perhaps in dry weather, is little more than a burn; but when I was near it, and in a violent rain, it was roaring through its deep channel with prodigious violence, resembling a large river; indeed the whole was a scene of wild mountains, and deep dark glens, covered with foaming torrents as far as the eye could see. At the top of the hills, between Loch Awe and Inveraray, I perceived many grand cataracts; but one above the rest, amongst the mountains, of the water I had crossed at Cladich, struck me with astonishment, though it was at least three miles from the road. I discovered it by its noise, and even from that distance it was very fine; what then must it be when near to it? I never

experienced such a day of rain; it was as though every flood-gate, both above and below, was opened to deluge the earth; and during the whole of the fifteen miles between Dalmally and Inveraray, particularly for the last ten, it was the noise of a constant rushing violent cataract. No sooner had I quitted the torrents running to Loch Awe, than numberless others appeared, gushing from every chasm, and rolling down from rock to rock to form the river Aray; so that as the chaise descended to that river under hanging precipices, the water and spray from them continually dashed against the windows of the carriage, sufficiently to alarm a timorous mind. It was however to me a grand and awful scene that penetrated my soul; and I had not a drawback from perfect admiration, except the idea of danger and labour for the men and horses. As soon as the road touches the brink of the river Aray, notwithstanding the tremendous mountains on each side of the very narrow glen, the plantations of the Duke of Argyle shade the river, and creep up every mountain to its summit; and for the three miles before the entrance to Inveraray, the wood is nearly impenetrable on each side the good road leading to that town. About two miles from the Castle I heard the sound of a tremendous cataract; I stopped the carriage and got out; there was then a very short cessation from violent rain; a trifle did not stop me; I therefore followed the noise of rushing water, and came to a wooden bridge across the Aray, resting upon a ledge of rocks, over which the river was foaming with great violence, it being a high flood. I never saw a more picturesque fall; the scenery of wood about it is enchanting; and though it be made very accessible, not the least trace of art is visible, but chaste simplicity is preserved. How it happens that the bridge, slight as it looks to be, is not carried away by the raging flood, I cannot imagine. As I stood upon it, it absolutely vibrated from the violent shocks it incessantly sustained from the dashing foaming river. When once the water has escaped this fretting passage, it winds away most beautifully, bordered by thick wood, to the Duke's pleasure ground, passes very near to the Castle, and in front of one of its sides empties itself into Loch Fine; and over it, as it joins the lake, is a beautiful stone bridge. There is also another bridge over the Aray, on the north-side of the Castle, of one arch, and a very fine bridge it is, of dark grey stone; it is called Few's bridge. About half a mile above that bridge is a mill, close on the Aray, and by it a very picturesque fall; but not any thing like so grand as the one under the wooden bridge above. The ground around this mill is part of the Duke's farm; indeed he holds almost all the land about Inveraray in his own hands, as I was told, amounting to about two thousand pounds a year.

Very little corn is cultivated in that part of the country; its

produce chiefly consists of grass and sheep pasture. The small glens are extremely productive, particularly Glen Shyra; but, alas! the climate is so wet, the abundant crops of grass cannot, out of doors, be made into hay. To obviate this inconvenience, the duke has erected, from his own plans, barns, into which the grass, as soon as it is cut, is carried and there dried. These barns are very ornamental, as well as extremely useful; for they appear like so many noble castles, resembling in colour the inhabited mansion, with Gothic exteriors. Those parts of the barns which could not be built castle-like, are painted, so as to complete the resemblance.

Inveraray, to me, is the noblest place in Scotland; but the climate is unfavourable. I asked a lady if the streets were ever perfectly dry? She answered me, very seldom; nor is there a bit of fresh meat to be got in the town during the whole winter. Salted beef, mutton, and herrings are constantly prepared for the stock of food during that season; for there is not a fresh joint of any meat to be had for love or money. The duke, of course, has every thing he wishes; for having so much ground in his hands, he can kill from his own stock. At Inveraray, the herring fishery begins about July, and lasts till November; the herrings caught there are the finest I ever before either saw or tasted, and are often so cheap, that six score fish may be bought for sixpence.

The approach from Dalmally to Inveraray, is by no means so striking as that from the south. The castle and town are situated on the banks of a broad bay, on the north-west side of Loch Fine; and coming from the head of the lake, about five miles, the road turns short round a promontory, and the eye of a stranger is on a sudden presented with one of the grandest scenes that can be imagined. To the south-west, the broad surface of the lake sweeps away as far as the eye can see, skirted by mountains of every hue and form; some craggy and bare, others verdant to the tops, with small wooded glens running between them. The range on the west shore is so entirely covered with trees, that little else of the mountains, except now and then a craggy summit, is to be seen. The eye of the traveller at this turn is directed to the north-west. The broad salt lake is the immediate front, with two fine bridges at a considerable distance; the one over the Shyra, running from the glen of that name, the other over the Aray; beyond which is seen the Castle, constructed of dark bluish-looking stone. Its form is a quadrangle, with four round towers at the corners; the four sides of the fabric nearly resemble each other, with battlements upon the whole. All the windows, both in the towers and the sides, are large, and have Gothic tops to them. The roof may be said to be flat; on the centre of which rises another quadrangle of

Herring-fisheries on Loch Fine.

less dimensions, having two rows of battlements upon the top of it, and like the lower part of the Castle, it has on every side of it large windows, with Gothic tops to them, serving for sky-lights to the hall and staircases. The Castle stands about a quarter of a mile from the lake, on an extensive lawn (rising gradually from the Aray Bridge), of great variety of ground, of the richest verdure, with very fine timber trees of different sorts scattered charmingly over it; some single, others clustered; and groups of sheep adding greatly to the beauty of the scene. Rising from the Castle (to the traveller's eye on the right), is the lofty Dunacquaich hill; thick wood creeping nearly to its summit. Its shape is very uncommon; and being planted with a great variety of trees and shrubs, the tints on its sides are very striking. Towards the top of it some crags peep between the brush wood, gorse, and broom, forming a picturesque contrast with the foliage, and the verdant grass cap, which covers the summit, on which stands a watch tower. The river Aray, with an abundance of fine trees, surround its base. Behind, and on the left of the Castle, piles of mountains of all hues, shapes, and heights, seem to form an impassable barrier, both to screen and guard it from attacks, either of the boisterous elements, or the wild encroachments of man. To the traveller, on the opposite side of the loch, the white walls of Inveraray town appear along the shore; and in the time of the herring fishery, innumerable vessels and boats crowd the bay, and many are drawn on the beach before the houses. The inn, and its large arched gateway, is conspicuous, backed by the wood and avenues of very ancient trees, and high mountains, all finely planted, forming a part of the noble chain before-mentioned, on the west of the lake.

There is a beautiful drive from Inveraray to a romantic bridge of one arch, over the river Douglas; — the mill close to it — the trees weeping, and ivy creeping about it, and the rocks around, render this spot very picturesque. There are two roads to this delightful scenery, one on each side of the Douglas river; and I know not which is the most charming.

It is said that Inveraray Castle is a heavy building; it may be so; but it corresponds so well with the scenery in which it is placed, that the sublime effect of the whole would be lessened, were the Castle any other than it is.

There is a strong character in the jagged mountain tops of this part of Argyleshire, and particularly around Inveraray and Aroquhar. It is an odd idea, but a true one, that most of the points of the high crags seem like huge giants' heads laid flat, with their faces uppermost; the points forming a forehead, nose, and chin of a huge old man

Boats crowd the bay.

199

I quitted my kind host and hostess at Inveraray with great regret, for nothing could exceed the attentions of Captain and Mrs. Graham; nor can I forget the pleasant hours made so, by the good temper and never-ceasing cheerfulness of Mrs. Haswell.

When I turned the corner that screened me from the enchanting scene of Inveraray, I really was cast down, and the rain that came on did not raise my spirits. I crossed the river Fine at the head of the lake, and soon arrived at Cairndow inn, where, according to my usual custom, I eat my dinner in the chaise; the rain pouring all the time. I was near a very pretty place called Ardkinglass, where is a new modern house just then finished, situated at the foot of Glen Kinglass, with the river of that name falling in gentle cataracts, and winding round it. The head of Loch Fine is in front of the house, with tremendous mountains all around, which, in wet weather foam with high torrents not to be numbered.

At leaving Cairndow, the road leaps up a steep hill, on the margin of the Kinglass river, and immediately enters that narrow glen. At its entrance there is some wood; but a mile beyond Ardkinglass, not a tree is to be seen. The river and the road occupy the middle of the glen, and nearly fill the space between the mountains on each side of it; and notwithstanding broken pieces of rocks are thickly scattered throughout, it is sufficiently covered with verdure to afford good sheep pasture. This glen is of some length, and the head of it runs towards the head of Loch Lomond; to which, however, from Glen Kinglass, there is only a foot way. The carriage road in Glen Kinglass runs through it for about three miles and a half, then leaves the river and the glen, and turns to the right, up one of the most formidable as well as most gloomy passes in the Highlands, amongst such black, bare, craggy, tremendous mountains, as must shake the nerves of every timorous person, particularly if it be a rainy day. And when is there a day in the year free from rain, in Glen Croe? and on the hill called "Rest-and-be-Thankful?" no day; no not one! So says the Argyleshire almanack. As soon as I crossed the river Kinglass, and quitted that glen, I got out of the chaise, for then it became somewhat fair above, and turned my steps to the steep of the mountain; a torrent rolled on my right, towering black crags were to my left, and, at a short distance, a broad roaring cataract faced me, dashing over the huge masses of rock, which every where crowded this mountain hollow. For although I had ascended a tremendous steep mountain for about three quarters of a mile, I still found myself in a hollow, with rough, black, and craggy rocks, prodigiously high above me, in every form and direction, streaming with springs, and striped with numberless white

torrents. Some of the crags on the hollow top of this mountain, hang so concave over the pass as to present a scene of awful darkness; and there is a small lake in this mountain gap, so shaded by the black crags hanging over it, that the water of it appears to be really black. Advancing through this rough and craggy pass, I came to the edge of it, looking down into Glen Croe. Whether I looked around me, or in front to the glen, all was a scene of wildness that no pen can describe. It was sufficient to strike a timid mind with horror — to fill a contemplative one with wonder and amazement, and leading its reflections up to the Omnipotent Creator. An infinity of towering, convex, concave, and pointed tops of mountains surrounded me, and rose high above me; black, rough, and dripping. I then stood on the edge of an excessively rough eminence, hanging over a zigzag road (of at least a mile) down to the glen; cataracts dashing in every direction, along and across the road, and bursting from the chasms on every side. A river runs swiftly through the middle of the glen, with the road close to it; and there are rough mountains to an awful height, on each side of it, with tremendous gaps in the rocks, and huge loose fragments scattered thickly over the glen. One or two solitary huts are seen on the margin of the water, and some patches of verdure peep through the pieces of rocks, and creep up the mountains, wherever a small portion of soil is collected, producing a very scanty pasture for the sheep, seen hanging about the crags, and diminished by distance to the size of scotch caraway comfits. This spot appears in the highest degree of desolation; the cause of which seems to have been a hard shower of black rocks, poured upon it from the surrounding masses; and although the fragments lie almost as thick as hailstones, yet not visibly have these mountains been decreased either in height or in bulk. This glen, when viewed from above, or within it, seems as if it were the ne plus ultra of all things; but wild as it is, Glen Croe, as well as Glen Coe, has charms for me, and I was sorry to lose sight of it. Had not night and rain been coming on, I should have loitered in this uncommonly wild region.

The reason why the hill above described, as well as the pass, is called "Rest-and-be-Thankful", is as follows. — In the year 1746, the 24th regiment, Lord Ancram Colonel, and Duroure Major of it, being employed in making that road to Inveraray, as I have been informed by a good friend of mine, who was then a young Lieutenant in that regiment; when they had completed the zig-zag to the top of the hill, they set up a stone like a tombstone, under a black rock, and engraved thereon the words, "Rest, and be thankful." The stone is still there, though not under a black rock; but it is raised upon a broken bank, and now contains, in addition to the old inscription of the 24th regiment, "repaired by the 23d regiment, in 1768."

The road out of Glen Croe towards Loch Long, is very narrow

and winding, amongst rough rocks, by the river's side, running from the glen to that salt water lake. As soon as the road joins Loch Long, it passes close by it on the north-west bank, under vast mountains towards its head, for near two miles from the descent out of Glen Croe. Soon after turning the head of the lake, the neat inn of Aroquhar will be found, facing the loch, and at the distance of about thirty yards from it. The house has been recently enlarged, and was converted into an inn chiefly for the accommodation of the Duke of Argyle, in going to Roseneath, another beautiful seat belonging to that nobleman. Travellers, who have neither time nor inclination to go farther than to see the beauties of Loch Lomond, should, from Dumbarton, sleep at Aroquhar instead of Luss; and as the distance is only two stages, they may, while the horses are resting at Luss, sail upon the lake, see the islands, &c. and still get to Aroquhar in one day. They would by that route see almost the whole of the beauties of Loch Lomond, and the next day return to Dumbarton by Roseneath; by which means they would also see a great part of the beautiful scenery about Loch Long, Loch Gare, with the broad mouth of the Clyde opposite Greenoch, and continue by that river to Dumbarton.

From Cairndow, a chaise containing three German gentlemen preceded mine, and in walking out of Glen Croe I overtook them, as they were also on foot. Human beings, in solitary tracts, soon become acquainted, and human beings meeting by chance in Glen Croe, is an event too rare to be passed unnoticed; I therefore soon learnt, according to the Highland curiosity, who they were, whence they came, and whither going. They had been in the island of Staffa, and were returning to London by Edinburgh. The two carriages arrived at Aroquhar inn in torrents of rain; but as the German gentlemen had permitted their servant, who was on horseback, to secure rooms for me, as well as for his masters, I soon made myself at home, notwithstanding the Germans requested to share my parlour as other company required theirs.

Here is a remarkable coincidence:— four years later in July 1800, when accompanied by Miss Jeffery of London, I visited Loch Catherine; my friend and I had not walked a hundred yards on Loch Catherine's side, before we saw behind us three active pedestrians, skipping amongst the rocks, with hammers in their hands, striking here and there for curiosities. It was not long before they joined us; and, like sojourners, in a distant land, we greeted each other with pleasure and freedom. The eldest was a clergyman, the Rev. John Leyden, accompanying two sprightly youths through the Highlands. They had a horse for their baggage, and one between the three gentlemen to ride on alternately. The youngest had thus early in his journey gotten his foot sadly cut by scrambling amongst the rocks, but his ardent spirit made him think lightly of his wound. Upon looking at his face I discovered his name, for he bore such a strong resemblance to his brother that I could not be mistaken. His brother was one of the German gentlemen whom I met in Glen Croe in the year 1796. It was singular enough that I should, at the distance of four years, meet another of the same family equally accidentally, and in fully as wild a region.

The next day was so adverse for moving, or seeing through the fog which accompanied the torrents of rain, that we were all weather bound at Aroquhar. I ventured out on the beach of the lake for a quarter of an hour, but the wind was too high to stand it longer, and the mist too thick to see any thing, except imperfectly; some black crags, and torrents raging down their sides, making themselves known by their whiteness and noise. The second evening that I as at Aroquhar, the weather became dreadful by rain, wind, and darkness, when a chaise stopped, containing a gentleman, his wife, and two young ladies. I opened my parlour to consult if room could be made, but it was not to be done; there was not even a shake-down to be had, as three of them were to be spread upon the carpet of the parlour I was in, after I should retire, for folks who had been in the inn all day. To see these strangers turned out was lamentable; and in such a night too! but as Tarbet inn was only one mile and a half further, by sending lanterns and guides they got safe to it: though they found sad accommodations there. I had the next day the pleasure of seeing this party at Luss, and dined with them at Dumbarton; when I learnt from them, that in the most dreary part of Glen Croe, they overtook a man whose horse had just dropped; that they did all they could to assist him, but to no effect. The horse was dying; and the man had taken the saddle upon his own back, and left the beast to die alone. What a deplorable state was that man in! I suppose he might get to one of the huts in Glen Croe. To walk back to Cairndow was impossible, loaded with the saddle; and in such a storm of rain, and wind, and darkness, into the bargain.

The morning I left Aroquhar was very tolerable; and as much as I could see of the view down Loch Long, it was pleasant and woody. To the head of it, is a cluster of black, jagged mountains, leading to the head of Loch Lomond, and towering over its western side; these mountains are called the Aroquhar Hills; they are extremely jagged, covered in appearance with old men's heads, and very high; but not so huge as Ben Lomond, opposite to them, on the east side of Loch Lomond. From the Aroquhar inn to Tarbet inn (better than a mile), is an opening between mountains, covered with trees; so as to form a fine grove, through which the road is made.

From Tarbet inn is a ferry to a house opposite, at the foot of Ben Lomond, built on purpose by the Duke of Montrose, for the accommodation of those who wish to go to the top of the mountain. A gentleman, I was told, had been waiting a week at Tarbet

for a favourable day to ascend, and was on that expedition the day I passed it. As it grew clear enough for me to see the top of that huge mass, I think he would not lose his labour; but on such occasions disappointment is often the case; the country below being seldom to be seen distinctly from such immense heights, even though at starting all appeared clear and cloudless below.

The drive from Tarbet to Dumbarton (21 miles) is superlatively beautiful. A few miles south of Tarbet, the road winds up a very steep hill, to a shelf hanging over the glassy lake; from that point, to the east and north, the sublimity of the scene is equal to the beauty of it. It is the narrow part of the lake, bounded by the Aroquhar hills and Ben Lomond, both sweeping precipitately to the water's edge, with rocky, verdant, and wooded promontories stretching into the lake, receding one behind the other towards its head, and finely reflected by the mirror beneath them. The southern view, (from this shelf), over Loch Lomond is enchanting; it includes the vast expanse of the lake, containing at least twenty-four islands, many of them large, enriched and beautified by wood and rocks, and every thing that can charm the sight. The mountains, the woods on the banks, and the cultivation as the mountains recede from the lake, with the high blue hills in the horizon to the south, all contribute to render this view, in point of beauty, equal to any in nature, when seen in a clear day, with a favourable light.

The town of Dumbarton has nothing striking in it; there are indeed two almost new towns near it; one on the west bank of the river, and the other on the east, by Balloch Boat, which proves the great increase of trade and population at and near Dumbarton. The rock on which the Castle is erected, is a very great curiosity; how such a prodigious mass of solid rock, and of great circumference and height, should rear its lofty rough head, and be insular on a perfect flat, without the least rising ground for a mile on any side of it, is very unaccountable. To this rock from the town is about three quarters of a mile, to the south; it rises on a peninsular of sand, washed by the Clyde, and the river Leven from Loch Lomond, which empties itself into the Clyde, at the base of the rock; at the top of which is a fine view. The Castle, in the light of utility as a defensive fortification, is a mere nothing; though a farcical fuss, in time of war, is made to gain admittance into it. The sketch and pencil of such an inoffensive draughtswoman as myself, was, with great solemnity, ordered to be left in custody, whilst I walked to the top of the Castle, lest I should run away with the plan of this important post of defence. I obeyed orders, but laughed in my sleeve at the prohibition of my innocent portfolio.

I found Glasgow greatly enlarged; I was there eleven years previous to this tour, and I could hardly believe it possible for a

I laughed in my sleeve!

town to be so increased, in size and improved as it was in 1796. Its situation is very fine; but like all other great manufacturing trading towns, the inhabitants are very rich, saucy and wicked.

CHAPTER EIGHT

I left Glasgow as soon as possible, and proceeded towards Hamilton, stopping at Bothwell Castle, where, by a rich feast of beauty and nature, I forgot the din of Glasgow, its pride, its wealth, and worldly ways; forgot my sleepless night; even hunger too (for I had not breakfasted) gave way to the delight the scenes of Bothwell afforded me. What a lovely walk is that by the river's side! How picturesque the ruin, and the wood! How enchanting the scene from the windows of the house! No drawback, except in a few spots; a little but very little of the slime of the Nature dressers, who shave too neatly for dame Nature's lovely honest face. Smooth lawns, the rose, the pink, the jessamine, the twining honeysuckle, and flower border, are sweet and lovely, but in some instances they are out of place.

Hamilton is a tolerable town. The Duke's palace, on the outside (I did not see the inside of it), is an old, and rather a forlorn-looking mass of building, attached by high walls to the worst end of the town. It stands on a flat; the ground rising I believe, on every side, and trees and woods every where about it; particularly at Chattelherault, where they are very fine. About one mile after I had passed the palace, I crossed the Avon Water, a considerable river, with a bed full of rocks; all around the bridge over it is beautifully romantic, particularly at a house on the edge of the water, about a quarter of a mile above. Soon after crossing the Avon, the road ascends a rough steep hill, by the side of Duke Hamilton's woods, and park pales, which is the road to Douglas Mill, from which the new road, by Clyde's side, to Lanerk, strikes off, and becomes a most beautiful drive, by the river's side all the way. Stone Biers Force is a very grand fall of the river Clyde, within three miles of Lanerk. The new bridge at the foot of the hill; the town of Lanerk high on the top of it; with the winding river, and noble woods of Boniton to the right; and those about Cartland Crags, and Lee Place, to the left; form a charming view, as the traveller advances towards the bridge.

Lee Place is ancient and venerable. One of its owners, Sir William Lockhart, was Embassador to France for the Republic of England, in Oliver Cromwell's time, and also in Charles the Second's. One of the Lockharts married a niece of Oliver's. There is at Lee a very fine picture of Cromwell, by Vandyke. Lee Place abounds with wood, and trees of all sorts, particularly an oak, which is in circumference, at the root, twenty-one feet three inches; and where the branches begin to expand at the top of the trunk, twenty-three feet. There are three large branches which arise from the trunk, one of them measures nine feet nine inches in circumference, another thirteen feet three inches, the third fourteen feet three inches. It is said to be 150 years since it was discovered that one of its branches had begun to decay, and though it has gone on decaying, still it is only the tops of the large branches that are now in a decayed state. By the tradition of the Lockhart family, this oak, in 1796, was 750 years old. A larch tree also, at Lee, which was planted when King George the third was born, measured, in 1782, ten feet four inches in circumference. There is also an avenue called the Velvet Walk, shaded by the finest ash and lime trees I ever saw; their spreading branches from a canopy over the walk, which entirely excludes the rays of the sun. The house is like the surrounding scene, very ancient (though not gloomy), with a face of calm dignity, repose, and quietness, suitable to the venerable aspect of age.

There is at Lee a curiosity of many virtues, called the Lee Penny. It is a stone of a dark red colour, and triangular shape; and its size about half an inch each side. It is set in a piece of silver coin, which (though much defaced,) by some letters still remaining, is supposed to be a shilling of Edward the First. The cross too is very plain on this shilling. It has been, by tradition, in the Lee family since the year 1320, that is, a little after the death of King Robert Bruce; who ordered his heart to be carried to the Holy Land, there to be buried. It was said, that one of the noble family of Douglas was sent with it, and the crowned heart in his arms, was from that circumstance; which is not so; for the person who really did carry the royal heart, was Sir Simond Locard of Lee. From Sir Simon being the person who carried the royal heart, he changed his name to Lockheart, as it is sometimes spelt, or Lockhart. Sir Simon having taken a Saracen prince prisoner, his wife came to ransom him; and on counting the money and jewels, a stone fell out of her purse, which she hastily snatched up; this, and her confusion being observed by Sir Simon, he insisted upon having the stone, or else he would not give up his prisoner. Upon this the lady remonstrated, but in vain; and she gave it to him, and told him its many virtues; videlicet, that it cured all diseases in cattle, and the bite of a mad dog both in man and beast. It is used by dipping the stone in water, which is given to the diseased cattle to drink; and the animals are to have the wounds, or parts infected, washed with the water. There are no words used in the dipping of the stone, nor any money taken by the servants, without incurring the owner's displeasure. Many are the cures said to be performed by it; and people come from all parts of Scotland, and even as far in England as Yorkshire, to get the water in which the stone has been dipped to give to their cattle, especially when ill of the murrain and blackleg.

It is said, when the plague was at Newcastle upon Tyne, the inhabitants sent for the Lee Penny, and gave a bond for a large sum of money in trust for the loan of the stone; and they thought it did so much good, that they offered to pay the value of the bond if they might keep the Penny; but the laird would not part with it.

The most remarkable cure performed upon a human being was on the person of Lady Baird of Sauchtenhall, near Edinburgh; who having been bit by a mad dog, was come to the length of the hydrophobia; upon which having begged that the Lee Penny might be sent to her house, she used it for some weeks, drinking and bathing in the water it was dipped in, and was quite recovered. This happened about the year 1700; and the fact is very well attested by the Lady of the Laird of Lee at that time; relating also that she and her husband were entertained at Sauchtenhall by Sir — Baird and his lady, for several days, in the most sumptuous manner, on account of the lady's recovery by the Lee Penny. (N.B. The Lee Penny has been examined by a lapidary, and found to be a stone, but of what kind he could not tell.)

The Lady of Lee, so entertained at Sauchtenhall, had not been dead more than thirty years when I saw the Lee Penny. At Lee, I was treated with the utmost politeness by Mrs. Lockhart; and the ceremony of the dipping of the Penny three times, and the three times twirl in the glass of wine I drank, was performed with all due solemnity; but as neither disease existed, nor faith accompanied the operation, no effect was produced from it upon me. A gentleman in company, though no enthusiast, and who was in the last stage of a consumption, like a drowning person catching at a reed, looked eagerly at his enchanted glass of water; and although his voice laughed at the fable, his heart silently though feebly hoped; I saw it by the turn of his eye as he swallowed the draught; but, alas! on him it had no effect.

During my visit to the amiable family at Carstairs house, I also saw Boniton and its beauties in perfection, both in fine weather and in a flood. The banks of the Clyde, from the cotton works to the Boniton falls, are very beautiful. The mill at Corie Lin, the ruin of the old house of Corie on the summit of the rocks hanging over the Lin, Wallace's seat at the top of the Lin, the noble masses of projecting rock, the rich wood on every side, with the grand fall of the Lin in the centre, which rolls from a prodigious height, and dashes to a great breadth, altogether produce a wonderful effect. The carriage stopped under fine single trees, at the entrance of a beautiful wood; The noise of the Lin pointed out the way by a winding path to a very thick part of the wood, facing the cataract, which at once astonishes and delights. Lady Ross has made many judicious cuts in the wood to open the fall. But if her ladyship would make a rough and winding way, scarcely to be seen, or even steps in the rocks, from the first station on her side of the river to the bottom of the fall, I am sure the effect of looking up at the Lin would be wonderfully grand.

Nothing can be more beautiful, romantic and rich, than the terrace hanging over the river, from the seat opposite the Corie Lin to the square stone stand erected to view the Boniton falls. The masses of rock confining the river on each side; the wood branching, feathering, and hanging over and down them in every form, beautified by the greatest variety of tints; and the river in its deep and narrow bed, rushing furiously amongst broken rocks; in short, it is one of the most enchanting walks of half a mile that can any where be met with. The traveller must not be satisfied with viewing the Boniton falls from the square erection, he must get close to and under those falls; they are three in one, and very charming. Every part of Boniton is well worth seeing; the prospects are not of the extensive kind, but they are delightful to a painter's eye. Were I to break the tenth commandment, most undoubtedly it would be in coveting Lady Ross's house and possessions at Boniton.

The town of Lanerk is sweetly situated; but all to the east of it, except just on the banks of the Clyde, is wild and dreary. Within half a mile to the north of Lanerk runs the Mouse, a very wild small river; on its banks are many romantic spots, particularly one called Borronauld, close to the Cartland Crags. A neat

small house stands in the hollow of a hill, high above the Mouse; in front, below the dwelling, is a lovely sweep of the river; over which, at a little distance, is a simple one-arched bridge of grey stone, so mellowed by the green and yellow tints of time and weather, that it was beautiful. I hope I saved it the torture of a white face-washing. A soft meadow is on the near side of the bridge, and rocks and wood wind on the river's southern bank before and behind the arch. To the left of the house is a rising hill, clothed with thick wood, through which, one winding path leads to the top of high crags hanging over the Mouse, and another down to the bottom of them; these are Cartland Crags. The river, when I was there, was fortunately low; and the polite owner of Borronauld took the trouble of accompanying one of my amiable young friends and me, through the bed of the river, for about three quarters of a mile. It is impossible to describe the sublimity, beauty, richness, and variety of that spot. We first crossed the river from Borronauld, by stepping from one great piece of rock to another, and landed on the small meadow not far from the bridge, from whence the opening into the crags is strikingly grand; but as the view of a small part was only increasing my desire to see the whole, we ventured to follow our good guide through the extent of the craggy passage. The rocks on each side, though covered with wood, are too steep and broken, at the edge of the water, to bear a path to be made, or to be preserved if made, by reason of the violence of the water in hard rains; we were therefore obliged to step from stone to stone, in the middle of the water; and at the sides, to creep along, and round the points of rocks, where huge flat stones are heaped one upon another, with beautiful trees sprouting from every crevice. Towers of rocks boldly rise to a considerable height on each side, with chasms and mouths of caves gaping and pouring forth never-ceasing streams; the gay, red-berry mountain ash, the alder, maple, thorn, and young oak, creeping up every side, and brightening the dark recesses that at every ten yards present themselves. In the caves of Cartland, Wallace frequently concealed himself from his enemies. There is a great variety of strata in the crags of Cartland; it was autumn when I saw them; and the plants, weeds, and trees, exhibited a rich variety of tints, hanging about the huge masses of Barytes, or ponderous earth, rising to prodigious heights; and as the sun shone on them, they resembled the finest blocks of polished red and white marble, ornamented with the most beautiful tints which vegetation in its autumnal pride can bestow. Every turn of the scene (and it is nothing but windings) presents a new and different beauty from the former. I was extremely sorry to quit this charming and enchanting spot, where I knew not what to admire most, the water, or its bank'

One of the most enchanting walks.

We pursued its course till we were within sight of the bridge over the Mouse, near its junction with the Clyde; we then climbed up its banks, through the wood, and returned to Borronauld, where we again joined the rest of our good friends of Carstairs; who imagined, by our long absence, that one of us at least had been swallowed up by the Mouse, as we were skipping from rock to rock.

On another day from Carstairs, we visited Douglas Castle, which is in a very fine unfinished state. It stands low, near a sluggish small river; no view at all from it; but it is shaded by an abundance of fine old and very large trees, particularly ash; on some of which, in times of old, offenders were tucked up without the assistance of either judge or jury. These execution-trees were shewn us within a stone's throw of the castle. There is only the ruin of one round tower remaining of the old building. It is said that one of the Dutchesses of Douglas set it on fire to get the Duke from it. Had he lived, another castle would have been completely raised on the same spot. The plan of the castle begun, if one may judge from what exists, was intended to be a square, only one side of which is built. Had the whole been finished, it must have been a prodigious pile, though, by the specimen of what is erected, it could never have been otherwise than heavy, inconvenient, dark and gloomy. We went up to the top of the castle first; and I never ascended, at once, so many stairs before; at least a hundred and fifty. At such a height, there is from the leads rather an extensive view to the west, over the town of Douglas. The round towers at the corners of the building, carried from the bottom to the top, are the pleasantest rooms by far in it. There are few spacious appartments, and those gloomy; the passages, and anti-room to them, from the staircase, are totally dark. There is no furniture in the castle, except two beds, and a few pictures, &c. The exhibitor diverted me by her imperfect lesson on the subjects of the pictures. A large modern piece caught our eyes; and we asked without examining, "What is this?" — "Lord Douglas's picture, with his nurse!" — What should this prove, but an emblem of his Lordship's great cause; his head, and Justice at full length trampling upon Discord, &c. — The figure of Justice, the good woman had transformed into that of his Lordship's nurse.

I left Carstairs House on the 10th of October, 1796, with a very heavy heart. So hospitably, and so kindly had I been treated by the whole of that amiable family, that it was with the utmost regret I quitted them.

It was a bad day; snow covered the top of Tinto Hill; and the rain thickened and continued, with some few intervals, till I arrived at Moffat, in the dusk of the evening. Moffat lies at the head of Annandale; which, though wild, possesses many beauties. The Spa, similar to the German Spa, is within a mile of the town. It is tolerably frequented, and is on the side of a hill, with a torrent rushing near it; at the head of which is the cataract called the Grey Mare's Tail. There are vast ranges of high mountains around the head of Annandale, from which rise fine rivers, running in every direction; such as the Clyde, the Tweed, the Yarrow, the Ettrick, the Esk, and the Annan.

During the night which I passed at Moffat it had poured with rain, so that in the morning every torrent was roaring as I pursued my journey, and the rivers had swollen beyond their bounds. At about two miles south of the town of Moffat, I crossed a branch of the Annan by Duncrief House, finely shaded by wood, and the water dashing furiously close to it. Cornal Tower is on the other side of the water, and is also surrounded by thick wood, at the base of vast mountains. The drive through Annandale is very pleasant, as the river is a very fine one; and is for the most part ornamented by wood, and some rocks on its banks, with a great diversity of mountains bounding the vale; but in twelve miles after I left Moffat, I quitted the beautiful Annan river for the dreary road to Lockerby, Ecclefechan, Gretna and Longtown.

ALSO AVAILABLE FROM BYWAY BOOKS

Northern Lights

or

a voyage in the Lighthouse Yacht
to Nova Zembla and the Lord knows where
in the summer of 1814

by
Sir Walter Scott

Scott's journal of his voyage to Orkney, Shetland, the Hebrides
and the north coast of Ireland in the company of the Commiss-
ioners for the Northern Lighthouses and their Surveyor-Viceroy,
Robert Stevenson — grandfather of Robert Louis Stevenson —
together with letters written before, during and after the voyage
and Stevenson's memoir of Scott.

ISBN 0 907448 01 1
160pp paperback £2.50

Highland Tours

by
James Hogg

The Ettrick Shepherd's travels in the Scottish Highlands and
Western Isles in 1802, 1803 and 1804 with an Introduction by
Sir Walter Scott. A classic portrayal of Scotland in transition,
peppered with stimulating comments and a unique insight into
Scottish history, culture, social and political life.

ISBN 0 907448 00 3

160pp paperback £1.95

Byway Books are illustrated from 19th Century engravings,
include simple maps and make perfect gifts. They are available
from all good bookshops, but in the case of difficulty may be
ordered direct from

Byway Books

9 Maxton Court
Hawick TD9 7QN

please add 40p per item for post and packing.